Legal Writing I & II

Legal Research and Writing &
Introduction to Litigation Practice

Ben L. Fernandez

The paperback version of this work is available at low cost at Amazon.com.

ISBN 9798746520340

Image credits: Green Chameleon (cover), Day of Victory Studio (preface), Green Chameleon (intro), Giammarco Boscaro (chapter 1), RH (chapter 2), M (chapter 7), David Mark (chapter 18), and David Veksler (chapter 20) on Unsplash, Pixabay, StockSnap and Shutterstock.

CONTENTS

Copyright

Preface

Introduction

Part I: Objective Writing   1

1. Sources of Law   2

2. Legal Research   19

3. Briefing Cases   36

4. Applying Cases and Analogical Reasoning   53

5. Analyzing Statutes and Marshaling Facts   77

6. Citation   94

7. IRAC   106

8. Objective Legal Memoranda   123

9. Other Examples of Legal Writing   136

10. Improving Your Writing   143

Part II: Persuasive Writing   147

11. Credibility   148

12. Bias   153

13. Ethical Rules for Advocacy   160

14. Civil and Appellate Procedure   166

15. Requirements for Civil Motions and Standards for Appeals   171

16. Persuasive Writing 176

17. Memoranda in Support of Motions 186

18. Motion Session 202

19. Appellate Briefs 207

20. Oral Argument 223

Apppendix 227

CASE BRIEFING EXERCISE 231

Clampitt v. Spencer 232

Eppler v. Tarmac 244

SAMPLE CASE BRIEFS 261

Clampitt v. Spencer Brief 262

Eppler v. Tarmac Brief 264

CASE ANALOGY EXERCISE 266

Malczewski v. Florida 269

SAMPLE CASE ANALOGY 275

IRAC EXERCISE 278

Young v. Kirsch 281

State Farm v. Mosharaf 291

Southland v. Thousand Oaks 305

SAMPLE IRAC 310

LEGAL MEMORANDUM EXERCISE 314

SAMPLE LEGAL MEMORANDUM 317

About The Author 323

PREFACE

Law schools have been teaching legal writing for a long time; and a lot of books on the subject have already been written. So why would anyone write another book on legal writing? I did it because I've been teaching legal writing (and contract drafting) for twelve years (after having practiced law for over twenty years), and I've found the way this subject is typically presented is often not very effective. Too many law students finish their first year having a passing familiarity with a great many topics, but a lacking competence with the most basic skills they need to practice law after graduation. I think the primary reason that happens is because students are flooded with too much to read and too much information to absorb. They are assigned multiple texts and 4 credits worth of information for a 2 credit course. As a result, they don't have enough opportunity to practice the most important skills they need to learn.

This book presents the subject of legal writing in a different way. It contains a much more concise discussion of each of the topics typically covered in first and second semester courses. Each chapter emphasizes the basics and leaves out the minutiae. Also the topics in this book are discussed one at a time, in logical order, with each chapter building on the discussion in the preceding chapter.

A more concise presentation gives you more time to practice.

That is important because you learn these skills by practicing them. You can't just read about how to write a legal memo and then write one. You need to practice writing one yourself, and you need to do that more than just once. The same is true for legal research, citation and all the other skills associated with a legal writing course. You need to practice them to become competent. So the book you use should not force you to spend most of your time reading. It should give you the opportunity to do what you need to do to learn these skills.

A discussion that focuses on the basics ensures that you do not spend too much time learning things that are less important. In a first semester course the skill you really need to develop is legal analysis (i.e. how to analyze cases and statutes and apply the rules they contain to a set of facts). A legal memo that has is comprised of all the customary parts and has no typographical errors and perfect citations, but contains an analysis that is either too superficial or otherwise flawed, is of no use to anyone. Legal analysis is the most important skill to learn from the first part of this book. You should get as much as you can out of this subject, but the most effective way to do that is by prioritizing the most important topics and then building on that foundation.

Taking these topics one step at a time also gives you the chance to master each skill before proceeding to the next step. There is a logical order to the topics presented in a legal writing course. In my opinion, those topics should be organized so that the discussion of each topic builds on the presentation before it.

I will start by introducing the chapters of the book and giving you some general advice about how to do well in law school.

INTRODUCTION

The first two chapters of this book are on the sources of law and legal research because you have to know what the sources of law are to know where to look to research a legal issue; and you need to be familiar with both those topics to find the statutes and cases you need to analyze in the next few chapters.

The components of a case brief are discussed next, and then the book explains how to apply a case to a fact pattern using the components of a brief. The next chapter is on how to determine a statutory rule, and then the book explains how to marshal the facts to the elements of a rule using a statutory rule as an example.

The next topic is legal citation which is how you reference the cases and statutes you worked on in the previous chapters. After that I discuss how to organize your analysis of each legal issue with "IRAC" and, finally, how to organize your discussion of the issues into the sections of a legal memorandum. At the end of the first part of this book I also briefly cover client communications and provide some suggestions for improving your writing.

The second half of this book contains the topics covered in a second semester course on legal writing. It covers the legal and ethical rules applicable to litigation, drafting a memorandum in support of a trial court motion, drafting of an appellate brief and oral advocacy. Like the first half, the presentation of each topic is brief, highlighting the basics and building on what was presented in the previous section. The most important skill to learn from the second part of this book is persuasion, and the most effective thing you can do to learn that that skill is to practice as much as you can.

To be successful in law school, you need to do things differently than you have done them in the past. For one thing, you have to be more disciplined and diligent than you may have been as an undergraduate. There is a lot more competition in law school. Everyone is a good student, so just being a good student makes you average. If you want to score higher, you have to up your game. The further you go in education, the harder you have to work if you want to be the leader of the pack.You will probably find that the reading assignments in many of your substantive courses are lengthy. To digest all the reading material you need to change the way you study for school. First, you need to prioritize your reading. Some things you are assigned to read are more important than others. For example, in a common law textbook, the cases are more important than the commentary. So you need to read the cases more carefully.

Second, you need to read purposefully. You don't read a case like you would read a novel, sitting back in an easy chair or lying in bed and passively taking it all in. You should be sitting up with pen or pencil in hand, looking for the rule applicable to the issue you are studying or researching. The case will usually involve an application of that rule to a set of facts; and sometimes the court will explain why they applied the law the way they did. Those are the things you should be looking for.

Third, when you find the rule and the application of the rules to the facts, slow down and read that information more carefully than you otherwise would. Pay attention to the specific language of the rule and the facts of the case. Think about why the court decided the way they did, even if they didn't give an explanation. And consider how they might decide the case differently if the facts were different.

Fourth, take as many notes as you can. If you don't want to use pen and paper, then type your notes into a laptop. It doesn't matter so much how you do it but rather that you go through the process of putting what you learned into your own words, and into the context of the other things you are learning in the course. In law school you will have to digest way too much information to rely on your memory when it is time for exams. You have to take a lot of notes to do well.

And fifth, as the course progresses, gradually synthesize the different concepts you have learned, and further distill your notes into a detailed outline of what was covered. You should have notes from the materials you read, and you should also have notes from the classes you attended. If you are sitting in class just passively listening like you are watching a TV show, you won't learn as much as you need to do well. You will do much better if you go through the process of taking those notes and then distilling them down into an outline to prepare for exams.

There are shortcuts you can take but there is always a cost for going that route. You won't learn as much if you don't take the time to brief the cases. And you will always be behind the students who did what was necessary to learn the material. Instead of always looking for corners you can cut, take the ball and run as far as you can. Do that and I bet you will be surprised at how much you can accomplish.

With that introduction, let's take the first step by learning what the sources of law are.

PART I: OBJECTIVE WRITING

1. SOURCES OF LAW

L aw school is not about learning what all the laws are. The Unites States has far too many laws for anyone to learn. For example, according to one recently published estimate, there are about 4,500 federal criminal statutes alone in the United States Code. *Mass Incarceration: The Whole Pie 2020*, Wendy Sawyer & Peter Wagner (Prison Policy Initiative March 24, 2020). Plus each of the fifty states also has its own criminal statutes, and that's where most of the criminal statutes are located. So the 4,500 federal criminal laws are really just the tip of the iceberg.

Not surprisingly, no one has ever been able to count all

of the laws in the United States, let alone learn what they all are. The job of a law student then is not to learn what all thes laws are. It is to learn what all the sources of law are, how to find laws on a particular topic, how to apply the law to a set of facts and analyze legal problems, and how to write about the result. To begin the process, let's get an overview of all the sources.

There are basically four sources of law in the United States: (1) local town bylaws and city ordinances, (2) state statutes, regulations and cases, (3) federal statutes, regulations and cases, and (4) international treaties, compacts and agreements. What you need to know about those sources is where to find them, and how to apply the rules they contain to the facts of your case. You need to have the big picture in your head so that when you do legal research you will be able to develop a comprehensive strategy that ensures you are able to find all the rules that apply.

A. Local Ordinances and Bylaws

Local law is the first source of law we will discuss. Local law consists of city ordinances or town bylaws. In Gainesville, Florida, for example, they are called the Code of Ordinances for the City of Gainesville. Topics covered include economic development, alcoholic beverages, animal control, cemeteries, fire prevention, health and sanitation, building codes, nuisances, parks and recreation, police, traffic, utilities and the land development code (the zoning code).

Real estate lawyers spend a lot of time looking at local law because the city ordinance or town bylaw is usually where the zoning code is found. The zoning code contains the dimensional and use requirements for house lots. Dimensional requirements include minimum lot size, front rear and side yard requirements and other similar matters. And use requirements are often shown on a zoning map where, among other things, residential districts are separated from commercial areas.

It is important to understand, however, that local law is usually trumped by state law, which is discussed next. So if there is a conflict between a local law requirement and a state law requirement, then the state law requirement governs. The reason is because of the authority given to localities in the state constitution. And the discussion of that topic is far beyond the scope of this book. For the purposes of a law school course on legal writing you should just be aware that local law is the lowest priority of all the four sources of law.

For that and other reasons, law school students usually aren't taught about local law, and it isn't on the bar exam either. In fact, you likely will not have the need to deal with any local laws until you start practicing; and, depending on the type of practice you have, you may never have to deal with local law. But you still need to be aware of it, since it is one of the four potential sources of law applicable to a legal issue.

B. <u>State Statutes, Regulations and Cases</u>

State law is the second source of law. Every state has its own constitution, and the constitution is the source of all the state's laws, including statutes enacted by the legislature and regulations promulgated by administrative agencies, cases of all the state courts in the state's judicial system, and executive orders issued by the state's executive branch.

Law students are also not typically taught the law of any one particular state. The courses offered in law school usually include examples of various state statutes and cases, but it is not until law students study for the bar exam that they begin to learn the laws of the state they intend to practice in.

In Florida the state statutes are divided into "titles" and "chapters" on various topics, including, the rules for the legislative, judicial and executive branches, the rules for civil practice and evidence, statutes of limitation, elections, municipalities, public lands, ports and harbors, motor vehicles, public health, social welfare, labor, regulation of professions and occupations, regulations of trade and commerce, agriculture, insurance, banking, real and personal property, estates and trusts, domestic relations, civil rights, torts and crimes.

Florida regulations are published in the Florida

Administrative Code, and they are organized by the administrative department that issues them, including the Administration Commission, Board of Governors, Commission on Ethics, Department of Agriculture and Consumer Services, Department of Banking and Finance, Department of Business and Professional Regulation, Department of Children and Families, Department of Corrections, Department of Education, Department of Environmental Protection, Department of Health, Department of Highway Safety and Motor Vehicles, Department of Law Enforcement, Department of Professional Regulation, Department of the Lottery, Fish and Wildlife Conservation Commission. Florida State Fair Authority, Joint Administrative Procedures Committee, Marine Fisheries Commission, Public Service Commission, Regional Planning Councils, State Board of Administration and Water Management Districts.

Whenever you are analyzing a statutory issue remember to also check to see if there are any regulations on point. Often the statute sets forth the general rule, and the details of the rule are in the regulations. The legislature enacts the statute, then empowers an administrative agency to promulgate regulations under the statute. It doesn't always work that way, but when it does, you need to review the regulations in addition to the statute to determine how the statutory rule applies in any given situation.

In addition to state statutes and regulations, case decisions by state courts are also law. The reason is because the American legal system follows a principle called "stare decisis," which is Latin for "to stand by things decided." What that means is that lower courts must follow prior precedents in higher court decisions. For example, if a higher state court decides to recognize the tort of negligent infliction of emotional distress, then that becomes the law of the state for all the lower courts, and all the lower courts must also recognize that tort. In that circumstance the precedent is called "binding."

Binding precedent consists of case decisions from an

appellate court higher in authority than the court hearing the matter. In most states, there are two levels of appellate courts. The highest appellate court is usually called the supreme court. Under the supreme court are typically multiple additional courts of appeal. And at the bottom of the hierarchy are the trial courts. (Sometimes there are regional trial courts and then additional local trial courts below that level.) So published decisions of the supreme court are binding on the courts of appeal, and decisions of the supreme court and the courts of appeal are binding on the trial courts. That means the appellate courts must follow supreme court precedents, and trial courts must follow the decisions of the supreme court and the appellate courts.

However, the decision of one appellate court is not binding on other appellate courts on the same level in the federal or state hierarchy. So, if your case is pending before an appellate court, instead of a trial court, then decisions of the other appellate courts on the same level (not the supreme court) are merely "persuasive." That means the appellate court you are before doesn't have to follow the decisions of the other appellate courts at the same level. You can still use other appellate court cases to try to persuade the court to rule one way or another. But if the court doesn't agree with the decisions in those cases, it is free to disregard them. And if there are disputes among the appellate courts as to an issue, then it is up to the supreme court to resolve the issue one way or another.

In addition, the higher court has to be in the same jurisdiction for a decision to be binding. So if you have a case before a state court in Florida, then decisions from the Florida appellate courts are binding, not decisions from any other state appellate courts. Also, the decision has to involve the same type of issue. So it is decisions on Florida state law that are binding in that situation, not decisions on the law of other states.

In Florida there is one Supreme Court, five District Courts of Appeal, twenty Circuit Courts (the regional trial courts) and sixty-seven County Courts (the local trial courts). Opinions of the trial courts, including the County Courts and Circuit Courts are usually not published. So reported cases in Florida consist primarily of decisions by the Florida Supreme Court and the District Courts of Appeal. The reporter for those cases is called "Florida Cases." They are also published in a regional reporter called the "Southern Reporter."

In law school students spend most of their first year studying tort law, contract law and property law. All of that law is contained in state court cases, and is called "common law." Because common law is state law, the principles of tort law, contract law and property law vary from state to state. Again, students don't learn the common law of any one state in law school. Students are taught common law by reading examples of cases in different states. After law school, when students study for the bar exam, they learn the common law of the state they are seeking to practice in.

There are also state executive orders, which are really not "law," but which are nonetheless mandatory rules citizens of the state are required to follow. Unlike statutes, regulations and case decisions, executive orders are usually not codified or published. However, you can access them through the executive office or on line. For example, the state executive orders for Florida are available on line at the Florida government website.

C. Federal Statutes, Regulations and Cases

The third source of law is federal law. At the federal

level, there is the U.S. Constitution, which is the source of federal law, as well as federal statutes and regulations, federal court cases, and executive orders. Federal statutes are codified in the United States Code. Each volume of the code is called a "title," and each title deals with a different topic. Here is a list of the titles of the United States Code:

Title 1—General Provisions
Title 2—The Congress
Title 3—The President
Title 4—Flag And Seal, Seat Of Government, And The States
Title 5—Government Organization And Employees; and
      Appendix
Title 6—Domestic Security
Title 7—Agriculture
Title 8—Aliens And Nationality
Title 9—Arbitration
Title 10—Armed Forces
Title 11—Bankruptcy; and Appendix
Title 12—Banks And Banking
Title 13—Census
Title 14—Coast Guard
Title 15—Commerce And Trade
Title 16—Conservation
Title 17—Copyrights
Title 18—Crimes And Criminal Procedure; and Appendix
Title 19—Customs Duties
Title 20—Education
Title 21—Food And Drugs
Title 22—Foreign Relations And Intercourse
Title 23—Highways
Title 24—Hospitals And Asylums
Title 25—Indians
Title 26—Internal Revenue Code
Title 27—Intoxicating Liquors
Title 28—Judiciary And Judicial Procedure; and Appendix

Title 29—Labor

Title 30—Mineral Lands And Mining

Title 31—Money And Finance

Title 32—National Guard

Title 33—Navigation And Navigable Waters

Title 34—Crime Control And Law Enforcement

Title 35—Patents

Title 36—Patriotic And National Observances, Ceremonies, And Organizations

Title 37—Pay And Allowances Of The Uniformed Services

Title 38—Veterans' Benefits

Title 39—Postal Service

Title 40—Public Buildings, Property, And Works

Title 41—Public Contracts

Title 42—The Public Health And Welfare

Title 43—Public Lands

Title 44—Public Printing And Documents

Title 45—Railroads

Title 46—Shipping

Title 47—Telecommunications

Title 48—Territories And Insular Possessions

Title 49—Transportation

Title 50—War And National Defense; and Appendix

Title 51—National And Commercial Space Programs

Title 52—Voting And Elections

Title 53—[Reserved]

Title 54—National Park Service And Related Programs

BEN L. FERNANDEZ

About the United States Code

The United States Code is the codification by subject matter of the general and permanent laws of the United States. It is divided by broad subjects into 53 titles and published by the Office of the Law Revision Counsel of the U.S. House of Representatives. The U.S. Code was first published in 1926. The next main edition was published in 1934, and subsequent main editions have been published every six years since 1934. In between editions, annual cumulative supplements are published in order to present the most current information.

This site contains virtual main editions of the U.S. Code. The information contained in the U.S. Code has been provided to GPO by the Office of the Law Revision Counsel of the U.S. House of Representatives. While every effort has been made to ensure that the U.S. Code on this site is accurate, those using it for legal research should verify their results against the printed version of the U.S. Code available through the Government Publishing Office.

Of the 53 titles, the following titles have been enacted into positive (statutory) law: 1, 3, 4, 5, 9, 10, 11, 13, 14, 17, 18, 23, 28, 31, 32, 35, 36, 37, 38, 39, 40, 41, 44, 46, 49, 51, and 54. When a title of the Code was enacted into positive law, the text of the title became legal evidence of the law. Titles that have not been enacted into positive law are only prima facie evidence of the law. In that case, the Statutes at Large still govern. Note: Title 52 is an editorially-created title, and Title 53 is currently reserved. For the current list of titles, see http://uscode.house.gov or

The U.S. Code does not include regulations issued by executive branch agencies, decisions of the Federal courts, treaties, or laws enacted by State or local governments. Regulations issued by executive branch agencies are available in the Code of Federal Regulations. Proposed and recently adopted regulations may be found in the Federal Register. Read More

Federal regulations are published in the Code of Federal Regulations. Like federal statues, federal regulations are organized by title. Here is a list of the titles (topics) included in the Code of Federal Regulations:

Title 1 - General Provisions

Title 2 - Grants and Agreements

Title 3 - The President

Title 4 - Accounts

Title 5 - Administrative Personnel

Title 6 - Domestic Security

Title 7 - Agriculture

Title 8 - Aliens and Nationality

Title 9 - Animals and Animal Products

Title 10 - Energy

Title 11 - Federal Elections

Title 12 - Banks and Banking

Title 13 - Business Credit and Assistance

Title 14 - Aeronautics and Space

Title 15 - Commerce and Foreign Trade

Title 16 - Commercial Practices

Title 17 - Commodity and Securities Exchanges

Title 18 - Conservation of Power and Water Resources

12

Title 19 - Customs Duties

Title 20 - Employees' Benefits

Title 21 - Food and Drugs

Title 22 - Foreign Relations

Title 23 - Highways

Title 24 - Housing and Urban Development

Title 25 - Indians

Title 26 - Internal Revenue

Title 27 - Alcohol, Tobacco Products and Firearms

Title 28 - Judicial Administration

Title 29 - Labor

Title 30 - Mineral Resources

Title 31 - Money and Finance: Treasury

Title 32 - National Defense

Title 33 - Navigation and Navigable Waters

Title 34 - Education

Title 36 - Parks, Forests, and Public Property

Title 37 - Patents, Trademarks, and Copyrights

Title 38 - Pensions, Bonuses, and Veterans' Relief

Title 39 - Postal Service

Title 40 - Protection of Environment

Title 41 - Public Contracts and Property Management

Title 42 - Public Health

Title 43 - Public Lands: Interior

Title 44 - Emergency Management and Assistance

Title 45 - Public Welfare

Title 46 - Shipping

Title 47 - Telecommunication

Title 48 - Federal Acquisition Regulations System

Title 49 - Transportation

Title 50 - Wildlife and Fisheries

Federal law trumps state law in the same way that state law trumps local law. In the case of federal law, the reason is because of the supremacy clause of the U.S. Constitution. The supremacy clause states that the federal constitution, federal laws made pursuant to it, and treaties made under its authority, constitute the "supreme law of the land", and thus take priority over any conflicting state laws. So if you find a federal law and a state law on the same topic, and the two laws are in conflict, the federal law takes precedence over the state law.

Like state cases, federal cases are also considered law because of the principle of stare decisis. Opinions of the federal court of last resort, the U.S. Supreme Court, are published in three places: "U.S. Reports," "Supreme Court Reports," and "Supreme Court Reports, Lawyers' Edition." The official reporter is U.S. Reports; Supreme Court Reports is published by West and includes something called "case headnotes," a research tool I'll explain later.

Decisions of the federal appellate courts, called the U.S. Circuit Courts, are published in a publication called the "Federal Reporter." Unlike state trial court cases, opinions of the federal trial courts are also published. The trial courts are called U.S. District Courts, and decisions of those courts are published in a reporter called the "Federal Supplement." Notably, the decisions in the Federal Supplement are persuasive not binding.

There is obviously only one U.S. Supreme Court, but there are thirteen U.S. Courts of Appeal (there are twelve circuits plus the federal circuit), and there are ninety-four U.S. District Courts (i.e. trial courts).

There are also federal executive orders, which, like state executive orders, are really not "law." However, unlike state executive orders, federal executive orders are published in a publication called the "Federal Register," and they are also available at the Register's website.

D. International Treaties, Compacts and Agreements

Last but not least are international treaties, compacts and agreements. Obviously, an in depth discussion of international law would be far beyond the scope of this book. For our purposes, you should just be aware of the existence of these materials and their potential applicability to cross border transactions. If a client ever hires you to work on a case involving trade, transactions or other conduct extending beyond the U.S. border, then that is a situation where you will have to get up to speed on international law.

International laws can be found at the website for the U.S. Office of Treaty Affairs (OTA). The OTA compiles and publishes treaties and international agreements to which the United States is a party in the Treaties and International Acts Series (TIAS), which is only available to the public on line. Also, HeinOnline has a library of U.S. Treaties and Agreements.

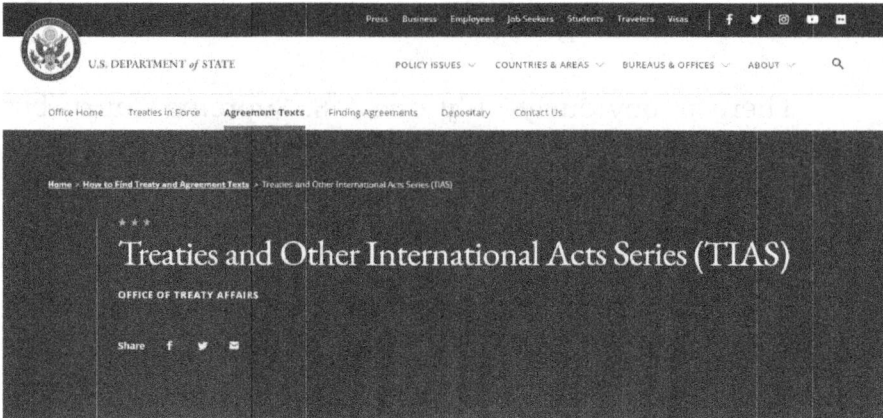

Those are the sources of law in the American legal system. It is important to have that information in your head because there are often laws on multiple levels applicable to a legal issue. For example, suppose you were trying to determine what laws apply to the bottling and sale of beer by a local microbrewery. You would start with local laws applicable wherever the operation is because they would likely have licensing and other requirements that have to be met. You would then look at state and federal laws on labeling and other bottling requirements. You may find, for example, that the basics are required by federal law, and state law adds some additional requirements of its own. And you would make sure to check any regulations promulgated under the federal and state statutes. If your client was planning to sell the beer over the border in Mexico, you would also research any international laws applicable to trade with Mexico. In that situation, you need to know to look in all four places. So it is important to have the big picture.

It is also important to know who publishes the paper version of those sources. One reason for that is because you refer to the sources by referring to the books they are published in. For example, if you are referring to a federal case, you must indicate whether it is published in the Federal Reporter or the Federal Supplement. You can't just give someone the internet address or "URL." You may have read the case on line, not in print, but when you refer to it in a memo, or a brief, you will have to state the name of the book it is published in, as well as the volume and page number. Even if you do everything on line, you still have to refer to the books. I'll explain this more in the chapter on citation.

Lawyers don't need to know what all the laws are. Lawyers need to know what laws are out there and where to look for them. There are basically four (4) sources: local, state, federal, and international. Within state and federal laws there are three (3) subcategories: statutes and regulations, cases, and executive orders. And there are three (3) different types of courts issuing decisions: supreme courts, appeals courts, and trial courts. Here is a brief chart of showing all the different sources of law in the American legal system:

International Law	Treaties, Compacts, Agreements	Office of Treaty Affairs, Treaties and International Acts Series HeinOnline
Federal Law	Statutes	United States Code
	Regulations	Code of Federal Regulations
	Supreme Court Cases Appellate Court Cases (U.S. Circuit Courts) Trial Court Cases (U.S. District Courts)	U.S. Reports, Supreme Court Reports, Lawyer's Edition (U.S. Supreme Court) Federal Reporter (U.S. Circuit Courts) Federal Supplement (U.S. District Courts)
	Executive Orders (U.S. President's Office)	
State Law	Statutes	Florida Statutes
	Regulations	Florida Administrative Code
	Supreme Court Cases Appellate Court Cases (Florida District Courts) Trial Court Cases (Florida Circuit Courts)	Florida Cases Southern Reporter
	Executive Orders (Florida Governor's Office)	
Local Law	City Ordinances	Code of Ordinances for the City of Gainesville
	Town Bylaws	

Knowing what all the sources of law are is the first step on the long road to being able to practice law well. Knowing how to find specific laws within those sources (i.e. legal research) is the second. And that is the subject of the next chapter.

2. LEGAL RESEARCH

Y ou may be surprised to learn that many of the skills you need to do legal research well are skills you already have. Just like every textbook you have ever read, compilations of statutes, regulations and cases each have their own table of contents in the beginning, and an index at the end. You know pretty much any information that appears in print is also available in digital form on the internet or on a CD-ROM or a flash drive. And you already have experience searching for information stored that way by using a search engine on a computer.

I remember a long, long time ago, when I first started

using the internet, I thought searching the web was just like doing legal research on the computer. Lawyers were using Westlaw and Lexis before consumers started using the World Wide Web. For you the experience will likely be the other way around. You will likely find doing legal research with a computer is just like searching for information on the internet. The process is not exactly the same but the skills you need are very similar to the ones you already have.

The two big differences between internet searching and legal research are first that you have to identify the source you want to search before you start doing legal research. And there are two types of sources: primary sources (e.g., statutes, regulations, cases) and secondary sources (e.g., treatises, encyclopedia, textbooks). Second, you can construct more sophisticated search queries when you use a legal research website. Among other things, there are Boolean terms and connectors you can use to tell the search engine more precisely what you are looking for, including the following:

/s	In same sentence	
+s	In same sentence and in same order	
/p	In same paragraph	
+p	In same paragraph and in same order	
/[n]	Within n (1-255) terms of	
+[n]	Within n (1-255) terms of and in same order	
%	But not	
[SPACE]	OR connector	
&	AND connector	
!	Root expander suffix for variant endings	
*	Universal single character(s)	

> (cannot start term)
>
>   #   Prefix to turn off plurals and equivalents

I'll discuss how to research primary sources first (e.g., statutes, regulations and cases), then I'll turn to secondary sources (treatises, restatements, encyclopedia).

A. Primary Sources

(i) Statutes and Regulations

There are three options for researching statutes and regulations: browse the table of contents for the publication you are using, look up your topic in the index and do a word or phrase search using a search engine on a website. The first two options are available in print and on-line; the third option is only available on-line or when the source is in digital form. If you choose to do the research on line, there are paid services you can use, like Westlaw, Lexis and Bloomberg Law. And there are also free services, like the U.S. Government Publishing Office website "GovInfo."

So, for example, if you were looking for the federal law prohibiting employers from discriminating against employees on the basis of age, you might start by looking in the table of contents for the United States Code, either on line or in print. Here is an excerpt of what you would find:

TITLE 20 - EDUCATION
TITLE 21 - FOOD AND DRUGS
TITLE 22 - FOREIGN RELATIONS AND INTER COURSE
TITLE 23 - HIGHWAYS
TITLE 24 - HOSPITALS AND ASYLUMS
TITLE 25 - INDIANS
TITLE 26 - INTERNAL REVENUE CODE
TITLE 27 - INTOXICATING LIQUORS
TITLE 28 - JUDICIARY AND JUDICIAL PROCED URE
TITLE 28a - JUDICIAL PERSONNEL FINANCIAL DISCLOSURE REQUIREMENTS
TITLE 29 - LABOR
TITLE 30 - MINERAL LANDS AND MINING
TITLE 31 - MONEY AND FINANCE
TITLE 32 - NATIONAL GUARD
TITLE 33 - NAVIGATION AND NAVIGABLE WATERS
TITLE 34 - CRIME CONTROL AND LAW EN FORCEMENT
TITLE 35 - PATENTS
TITLE 36 - PATRIOTIC AND NATIONAL OBSERVANCES, CEREMONIES, AND ORGANIZATIONS
TITLE 37 - PAY AND ALLOWANCES OF THE UNIFORMED SERVICES
TITLE 38 - VETERANS' BENEFITS

TITLE 39 - POSTAL SERVICE
TITLE 40 - PUBLIC BUILDINGS, PROPERTY, AND
WORKS

Title 29, which contains federal labor laws, seems the most likely to contain what you are looking for. If you then browsed through the table of contents for Title 29, you would find this:

CHAPTER 10—DISCLOSURE OF WELFARE AND PENSION PLANS (§ 301)
CHAPTER 11—LABOR-MANAGEMENT REPORTING AND DISCLOSURE PROCEDURE (§§ 401 – 531)
CHAPTER 12—DEPARTMENT OF LABOR (§§ 551 – 568)
CHAPTER 13—EXEMPLARY REHABILITATION CERTIFICATES (§§ 601 – 607)
CHAPTER 14—AGE DISCRIMINATION IN EM

CHAPTER 14-AGE DISCRIMINATION IN EMPLOYMENT (§§ 621 – 634)

CHAPTER 15—OCCUPATIONAL SAFETY AND HEALTH (§§ 651 – 678)
CHAPTER 16—VOCATIONAL REHABILITATION AND OTHER REHABILITATION SERVICES (§§ 701 – 797)
CHAPTER 17—COMPREHENSIVE EMPLOYMENT AND TRAINING PROGRAMS (§§ 801 – 991)
CHAPTER 18—EMPLOYEE RETIREMENT INCOME SECURITY PROGRAM (§§ 1001 – 1461)
CHAPTER 19—JOB TRAINING PARTNERSHIP (§§ 1501 – 1792)
CHAPTER 20—MIGRANT AND SEASONAL AGRICULTURAL WORKER PROTECTION (§§ 1801 – 1872)

Chapter 14 is on age discrimination in employment,

so you would then look at subsections 621 through 634 in Chapter 14. Here is an excerpt of what you would find next.

§ 621. Congressional statement of findings and purpose
§ 622. Education and research program; recommendation to Congress

§ 623. Prohibition of age discrimination

§ 624. Study by Secretary of Labor; reports to President and Congress; scope of study; implementation of study; transmittal date of reports
§ 625. Administration
§ 626. Recordkeeping, investigation, and enforce ment
§ 627. Notices to be posted
§ 628. Rules and regulations; exemptions
§ 629. Criminal penalties

Section 623 appears to be what you are looking for. That section provides, in pertinent part, as follows:

(a) Employer practices. It shall be unlawful for an employer—

(1) to fail or refuse to hire or to discharge any individual or otherwise discriminate against any individual with respect to his compensation, terms, conditions, or privileges of employment, because of such individual's age;

(2) to limit, segregate, or classify his employees in any way which would deprive or tend to deprive any individual of employment opportunities or otherwise adversely affect his status as an employee, because of such individual's age; or

(3) to reduce the wage rate of any employee in order to comply with this chapter.

In the alternative, if you had started by looking in the index for the Code under "discrimination" (again, either on-line or in print), you would have found, among other things, this reference:

Discovery
Discovery Science and Engineering Innovation
Institutes
Discretionary Fund
Discrimination
Discs (Corporations)
Domestic International Sales Corporations
Disease Prevention and Health Promotion Office
Diseases
Disfigurement
  Mayhem
Dishes

Searching under discrimination, would have then taken you to this:

Civil Rights
Abortion, Education: 20 USCA § 1688
Actions and Proceedings
Adoption: 42 USCA § 1996b
Advancement of Women and Minorities in Science, Engineering, and Technology Development Commission: 42 USCA § 1885a NT
Age
Aged Persons
Agricultural and Mechanical Colleges: 7 USCA § 323
Agricultural Products, Unfair Trade Practices:

7 USCA § 2303
Agriculture, Socially Disadvantaged Farmers and Ranchers, Disclosure: 7 USCA § 2279-1
Agriculture Department, Loans: 7 USCA § 2279d

And then, looking under "age," would have led you to this:

Compensation and Salaries: 29 USCA § 626, 29 USCA § 633a
Congress, Officers and Employees, Actions and Proceedings: 2 USCA § 1311
Domestic Violence, Federal Aid: 42 USCA § 10406
Health Insurance: 42 USCA § 18116

Labor and Employment: 29 USCA § 621 et seq.

Federal Aid: 42 USCA § 6101 et seq.
President of the United States, Executive Office, Officers and Employees
3 USCA § 454, 3 USCA § 411

You could have also found the prohibition against age discrimination in employment by doing a word search on one of the paid databases, like Westlaw, Lexis or Bloomberg Law. If you just searched generally under "age discrimination" in Westlaw your search would have yielded far too many results. But if you started by narrowing your search to just the U.S. Code database, you would have located the prohibition at 29 U.S.C. § 623(a). Using a paid database is always the most expensive option, but in this case, doing a word search would have been the quickest method for finding what you are looking for.

(ii) Cases

Researching cases is different than researching statutes

and regulations. A West publication called the "Digest" contains a very detailed and lengthy outline of all the topics discussed in the cases, as well as an index of all those topics. (There are separate digests for federal cases and the cases in each state.) Each topic in the Digest has a number assigned to it, which Westlaw calls a "Key Number." (Lexis and Bloomberg Law have their own digests and a little different ways of organizing the information they contain, but the method they use is basically the same). Also, the list of topics in the Digest is annotated with multiple cases and a highlight of the discussion of the topic in each case called a "headnote." So you can get a quick idea of what is in each case (and whether the case is something you want to read further) by reading the headnote.

The Digest is not a table of contents and the index is not an index to the cases (it is an index to the table of contents), but it can still be useful to think of the Digest as containing the table of contents and index for the cases in a particular jurisdiction. With statutory research the table of contents, the index and the statutes are all in the same publication. With case research the table of contents and the index (the Digest) are in one publication and the cases are in a different publication. Also, with statutory research the table of contents and the index refer you to the rules. With case research the Digest refers you to the cases, and the rules are in the cases.

THOMSON REUTERS
WESTLAW EDGE

West Key Number Hea... ▾   Search West Key Number Headnotes

Home

🔑 West Key Number System

☆ Add to Favorites   ⊖ Copy link

Search for Key Numbers relevant to your issue ⓘ

Q▾ Enter terms e.g., landlord duty of care to trespassers

Jurisdiction selected: All Federal · Change Jurisdiction

☐ Select all content · No items selected · Clear Selection

☐ 1	ABANDONED AND LOST PROPERTY		☐ 141E	EDUCATION
☐ 2	ABATEMENT AND REVIVAL		☐ 142	EJECTMENT
☐ 4	ABORTION AND BIRTH CONTROL		☐ 142T	ELECTION LAW
☐ 5	ABSENTEES		☐ 143	ELECTION OF REMEDIES
☐ 6	ABSTRACTS OF TITLE		☐ 145	ELECTRICITY
☐ 8	ACCORD AND SATISFACTION		☐ 146	EMBEZZLEMENT
☐ 9	ACCOUNT		☐ 148	EMINENT DOMAIN
☐ 10	ACCOUNT, ACTION ON		☐ 149	ENTRY, WRIT OF
			☐ 149E	ENVIRONMENTAL LAW

So, as another example, suppose you were looking for cases involving claims against a landlord or a tenant for tortious interference with contractual relations. You might start with the table of contents for the Digest (on line or in print), and go to the section that covers torts:

373 TENANCY IN COMMON
374 TENDER

375 TERRITORIES
377E THREATS, STALKING, AND HARASSMENT
378 TIME

379 TORTS

380 TOWAGE
381 TOWNS
382T TRADEMARKS
384 TREASON
386 TRESPASS

Under torts, you would find, among other things, a section on tortious interference:

III. TORTIOUS INTERFERENCE, k200-k324
  (A) IN GENERAL, k200-k209

(B) BUSINESS OR CONTRACTUAL RELATIONS, k210-k288

    (C) WILLS, INHERITANCES, TRUSTS AND GIFTS, k289-k299
      (D) OBSTRUCTION OF OR INTERFERENCE WITH LEGAL REMEDIES; SPOLIATION, k300-k324

The section on Business or Contractual Relations would then include this:

(B) BUSINESS OR CONTRACTUAL RELATIONS, k210-k288
1. IN GENERAL, k210-k239

2. PARTICULAR CASES, k240-k249

3. ACTIONS IN GENERAL, k250-k255
4. EVIDENCE, k256-k269
5. QUESTIONS OF LAW OR FACT, k270-k279
6. INSTRUCTIONS, k280-k286
7. VERDICT AND FINDINGS, k287-k288

And, under Particular Cases, you would find this:

2. PARTICULAR CASES, k240-k249
Key Number Symbol 240 In general
Key Number Symbol 241 Business relations or economic advantage, in general
Key Number Symbol 242 Contracts in general

Key Number Symbol 243 Landlord and tenant

Key Number Symbol 244 Insurance in general
Key Number Symbol 245 Physicians and health care; health insurance
Key Number Symbol 246 Attorneys

The result: cases involving claims against a landlord or a tenant for tortious interference with contractual relations are collected in the Digest under Key Number 379k243. (You could have also found the applicable key symbol by using the index, but the index is apparently only available in print, not on line.)

An alternative to using the Digest is doing a word search on Westlaw, Lexis, Bloomberg Law, which are all paid sites, or Google Scholar, which is free.

Google Scholar

⬤ Articles ◯ Case law

⬤ Federal courts ◯ Florida courts Select courts...

Articles about COVID-19

CDC	NEJM	JAMA	Lancet	Cell	BMJ
Nature	Science	Elsevier	Oxford	Wiley	medRxiv

Stand on the shoulders of giants

If you searched Westlaw under "landlord tenant tortious interference contractual relations," your search will likely retrieve too many results. Among other things, the search engine will produce landlord tenant cases that have nothing to do with tortious interference, and tortious interference cases that don't involve a landlord or a tenant.

If you revised your search on Westlaw to something like this: "landlord tenant /p tortious /s interference /s contractual /s relations," you would get much closer to the desired result, including cases that mention the words tortious, interference, contractual and relations in the same sentence, and either landlord or tenant in the same paragraph as those sentences. But why would you do that when the publisher already sorted and filed the cases you are looking for under Key Number 379k243? Computer searching can be very effective, but in this situation, I would use the Digest. Or, better yet, search both ways!

Once you have found what you are looking for you need to make sure the applicable statute or regulation is the version that was in effect when the facts at issue occurred. If you are relying on a case, you also need to make sure it has not since been overruled by some higher authority. In other words, it is still good law. That process used to be called "shepardizing," using a service called "shepards." Today, it is more often done on computer using Westlaw, Lexis or Bloomberg Law. For example, if you reading a case in Westlaw, you will see on the top of the screen what other cases have cited the case you are reading, and whether there has been any negative treatment.

B. <u>Secondary Sources</u>

When you are first starting out, and you are unfamiliar with an area of law, it usually doesn't make sense to go directly to a primary source. In that situation, you need to get an overview of the topic, and make yourself familiar with the terminology and the issues, before you can start looking through specific statutes and cases. And the best way to do that is by starting with a secondary source. A secondary source is a summary, discussion or commentary of the law by some expert in the field. You use a secondary source to do legal research the same way you use primary sources. Look in the table of contents or the index, or do word or phrase search using a search engine.

Examples of popular secondary sources used by practitioners include treatises, like Corbin on Contracts and Prosser and Keaton on Torts. A treatise is a book or, more likely, a series of books containing all the legal principles relating to a particular area of law. Restatements are secondary sources that "restate" the legal rules that constitute the common law in a particular area. There are restatements of tort law, property law and contract law written by the American Law Institute. Another useful secondary source is a legal encyclopedia, like Corpus Juris Secundum and American Jurisprudence (affectionately known by law students as "CJS" and "AmJur"). Legal encyclopedias cover multiple topics and usually span many volumes of text. CJS and AmJur are national in scope. There are also similar state specific resources, like Florida Jurisprudence. Try a secondary source first to get the lay of the land, and then your searches in primary sources like cases and statutes will likely be more efficient.

Of course, secondary sources are persuasive not binding, so it is primary sources you will ultimately want to rely on in your memoranda (and even primary sources are not always binding). The main purpose of secondary sources is to educate lawyers on a specific topic, and help lawyers research specific issues relating to that topic. When you are dealing with an unfamiliar topic, a secondary source will help you get up to speed and more efficiently research the specific issues involved in your case.

C. Paper Research v. Computer Research

When you are thinking about the mechanisms that are out there for doing legal research, don't fall into the trap of dividing the topic into "paper research" and "computer research." The options aren't to turn on a computer or open a book. The options are to do a word or phrase search, search using a table of contents, or look up a topic in an index. When you do a word search, it is a computer that is compiling the search results for you. When you us a table of contents or an index (which you could do in paper or on a computer), the search results are compiled by a human being who has actually read the source material. And that extra person's help is often a plus.

If you research with something like the Digest – whether on a computer or in a book - you will also have the advantage of being able to see the topic in context. If you look up a slip and fall case, you will see that is part of the subject of premises liability, which is under tort law. Also, for each topic, there are headnotes of cases that have been read and quoted or paraphrased by a human being.

The index of a case Digest has similar advantages. An index also tells you what topics are included in a series of books or databases, but it is organized alphabetically instead of by topic. And there are usually cross-references to related or similar subjects. Again, the topics are filed and sorted by people not computers. A person can discern the meaning of language, not just identify a literal match. So you are less likely to retrieve irrelevant and useless information using table of contents or an index instead of doing a word search.

You may be more comfortable doing legal research by doing word or phrase searches. For most of the non-legal searching you do on line, search engines like Google and Yahoo work great. Also, if you are doing legal research, and you are looking for a "needle in a haystack," there is nothing better than to do a word or phrase search on Westlaw or Lexis. But you need to be able to use all three methods of searching. If you don't, someone who does will always have an advantage over you. In an adversarial system like the legal system, that is really not what you are going for.

I once had an auto theft case that involved a juvenile. What was odd about the case was that, after the juvenile stole the car and drove around in it, he returned it to the place where he found it. Initially, I thought the fact that he returned the car would be relevant to intent, and I started looking for intent cases on Westlaw but I found nothing. Then I used the digest and looked under the different types of auto theft cases it had listed, and I found cases organized under a topic labeled "joyriding." It turns out that is the term for this type of crime. And Westlaw had all the cases I was looking for sorted and kept in one place. Once I found the applicable Key Number, it was easy to find something on point. But it was the digest that saved me, not a word search.

Another time I was researching the issue of whether the presence of second hand smoke in an apartment could support a claim for breach of the implied warranty of habitability. I looked in the digest first and found lots of warranty of habitability cases, but nothing that specifically involved second hand smoke. Then I did a word search on Westlaw using "smoke" or "smoking" and "warranty of habitability" as a search terms, and all the state reporters for the entire country as a database and bingo! I found what I was looking for. The digest didn't help me, but Westlaw saved the day.

Whether you do the work using a computer or pages in a book is not what matters. Legal research is not divided into computer research and paper research, it is divided into primary sources and secondary sources, each of which can be researched doing a word or phrase search, or using a table of contents or index. That means there are always at least 9 places to look when you are researching a legal issue. There are cases that can be researched using (1) the table of contents, (2) the index or (3) a search engine; there are statutes and regulations that can be researched using researched using (4) the table of contents, (5) the index or (6) a search engine; and there are secondary sources that can also be researched using (7) the table of contents, (8) the index or (9) a search engine. What works best depends on the circumstances.

Now that you know how to find cases, we can discuss how to brief them and then how to apply the legal rules they contain.

3. BRIEFING CASES

I f all you have in your class notes is "black letter law," you are unlikely to do well on your final exams. You need the information in case briefs to apply the legal principles you learn in each law school class. That is why law students have been briefing cases since Christopher Columbus Langdell first invented the casebook method of legal education. *The Proliferation of Case Method Teaching in American Law Schools: Mr. Langdell's Emblematic "Abomination,"* 1890-1915, Bruce A. Kimball, History of Education Quarterly Vol. 46, No. 2 (Summer, 2006), pp. 192-247.

Case briefs vary in style and format. (Actually, you don't really brief a case; you brief an issue. If the case has multiple issues, and you want to analyze all of them, it is usually best to brief the issues separately.) A typical brief will at least contain the name of the case, the relevant facts, the issue before the court, the rule applicable to that issue, the holding and the court's reasoning or rationale. Often, the procedural history and ultimate disposition are also included. Those are also the things you should be looking for when you read a case, whether you write them down or not. In other words, when you are reading a case, you should be actively looking for the relevant facts, the issue, the rule, the holding, and any rationale.

I'll use the Massachusetts case of <u>Commonwealth v. Sexton</u> to demonstrate how to write a case brief. This is an example of a case you might read in a criminal law textbook in a chapter on assault and battery with a dangerous weapon. You might also find this case in a case digest or a secondary source on criminal law if you were researching the elements of assault and battery with a dangerous weapon. Either way, you would read this case purposefully to determine, among other things, how the rule is applied to the specific facts of the case, as well as all the other elements of a case brief.

The case starts off with the caption identifying the court, the parties and the date:

Supreme Judicial Court of Massachusetts, Hampden.

COMMONWEALTH v. Everett SEXTON.

Decided: June 05, 1997

Before WILKINS, C.J., and ABRAMS, LYNCH, GREANEY and FRIED, JJ. Marcia B. Julian, Assistant District Attorney, for the Commonwealth. Timothy M. Farris, Springfield, for defendant.

The name of the court that decided the case is stated first. The Supreme Judicial Court is the court of last resort – the highest appeals court – in the Commonwealth of Massachusetts. The parties are the Commonwealth of Massachusetts and Everett Sexton (it's a criminal case). The case was decided on June 5, 1997. The names of the judges who heard the case and the attorneys who argued it are also stated. To brief this case, at least start off with the case name, like this:

Com. v. Sexton

In this case, the court has included a brief introduction before the opinion. The introduction would be helpful if you were doing legal research. You could tell by reading it if this is the type of case you are looking for. But I wouldn't include it in the case brief since you will be reading the rest of the case anyway.

> The defendant, Everett Sexton, was convicted on a joint venture theory of assault and battery by means of a dangerous weapon and willful and malicious destruction of property. On appeal, the Appeals Court affirmed his conviction of willful and malicious destruction of property, but reversed his conviction of assault and battery by means of a dangerous weapon on the ground that concrete pavement, the instrumentality at issue, is not a dangerous weapon. *Commonwealth v. Sexton*, 41 Mass. App. Ct. 676, 678-680, 672 N.E.2d 991 (1996). We granted the Commonwealth's application for further appellate review and affirm the conviction by the Superior Court.

After the introduction the court states the facts of the case. As you will see, most of these facts are not relevant to the issue the court is deciding.

> On the evening of August 28, 1992, Jeffrey Czyzewski and a female companion went to a bar in Holyoke. At the bar, Czyzewski played a game of pool with the wife of Donald Sexton. Czyzewski briefly left the pool table. On his return, he accused Sexton's wife of cheating by moving the pool

balls during his absence. Ending the game, Czyzewski left the pool table and was thereafter approached three separate times by an agitated Donald Sexton, who demanded an apology. Czyzewski testified that after the second request, the defendant, Everett Sexton, the brother of Donald Sexton, approached Czyzewski and said that he would stand by his brother if anything happened. On the third occasion, Donald Sexton smashed a beer bottle on the bar, but was restrained before he could threaten Czyzewski further. Following this incident, the defendant, his brother, and his brother's wife left the bar.

Shortly thereafter, Czyzewski and his companion went out to the parking lot and got into their car. Immediately a van pulled up alongside them and the defendant, his brother, and a third man got out. The defendant and his brother kicked in the window on the passenger side where Czyzewski was sitting. The defendant reached through the shattered window to grab Czyzewski, attempting to pull him through the window. At that moment, Czyzewski's companion was able to start the car and drove out of the parking lot. As they pulled out, the Sextons said, "Let's go get him," and returned to the van to follow Czyzewski. Because their car was about to run out of gas, Czyzewski and his companion were forced to return to the parking lot, with the van following behind. Czyzewski left the vehicle and Donald Sexton, the defendant, and their companion left their van. The defendant and his brother immediately approached Czyzewski; they began to push and shove him. The defendant restrained Czyzewski by lifting Czyzewski's jacket over his head and the brothers threw Czyzewski to the ground. On the ground, Donald Sexton banged Czyzewski's head against the pavement a number of times while the defendant repeatedly kicked him. The beating was interrupted by the bar owner and another man. The Sexton brothers left before the police arrived.

To brief this case, you would outline the facts, not copy them; and you would eliminate unnecessary or irrelevant facts. Here is an example:

Facts: *This case involves a fight that occurred in a parking lot outside a bar in Holyoke, Massachusetts. Sexton and his brother pushed and shoved Czyzewski. They lifted Czyzewski's jacket over his head and threw him to the ground. On the ground, the brother banged Czyzewski's head against the pavement a number of times while Sexton repeatedly kicked him.*

After the facts, the court describes the procedural history and the rationale for the lower court's decision.

The Appeals Court held that the defendant possessed the requisite intent and knowledge to be guilty of assault and battery by means of a dangerous weapon on a joint venture theory, but reversed this conviction on the ground that "concrete pavement" is not a dangerous weapon under G.L. c. 265, § 15A. *Commonwealth v. Sexton, supra* at 678-679, 672 N.E.2d 991. At trial, the judge had instructed the jury that "concrete pavement" could be considered a dangerous weapon if the jury found that it was "used in such a way that [it was] capable of causing death or serious[] bodily injury to a person." While the Appeals Court agreed that "ordinarily the determination whether an object that is not dangerous per se is a dangerous weapon under § 15A is a question of fact for the jury," *Commonwealth v. Sexton*, 41 Mass. App. Ct. 676, 679, 672 N.E.2d 991 (1996), *citing Commonwealth v. Appleby*, 380 Mass. 296, 305, 402 N.E.2d 1051 (1980); *Commonwealth v. Marrero*, 19 Mass. App. Ct.

921, 922, 471 N.E.2d 1356 (1984), concrete pavement did not fit the statutory definition and thus "[did] not qualify as a dangerous weapon[ ] under § 15A as a matter of law." *Id., citing Commonwealth v. Shea,* 38 Mass. App. Ct. 7, 15, 644 N.E.2d 244 (1995) (ocean); *Commonwealth v. Davis,* 10 Mass. App. Ct. 190, 193, 406 N.E.2d 417 (1980) (human teeth). The Appeals Court reached this holding by reading *Commonwealth v. Shea, supra,* to conclude that a dangerous weapon "is an object or instrumentality that the batterer is able to wield to inflict serious injury or death upon another." *Commonwealth v. Sexton, supra.* Because the pavement was not an item with which the defendant "could arm himself," but was instead "simply part of the surroundings in which the defendant found himself while perpetrating an assault," *id.*, the Appeals Court rejected the Commonwealth's argument that, in the circumstances, the pavement met the statutory requirements because it was "used in a manner that was capable of producing serious bodily harm."

The Appeals Court also supported its decision by noting that "it is a well settled principle of statutory construction that criminal statutes are to be strictly construed." *Commonwealth v. Sexton, supra* at 679, 672 N.E.2d 991, *citing Commonwealth v. Campbell,* 415 Mass. 697, 699, 616 N.E.2d 430 (1993). In construing G.L. c. 265, § 15A, we note that the phrase "dangerous weapon" is not defined. Instead, we have consistently looked to our precedent in applying this label. We find nothing in our case law which precludes our holding today, *see Commonwealth v. Statham,* 38 Mass. App. Ct. 582, 584, 650 N.E.2d 358 (1995) (case law interpretation controls in absence of statutory definition), nor do we think it contravenes the intent of the Legislature, which chose to invoke greater penalties for assaults which threatened serious injury because an actor chose to employ a dangerous weapon.

Then the court states the issue and begins its analysis by summarizing prior opinions on this topic.

> This case presents an issue of first impression, in that we have not previously addressed whether stationary objects can be considered dangerous weapons in Massachusetts. The statute, G.L. c. 265, § 15A, does not define the term "dangerous weapon," but we have stated previously that there are things which are dangerous per se and those which are dangerous as used. *Commonwealth v. Appleby*, 380 Mass. 296, 303, 402 N.E.2d 1051 (1980). We have defined the former class as "instrumentalit[ies] designed and constructed to produce death or great bodily harm." *Id.* In the latter class are things which become dangerous weapons because they are "used in a dangerous fashion." *Id.* at 304, 402 N.E.2d 1051. In such cases it is generally "a question for the fact finder whether the instrument was so used in a particular case." *Id. Commonwealth v. Farrell*, 322 Mass. 606, 614-615, 78 N.E.2d 697 (1948). *See Commonwealth v. Davis, supra* at 193, 406 N.E.2d 417 (fact finder looks to the "circumstances surrounding the crime [including], the nature, size and shape of the object, and the manner in which it is handled or controlled"). In evaluating different situations, the determination has invariably turned on "use," and our courts have repeatedly held that ordinarily innocuous items can be considered dangerous weapons when used in an improper and dangerous manner. *See Commonwealth v. Scott*, 408 Mass. 811, 822-823, 564 N.E.2d 370 (1990) (gag); *Commonwealth v. Barrett*, 386 Mass. 649, 655-656, 436 N.E.2d 1219 (1982) (aerosol spray can); *Commonwealth v. Appleby, supra* at 304-305, 402 N.E.2d 1051 (riding crop); *Commonwealth v. Tarrant*, 367 Mass. 411, 418, 326 N.E.2d 710 (1975) (German shepherd dog); *Commonwealth v. Farrell, supra* at 615, 78 N.E.2d 697 (lighted

cigarettes); *Commonwealth v. Mercado*, 24 Mass. App. Ct. 391, 395, 509 N.E.2d 300 (1987) (baseball bat); *Commonwealth v. LeBlanc*, 3 Mass. App. Ct. 780, 780, 334 N.E.2d 647 (1975) (automobile door swung knocking police officer down). Our courts have also noted, with approval, decisions in other jurisdictions which have found otherwise innocent items to fit this classification when used in a way which endangers another's safety. *Commonwealth v. Appleby, supra* at 304, 402 N.E.2d 1051. *Commonwealth v. Davis, supra* at 192-193, 406 N.E.2d 417. *See United States v. Loman*, 551 F.2d 164, 169 (7th Cir.), *cert. denied*, 433 U.S. 912, 97 S.Ct. 2982, 53 L.Ed.2d 1097 (1977) (walking stick); *United States v. Johnson*, 324 F.2d 264, 266 (4th Cir.1963) (chair brought down upon victim's head); *People v. White*, 212 Cal.App.2d 464, 465, 28 Cal. Rptr. 67 (1963) (a rock); *Bennett v. State*, 237 Md. 212, 216, 205 A.2d 393 (1964) (microphone cord wrapped around victim's neck); *People v. Buford*, 69 Mich. App. 27, 30, 244 N.W.2d 351 (1976) (dictum) (automobile, broomstick, flashlight and lighter fluid may all be dangerous weapons as used).

To continue with the case brief, you would then state the issue, like this:

Issue: Whether concrete pavement can be considered a dangerous weapon.

You will notice my statement of the issue is more specific than the court's statement of the issue. I referred to the "concrete pavement" while the court just referred to "stationary objects." The issue usually involves the application of a legal principle to specific facts. Whether the court states the specific facts or not, you should state the issue as an application of law to specific facts in your case briefs.

It would be nice if all courts wrote case opinions in

a uniform way, and each of them specifically identified the relevant facts, the issue, the rule applicable to that issue, the holding and the reasoning for the decision. But it doesn't work that way. Case opinions may be used to educate law students, but judges do not write case opinions for that purpose. So you will often find the wording of the case needs to be translated for your case briefs. In addition, the court doesn't always explain its reasoning, so it is not unusual for you to have to extrapolate from what is there to determine what the reasoning must have been.

Next the court states its decision and, in this case, the court also explains the reasoning for its decision.

We do not agree with the Appeals Court that, to be a dangerous weapon, the defendant must be able to wield the item at issue, nor do we think it relevant that the pavement was present as part of the environment in which the defendant chose to participate in this assault. Prior to the Appeals Court's decision in *Commonwealth v. Shea, supra*, the only explicit restriction on our use-based categorization of dangerous weapons held that human teeth and other parts of the human body were not dangerous weapons because they are not "instrumentalities apart from the defendant's person." *Commonwealth v. Davis, supra* at 193, 406 N.E.2d 417. In *Shea*, a case in which the defendant pushed two women from his boat and sped off, leaving them five miles off shore, the Appeals Court found that, while "the ocean can be and often is dangerous, it cannot be regarded in its natural state as a weapon within the meaning of § 15A," because "in its natural state [it] cannot be possessed or controlled." *Commonwealth v. Shea, supra* at 15-16, 644 N.E.2d 244. We believe that this is too narrow a reading of the instrumentality and use language we have employed when we have defined dangerous weapons as "an instrument or instrumentality which, because of the manner in which it is used, or attempted to be used, endangers the life or inflicts great bodily harm." *Commonwealth v. Farrell, supra* at 615, 78 N.E.2d 697. While one might not be able to possess the ocean or exercise authority over it in a traditional sense, *Commonwealth v. Shea, supra* at 16, 644 N.E.2d 244, one could certainly use it to inflict great harm, such as by holding another's head underwater.1

Likewise, it is obvious that one could employ concrete pavement, as the defendant and his brother did here, to cause serious bodily harm to another by banging the victim's head against the hard surface. As the Commonwealth points out, there would be no problem in convicting a defendant of assault and battery by means of a dangerous weapon if he used a broken slab of concrete to bludgeon his victim. We see no reason to hold that such a conviction cannot stand merely because the instrumentality in question is a fixed thing at the time of its dangerous use.

A number of other jurisdictions which have considered this question have also held that an object's stationary character does not prevent its use as a dangerous weapon. *United States v. Murphy*, 35 F.3d 143, 147 (4th Cir.1994), cert. denied, 513 U.S. 1135, 115 S.Ct. 954, 130 L.Ed.2d 897 (1995) (steel cell bars); *State v. Brinson*, 337 N.C. 764, 766, 448 S.E.2d 822 (1994) (cell bars and floor); *People v. O'Hagan*, 176 A.D.2d 179, 179, 574 N.Y.S.2d 198 (1991) (cell bars); *People v. Coe*, 165 A.D.2d 721, 722, 564 N.Y.S.2d 255 (1990) (plate glass window); *State v. Reed*, 101 Or. App. 277, 279-280, 790 P.2d 551 (1990) (sidewalk); *People v. Galvin*, 65 N.Y.2d 761, 762-763, 492 N.Y.S.2d 25, 481 N.E.2d 565 (1985) (same).2 As North Carolina recognized, an item's dangerous propensities "often depend [ ] entirely on its use," *State v. Brinson, supra* at 769, 448 S.E.2d 822, and not its mobility, for "[w]hether the pitcher hits the stone or the stone hits the pitcher, it will

> be bad for the pitcher." *State v. Reed, supra* at 280, 790 P.2d 551, quoting Cervantes, Don Quixote, Part II, ch. 43 (1615). We hold that one who intentionally uses concrete pavement as a means of inflicting serious harm can be found guilty of assault and battery by means of a dangerous weapon.

Sometimes you have to tease the holding, rule and reasoning from the court's opinion, as they are not often separately stated. In this case, however, the holding is stated at the end of the previous paragraph. To state it in a case brief, you would just paraphrase the language to track the language of the issue, like this:

> *Holding:* *Concrete pavement can be considered a dangerous weapon.*

As for the rule, the court refers to the rule in a number of places, and then clearly states it by quoting from the case of *Com.v. Farrell*.

> *Rule:* *A dangerous weapon is "an instrument or instrumentality which, because of the manner in which it is used, or attempted to be used, endangers the life or inflicts great bodily harm."*

Once you have stated the facts, the issue, the holding and the rule, you would then paraphrase the court's reasoning. Here is how I did it for this case:

> *Reasoning:* *The defendant does not have to be able to "wield" an item for it to be a dangerous weapon; and it is irrelevant whether the instrumentality is part of the environment. If the defendant used a broken slab of concrete to bludgeon his victim, the slab would be a dangerous weapon.*

The result should not be different "merely because the instrumentality in question is a fixed thing at the time of its dangerous use."

In the rest of the case the court dispenses with a second issue that is not relevant to the topic for this brief. (Even though they are called "case briefs" they are really briefs of a specific issue dealt with in a case, so the parts of the case that deal with other issues need not be included.)

> Finally, we agree with the Appeals Court that the jury were presented with sufficient evidence to find that the defendant possessed the requisite intent and knowledge to be guilty of assault and battery by means of a dangerous weapon under a joint venture theory. From the defendant's statements and actions it is apparent that he possessed the intent to engage in an assault and battery with his brother. While he may not initially have had knowledge that his brother intended to use the pavement to effectuate the attack, as the Appeals Court noted, "there is no need to prove an anticipatory compact between the parties to establish joint venture," *Commonwealth v. Sexton, supra* at 678, 672 N.E.2d 991, *citing Commonwealth v. Fidler*, 23 Mass. App. Ct. 506, 513, 503 N.E.2d 1302 (1987), if, "at the climactic moment the parties consciously acted together in carrying out the criminal endeavor." *Commonwealth v. Young*, 35 Mass. App. Ct. 427, 435, 621 N.E.2d 1180 (1993). The defendant continuously kicked and punched Czyzewski while his brother repeatedly slammed Czyzewski's head into the pavement. At no time during this conflict did the defendant seek to withdraw.

At the end of the case is the ultimate disposition, and the "footnotes" for the text of the opinion (they are really "endnotes" but the publishers usually call them "footnotes.").

The conviction of assault and battery by means of a dangerous weapon is affirmed.

So ordered.

FOOTNOTES

1.   While we take issue with some of the reasoning in *Shea*, we do not necessarily disagree with the result the court reached in that case.   In *Shea*, the danger posed by the ocean was not a result of the defendant bringing his victims into contact with that body of water, but rather the circumstances which followed when he deserted them, five miles from shore.   We contrast this to a situation in which a defendant might drop his victim into a vat of acid, in which the mere contact with the substance would directly pose the risk of serious bodily harm.

2.   While other jurisdictions have taken a contrary position, we do not find them sufficiently apposite.   In *Edwards v. United States*, 583 A.2d 661, 663-664 (D.C.1990), in determining whether bathroom fixtures could be considered dangerous weapons, the court was applying a statute which addressed crimes committed by a person "armed with or having readily available any pistol or other firearm . or other dangerous or deadly weapon," which went on to enumerate the types of specific instrumentalities the statute contemplated, carrying with its violation a possible life sentence.   Although the Supreme Court of Louisiana rejected concrete as a dangerous weapon, it did so in the context of a defendant striking his victim and "caus[ing] him to fall upon the concrete and sustain injuries," *State v. Legendre*, 362 So.2d 570, 571 (La.1978), a scenario quite different from the purposeful and deliberate use of the pavement as a means of beating another which we must examine.   Likewise, a Missouri appellate court found it "untenable to suggest that the dangerous instrument or deadly weapon components" of its statute were implicated

in a case where the defendant beat a woman against a door casing and plumbing fixtures, but only considered whether the defendant's fists met this definition, never addressing the defendant's use of stationary objects he employed. *State v. Johnson*, 770 S.W.2d 263, 269 (Mo.Ct.App.1989). Only *State v. Houck*, 652 So.2d 359, 360 (Fla.1995) (pavement and other passive objects not considered weapons as matter of law), directly contradicts our holding.

Here is what a finished case brief would look like:

Com. v. Sexton

Facts: This case involves a fight that occurred in a parking lot outside a bar in Holyoke, Massachusetts. Sexton and his brother pushed and shoved Czyzewski. They lifted Czyzewski's jacket over his head and threw him to the ground. On the ground, the brother banged Czyzewski's head against the pavement a number of times while Sexton repeatedly kicked him.

Issue: Whether concrete pavement can be considered a dangerous weapon.

Holding: Concrete pavement can be considered a dangerous weapon.

Rule: A dangerous weapon is "an instrument or instrumentality which, because of the manner in which it is used, or attempted to be used, endangers the life or inflicts great bodily harm."

> *Reasoning:*   *The defendant does not have to be able to "wield" an item for it to be a dangerous weapon; and it is irrelevant whether the instrumentality is part of the environment. If the defendant used a broken slab of concrete to bludgeon his victim, the slab would be a dangerous weapon. The result should not be different "merely because the instrumentality in question is a fixed thing at the time of its dangerous use."*

Case brief formats vary in the level of detail they include. As I said in the beginning, you could also include the original procedural history and ultimate disposition. If there is a dissenting opinion, you could summarize that as well. The most detailed case brief is likely the best, but taking that time to brief every case you read with a very high level of detail is not an option for many law students.

What some law students end up doing to save time is "margin briefing." For example, instead of figuring out what facts are relevant and writing them down, the student will just circle the fact section in the opinion and write "facts" in the margin. That works o.k. for some sections of the brief, and it definitely saves time. The problem is, again, the elements of a brief are often not specifically stated in an opinion; and you won't learn them if you don't take the time to figure out what they are. So you won't learn as much by briefing that way.

Once you have briefed all the cases, the semester is over and you are studying for an exam, you may want to distill the briefs even further to annotate your outline of what the course covered. In that situation, make sure you include, at a minimum, answers to the following three questions. What happened? What did the court decide? And why did the court decide the case that way? For example, if I were doing an outline of my criminal law course to study for the final exam, I would probably annotate my outline with case cites and brief summaries of what I learned from each case. In that situation, my summary of *Com. v. Sexton* might just be something like this:

> The defendant banged the victim's head into stationary concrete. The court held the defendant committed assault and battery with a dangerous weapon. Hitting someone over the head with a piece of concrete would have satisfied the elements of the crime; this was basically the same thing, except the other way around. Com. v. Sexton

I know that's really brief, but that does capture the essence of what was decided in that case. A more detailed brief would be better but I found I could only cram so much information into my head for a final exam. If the course only covered a few cases, then I would have done a more detailed summary. But a semester course in criminal law usually covers a lot of cases. My criminal law exam was closed book, so I had to commit to memory what I learned from each case. Plus criminal law wasn't the only course I took that semester. You may be able to do more, but I found I needed something more concise than a case brief to study for final exams.

When you start practicing law you will likely want to adopt an even more precise approach to reading cases. When I am doing research now, I initially skip the case headnotes, skim through the background information, the procedural history, and any discussion of prior cases. What I am looking for is how the court applied the rule to the specific facts of the case. That is at the precedent at the core of every case. I find that first and then decide whether the case is appropriate for whatever analysis I am doing. If it is then go back to see if there are other things in the opinion I can use or need to review to fully understand the decision.

In law school, the situation is different. You need to learn the process more than the rules; and your professor has already determined the cases you are asked to read are relevant and useful for understanding whatever subject you are being taught. So it would be mistake to just take notes on the "black letter law" in each case. You need to also understand the reasoning, and you need to be able to determine which facts are relevant and which are not. If you don't accomplish that you won't be able to apply the rule to an exam question or a research issue. That is why law students don't just read cases, they brief them. When it is time for finals you can further distill the information in your brief but that doesn't mean you should skip the process of briefing cases as you read them.

Having learned how to do a case brief, we have what we need to apply the cases to a legal issue, either by analogizing or distinguishing the relevant facts.

4. APPLYING CASES AND ANALOGICAL REASONING

When you are sitting in your torts class, or your property class, or your contracts class, listening to your professor talk about case decisions, you may wonder, as I did when I was in law school, why the professor doesn't just tell you what the rules are (i.e. what is the "black letter law"), like they do in supplements (in my day they were called "horn books"). Hundreds of years ago, when Christopher Columbus Langdell founded the Harvard Law School, he decided it would be best not to do that, but rather to train lawyers using the case book method.

If your tort professor just told you liability in a tort case depends on whether the party exercised "reasonable care," you wouldn't be able to do very much with that information. The legal rule is purposely vague. As a result, you can't apply it without looking at some examples. To put it another way, you need to read the cases – and pay particular attention to the facts of the cases - to fully understand what the rule is.

If you have a reported case that says a specific type

of conduct is unreasonable, and your case involves conduct that is similar, you analyze your case by drawing analogies to the reported case to support the inference that the judge in your case should come to the same result as the judge in the reported case. And in order to make those analogies, you need to know what all the characteristics of the reported case are, including, among other things, the facts, the holding and the rationale. A case brief is an outline of those characteristics. A case brief is an outline of the information you need to do a case analogy.

A. Analogizing a Case to a Fact Pattern

To demonstrate how to do a case analogy, I'll start with an example of a tort case. Suppose you have a client named Margaret Bradbury. Ms. Bradbury rents an apartment at "Ocean Park at Ponte Vedra," an apartment complex in Jacksonville Beach, Florida. She was injured recently when she fell in her shower, and she wants to sue her landlord for damages.

Ms. Bradbury tells you that she was taking a shower in her apartment, like she did every morning. Her back was sore as a result of some gardening she had done the day before. When she got out of the shower she needed a little support. There is a rail next to the shower door she had been using as a towel rack. As she exited, she grabbed the rail for support, and it ripped right out of the wall and caused her to fall. She couldn't tell by looking at it but the rail was apparently not securely attached to the wall. As a result of the fall, Ms. Bradbury suffered personal injuries, including a badly sprained ankle and wrist. She has medical expenses and lost wages, and she blames the landlord for what she feels was an unsafe condition in her apartment.

Now suppose you do some research and find a case that seems analogous to your case. The case says that a landlord has a duty to "reasonably inspect the premises before allowing the tenant to take possession, and to make the repairs necessary to transfer a reasonably safe dwelling unit to the tenant." The case is Fitzgerald v. Cestari. Read through the case to analyze Ocean Park's liability for transferring the unit to Ms. Bradbury with the allegedly unsafe rail in her shower; and brief the case as you read it. Also, assume for the purposes of this example that there is no violation of the building code in Ms. Bradbury's case.

---

569 So. 2d 1258 (1990)

Terry FITZGERALD, Etc., Petitioner,

v.

Jan CESTARI, et Ux., Respondents.

No. 75538.

Supreme Court of Florida.

November 8, 1990.

Kenneth R. Drake of Touby, Smith, Demahy & Drake, Miami, for petitioner.

Richard A. Sherman and Rosemary B. Wilder of the Law Offices of Richard A. Sherman, P.A., Fort Lauderdale, for respondents.

EHRLICH, Justice.

We have for review Fitzgerald v. Cestari, 553 So. 2d 708 (Fla. 4th DCA 1989), because of apparent conflict with the decisions of several district courts of appeal. We have jurisdiction, article V, section (3)(b)(3), Florida Constitution, and approve the decision below.

Petitioner, Terry Fitzgerald, filed suit against the

Cestaris seeking damages for injuries suffered by her seven-year-old daughter, Brandi, when Brandi ran through a sliding glass door in a single family dwelling owned by the Cestaris and leased by the Cavanaughs. The accident *1259 occurred while Brandi was visiting the Cavanaughs. The complaint alleges that the sliding glass door which was in the rear of the house and which previously had been opened was closed while Brandi was playing in the front yard. Brandi ran through the house, en route to her grandparents' house which was behind the house occupied by the Cavanaughs, colliding with the door. The glass door was not made of safety glass and had no decals or other markings on it. Count I of the amended complaint alleged that the Cestaris breached their duty of care to keep the premises in a reasonably safe condition and to give timely notice of latent or concealed perils, by failing to place decals or other markings on the sliding glass door, and by failing to inspect and repair the sliding glass door because it was not composed of safety glass, as required by the Southern Standard Building Code. Count II alleged that Brandi was a member of the class which was to be protected by the Southern Standard Building Code and, therefore, the Cestaris' failure to maintain their premises in conformity with the code constituted negligence per se.

The Cestaris filed a motion for summary judgment, asserting that the lack of safety glass was a latent defect that was not discoverable by them through normal inspection and that, under the doctrine of Slavin v. Kay, 108 So. 2d 462 (Fla. 1958), it was the negligence of the original builder of the premises, who installed the doors, that was the proximate cause of the injuries. In an affidavit filed in support of the motion for summary judgment, Jan Cestari asserted that the glass in the door was the original glass installed in the home when he purchased it; that he and his family were unaware of the type of glass that comprised the door; and that the type of glass in the door was not readily discoverable by his inspection.

The trial court granted summary judgment, finding that as a matter of law the Cestaris had no duty to investigate and determine the type of glass used in the doors and that the Cestaris had no duty to place decals or other markings on the door. A transcript of the deposition of Norman Spangler, [1] a sliding glass door expert, was filed in conjunction with Fitzgerald's motion for rehearing which was denied. Mr. Spangler testified that there are several types of safety glass, including tempered glass, laminated glass and wired glass which could be used in sliding glass doors. However, the only type of safety glass he had seen used in such doors was tempered glass. He testified that one cannot tell if a sliding glass door is tempered or untempered by the look of the glass. This can be determined by looking for markings in the corners of the glass. According to Mr. Spangler, tempered glass typically is imprinted with the manufacturer's name, the thickness of the glass and the fact that the glass is tempered. Mr. Spangler testified that to his knowledge, nonsafety glass has no markings at all. He further testified that a person not in the sliding glass door business would have to call a glass shop to learn that if there are no markings on the glass in a sliding glass door it is not tempered for safety.

On appeal, the Fourth District Court of Appeal affirmed. The court reasoned that, as a matter of law, the defect in the sliding glass door was a latent defect of which the Cestaris had no knowledge and which reasonable inspection would not have disclosed to them. The court held that under the Slavin doctrine it is the original builder who should be held accountable for the injury. 553 So. 2d at 709. The district court also rejected Fitzgerald's argument that a line of Florida cases, including Peppermint Twist, Inc. v. Wright, 169 So.

2d 330 (Fla. 3d DCA 1964) and <u>Canner v. Blank</u>, 152 So. 2d 193 (Fla. 3d DCA 1963), establish that cases involving sliding glass doors present factual questions for the jury. The district court concluded that those cases were not applicable because in those cases the unresolved issues being submitted to the jury involved the contributory negligence of the injured minor plaintiff and contributory negligence is not an issue in this case. <u>Id.</u>

*1260 As a starting point in our analysis, it is important to note that there are two distinct claims presented in this case: 1) that the Cestaris were negligent for failing to ascertain that the door was not made of safety glass and for failing to conform their premises to the Southern Standard Building Code which requires safety glass be used in sliding glass doors; and 2) that the Cestaris were negligent for failing to place decals or other markings on the door.[2] We agree that, on this record, summary judgment was properly entered on both of these claims.

Although it is not apparent from the decision below, the Cestaris were lessors of the subject premises rather than owners in possession. Each of the decisions which appear to conflict with the decision below involved a defendant who had possession and control of the premises at the time of the accident.[3] As we noted in <u>Mansur v. Eubanks</u>, 401 So. 2d 1328, 1329 (Fla. 1981), traditionally a landlord was not liable for injuries resulting from the condition of the leased premises. See Restatement (Second) of Torts § 356 (1965); and W. Keeton, Prosser and Keeton on the Law of Torts § 63 (5th ed. 1984). However, in <u>Mansur</u>, this Court extended a landlord's liability, holding that

the owner of a residential dwelling unit, who leases it to a tenant for residential purposes, has a duty to reasonably inspect the premises before allowing the tenant to take possession, and to make the repairs necessary to transfer a reasonably safe dwelling unit to the tenant unless defects are waived by the tenant...

After the tenant takes possession, the landlord has a continuing duty to exercise reasonable care to repair dangerous defective conditions upon notice of their existence by the tenant, unless waived by the tenant.

Mansur, 401 So.2d at 1329-30.

First, we agree with the district court that under this Court's decision in Slavin, the Cestaris are relieved from liability for failing to ascertain that the sliding glass door was not made of safety glass as required by the applicable building code. It is undisputed that the dangerous condition, in this case a lack of safety glass, was not discoverable through a reasonable inspection by the owners. Cf. Lubell v. Roman Spa, Inc., 362 So. 2d 922 (Fla. 1978). According to the deposition testimony of Mr. Spangler, while there are markings on tempered glass, which could be identified by one familiar with such markings, there are no markings on untempered glass. This testimony supports Jan Cestari's contention that the type of glass in the doors was not readily discoverable by his inspection. It is, therefore, undisputed that a reasonable inspection of the doors by the Cestaris would not have put them on notice of the dangerous condition. Cf. Becker v. IRM Corp., 38 Cal. 3d 454, 213 Cal. Rptr. 213, 698 P.2d 116 (1985) (summary judgment improper where glass causing injury was marked "untempered," because trier of fact could find reasonable inspection by landlord would have included visual inspection which disclosed the danger). As noted above, a lessor of a residential dwelling unit has a duty to reasonably inspect the premises before allowing the lessee to take possession. However, our decision in Mansur does not place a duty on a landlord to inquire of experts concerning the type of glass in sliding glass doors on the premises.

Likewise, while the Cestaris had a duty to reasonably inspect the premises for dangerous conditions and to transfer the premises in a reasonably safe condition, we *1261 agree with the trial court's ruling that, as a matter of law, they had no duty to place decals or other markings on the sliding glass door. An ordinary sliding glass door is not the type of "dangerous condition" which a landlord is in a better position than the tenant to guard against.[4] The presence of a sliding glass door on the leased premises was clearly apparent to the lessees who, upon taking possession, controlled the manner in which it was used. Whether a sliding glass door creates a hidden dangerous condition giving rise to a duty to warn generally depends upon the surrounding circumstances, i.e., location of the door, age of the injured party, lighting conditions, pattern of an open door, and activities on the premises. See, e.g., Giordano v. Mariano, 112 N.J. Super. 311, 271 A.2d 20 (1970); Shannon v. Butler Homes, Inc., 102 Ariz. 312, 428 P.2d 990 (1967). It therefore follows that the duty to warn Brandi of the hidden danger the closed door may have presented rested solely upon the lessees, who were in control of the premises. See Bovis v. 7-Eleven, Inc., 505 So. 2d 661 (Fla. 5th DCA 1987) (lessees of premises have duty to warn third parties of dangerous conditions on premises because such duty rests on right to control premises rather than on legal ownership of the dangerous area).

Accordingly, the decision of the district court affirming the entry of summary judgment in favor of the respondents is approved.

It is so ordered.

SHAW, C.J., and OVERTON, McDONALD, BARKETT, GRIMES and KOGAN, JJ., concur.

NOTES

[1] It appears this testimony was proffered at the hearing on the motion for summary judgment.

[2] Although Fitzgerald urges liability for failure to comply with section 83.51(1)(a), Florida Statutes (1983), which requires a landlord to maintain leased premises in compliance with the requirements of the applicable building code, this claim was not raised in the amended complaint or urged to the trial court and therefore will not be addressed by this Court.

[3] See Hannabass v. Florida Home Insurance Co., 412 So. 2d 376 (Fla. 2nd DCA 1981); Peppermint Twist, Inc. v. Wright, 169 So. 2d 330 (Fla. 3rd DCA 1964); Canner v. Blank, 152 So. 2d 193 (Fla. 3rd DCA 1963); McCain v. Bankers Life & Casualty Co., 110 So. 2d 718 (Fla. 3rd DCA), cert. denied, 114 So. 2d 3 (Fla. 1959).

[4] This claim must be analyzed as if the glass door were in compliance with the building code because it has already been determined that the Cestaris could not have discovered the lack of safety glass through a reasonable inspection. Further, it is alleged that it was the lack of decals not the lack of safety glass which caused the accident. The lack of safety glass merely affected the nature and extent of the injury.

Now use the information in your case brief to analyze the issue by doing a case analogy. Start by explaining Fitzgerald: tell the reader what happened, what the court decided and why. Here is an example,

In Fitzgerald v. Cestari, 569 So.2d 1258 (Fla. 1990), a tenant's visitor, Terry Fitzgerald, filed suit against the owners of the property the tenant rented, the Cestaris, seeking damages for injuries suffered by the visitor's seven-year-old daughter, when the daughter ran through a sliding glass door in the property. The daughter was playing in the front yard and ran through the house, colliding with the door. "The door was not made of safety glass and had no decals or other markings on it."

Based on these facts, the court held that the Cestaris did not fail to "reasonably inspect the premises" by not ascertaining that the sliding glass door was not made of safety glass. The dangerous condition, the lack of safety glass, was not discoverable through a "reasonable inspection" by the owners. According to the deposition testimony of an expert witness, "while there are markings on tempered glass, which could be identified by one familiar with such markings, there are no markings on untempered glass." Therefore, there was no breach of any duty to inspect the premises and deliver the unit in safe condition.

After you have explained the case precedent, apply the case to the fact pattern. Start by explaining what happened to Ms. Bradbury and comparing the fact pattern to the facts of Fitzgerald, then apply the reasoning of the reported case to the fact pattern, and come to a conclusion. If the facts are analogous and the reasoning applies, the conclusion should be the same as well.

Our case involves a claim by a tenant against a property owner for personal injuries suffered by the tenant during her occupancy of the unit. Our client, Margaret Bradbury, rented an apartment at "Ocean Park at Ponte Vedra," an apartment complex in Jacksonville Beach. Bradbury was injured exiting the shower in her apartment. Apparently, there was a rail on the wall next to the shower door. When Bradbury exited the shower she used the rail as support, and it ripped out of the wall. As a result, Bradbury fell and suffered personal injuries.

Bradbury's case is analogous to the Fitzgerald case.

In both cases the plaintiff was injured because of an allegedly defective condition in an apartment owned by the defendant. Like the owner in <u>Fitzgerald</u>, Ocean Park had a duty to reasonably inspect the premises before allowing Bradbury to take possession. However, the insufficiently affixed rail in Bradbury's case, like the untempered glass door in <u>Fitzgerald</u>, is not something that would have been discoverable through a "reasonable inspection" by the owner; it is not something Ocean Park would have discovered in an inspection of the unit. The Cestaris would not have been able to determine the glass door was untempered by looking at it. And Ocean Park would not have been able to determine the rail in Ms. Bradbury's shower was not sufficiently affixed to the wall by looking at it either. Therefore, a court will likely find that Ocean Park did not breach any duty to reasonably inspect the apartment and deliver it in safe condition.

That is an example of how you analogize a case to a fact pattern. Don't just state the rule and apply it to the facts. You need to explain the case first by describing the facts in particular. Then you apply the case by comparing the facts to the fact pattern. If they are analogous then the rule of the case should apply to the fact pattern the same way it applied to the facts of the reported case. The Bradbury case should come out the same way the <u>Fitzgerald</u> case did. In other words, Ocean Park will likely not be found negligent.

B. <u>Distinguishing a Case From a Fact Pattern</u>

Now let's look at another example, this one to demonstrate how to distinguish a case from a fact pattern. Suppose you have another client named Bill Haley. Mr. Haley lives on the famous Bourbon Street in New Orleans. He loves it there because of all the local restaurants. And his favorite place to eat is the Swine Depot, a local restaurant well known for its delicious pork ribs.

Last week Mr. Haley was eating a pulled pork sandwich at the Depot and had a bad experience. He took a bite of the sandwich and started coughing, like he had swallowed something that he couldn't digest. He could still breathe but his condition worsened, and he was taken to the emergency room. A doctor there performed an operation and removed a piece of pig bone that was lodged in Haley's throat. The bone was ¾ of an inch long. Mr. Haley blames the restaurant for not removing it from the sandwich and now wants you to file a lawsuit on his behalf.

After the complaint was filed you took the deposition of Billy Bob, the chef at the Depot. His testimony was that a pulled pork sandwich is made by pulling cooked pork into small strips by hand. He says "a piece of bone such as the piece ingested by Haley normally would be discovered and removed during his preparation of the meat." When asked why it was not, Chef Billy Bob could offer no explanation.

You then go to law library at the local courthouse to do some research. You could do it on your computer but it is a nice day and you enjoy getting out of the office. Anyway, as a result of your research, you find the Louisiana case of Porteous v. St. Ann's Cafe & Deli, which appears to deal with the issue at hand. According to Porteous, a chef has a duty "to act as a reasonably prudent man skilled in the culinary art" in preparing food, including removing injurious substances. Here is the case (I deleted the dissenting opinion to keep it relatively short):

713 So.2d 454 (1998)

Donald C. PORTEOUS, Jr.

v.

ST. ANN'S CAFE & DELI and Lafayette Insurance Company.

No. 97-C-0837.

Supreme Court of Louisiana.

May 29, 1998.

Geoffrey H. Longenecker, Madisonville, for Applicant.

Alexander Adam Lambert, John Thomas Holmes, Metairie, for Respondent.

*455 CALOGERO, Chief Justice.[*]

On January 22, 1995, Donald C. Porteous, Jr. was dining at St. Ann's Cafe & Deli. While eating the second half of an oyster poboy, he bit down onto a small, grey, and roughly round substance, which apparently was a pearl. When plaintiff bit onto the pearl, he broke a tooth and cracked it all the way down the shaft. The plaintiff reported the incident to a waiter. The waiter wrote an incident report and took possession of the remainder of the sandwich and the pearl. Two days later, plaintiff went to his dentist and thereafter underwent dental treatment, which included a root canal and placement of a crown atop the broken tooth. The plaintiff then sued St. Ann's Cafe & Deli and Lafayette Insurance Company, alleging that the defendant was negligent because of the lack of adequate food inspection procedures, which resulted in the presence of an injurious substance and his sustaining injury to his tooth.

In determining whether the defendant was liable for the plaintiff's injuries, the trial court applied the "foreign-natural" test. That test was adopted from the common law. Louisiana courts of appeal have used this common law test to determine the liability of a restaurant when a customer is injured by a harmful substance in the restaurant's food. Melady v. Wendy's of New Orleans, Inc., 95-913 (La. App.

5th Cir. 4/16/96); 673 So.2d 1094; Johnson v. South Pacific Canning Co., 580 So.2d 556 (La. App. 5th Cir. 1991); Riviere v. J.C. Penney Comp., 478 So.2d 965 (La. App. 5th Cir.1985); Title v. Pontchartrain Hotel, 449 So.2d 677 (La. App. 4th Cir.1984); Loyacano v. Continental Ins., 283 So.2d 302 (La. App. 4th Cir.1973); Musso v. Picadilly Cafeterias, Inc., 178 So.2d 421 (La. App. 1st Cir.1965). Under the foreign natural test, if the injurious substance is foreign to the food, then the restaurant is strictly liable. If the injurious substance is natural to the food, there is no strict liability. Rather, liability is imposed only if the restaurant was negligent in failing to discover and remove the harmful natural substance from the food.

After applying the foreign-natural test, the trial court held that although the injurious pearl was natural to the oyster, the restaurant was negligent, and therefore liable, because of the lack of adequate procedures to ensure that injurious substances, such as a pearl in the oyster, were not served on the po-boys. The plaintiff was then awarded damages plus costs and interest.

The court of appeal recited the facts found by the trial court and declared that the "trial court's determination of credibility and findings of fact will not be disturbed on appeal so long as they are reasonable in light of the record as a whole." The court of appeal concluded that the trial court's finding that the restaurant negligently failed to institute procedures to intercept harmful objects in the oysters was a reasonable finding and would not be disturbed on appeal. Thus, the trial court was affirmed in the court of appeal. Porteous v. St. Ann's Cafe & Deli No. 96-CA-2692 (La. App. 4th Cir. 3/5/97) (unpublished opinion).

We granted certiorari to determine if the law and the facts were properly applied in this restaurant-harmful food product case, a precise matter which has not been addressed in recent decades by this Court. For the reasons that follow, we find that the lower courts erred in applying the common law foreign-natural test. Rather, the proper analysis to determine the defendant's liability is to be found in Louisiana's substantive law as found in the Louisiana Civil Code in the articles relating to liability and damages for offenses and quasi offenses—the traditional duty risk tort analysis.[1] With the entire record now in hand, we hold that, under the *456 traditional duty risk tort analysis, the plaintiff has failed to prove that the defendant breached its duty to act as would a reasonably prudent restaurateur in selecting, preparing and cooking food, including removal of injurious substances. We therefore reverse the judgments of the lower courts.[2]

DISCUSSION

In the recent decades, this Court has not spoken on this issue and the Louisiana Courts of Appeal have borrowed the foreign natural test from the common law. We decline to adopt that test.[3]

The Civil Code is the chief repository of the substantive law of Louisiana, and as previously indicated, the theory of recovery available to an injured plaintiff to determine the liability of a restaurant in a case of this sort is the determination of negligence with the traditional duty risk tort analysis. See La. Civ. Code Ann. arts. 2315, 2316.

TORT CLAIM

Articles 2315 and 2316 are the codal bases for a claim in tort. Article 2315 states that "[e]very act whatever of man that causes damage to another obliges him by whose fault it happened to repair it." Article 2316 provides that "[e]very person is responsible for the damage he occasions not merely by his act, but by his negligence, his *457 imprudence, or his want of skill." To determine whether a defendant is negligent, the case usually requires proof of five separate elements: (1) duty; (2) breach of duty; (3) cause-in-fact; (4) scope of liability or scope of protection; and (5) damages. Roberts v. Benoit, 605 So.2d 1032, 1051 (La.1991) (on rehearing) (citing Fowler v. Roberts, 556 So.2d 1, 4 (La.1989) (on original hearing)). Relative to these five elements, the case at hand turns on two of the elements—the issue of the defendant's duty and the defendant's breach of duty—discussion regarding which follows.

Duty of the Defendant

A defendant's duty to conform his conduct to a specific standard may be express or implied, either statutorily or jurisprudentially. Faucheaux v. Terrebonne Consolidated Government, 615 So. 2d 289, 292 (La.1993). In Louisiana, there is no statute which expressly addresses a commercial restaurant's duty to serve food free of injurious substances. [4] There is, nonetheless, no doubt that there is and should be such a duty. We determine that the duty is the following: A food provider, in selecting, preparing and cooking food, including the removal of injurious substances, has a duty to act as would a reasonably prudent man skilled in the culinary art in the selection and preparation of food.[5]

Breach of Duty

Plaintiff alleges that the defendant restaurant breached its duty by acting unreasonably in the selection, preparation and cooking of the food because the restaurant lacked adequate inspection procedures to detect and remove injurious substances from the food served to its customers. The defendant, on the other hand, asserts that it did not breach its duty because it acted reasonably in the selection and preparation of the food product at issue.

In determining whether a restaurant breached its duty by failing to act reasonably in the selection, preparation and cooking of the food that contained a substance which caused injury, the court should consider, among other things, whether the injurious substance was natural to the food served and whether the customer would reasonably expect to find such a substance in the particular type of food served. [6]

In the present case, the plaintiff was injured when he bit onto a pearl while eating an oyster po-boy in the defendant restaurant. A pearl in an oyster is not entirely rare, but is, indeed, a naturally occurring phenomenon. So long as oysters are harvested and eaten, there will occasionally, though perhaps infrequently, be pearls found in oysters. Furthermore, when eating oysters, a customer should be aware of—and alert to the possibility—that a pearl may be found within the oyster.

Additionally, at trial, the restaurant manager, Ms. Marvez, testified that an accident like this had never occurred before in her restaurant. Ms. Marvez further stated that the restaurant buys its oysters pre-shucked, pre-washed, and pre-packed from a reputable seafood company. When Ms. Marvez was asked about the restaurant's procedures to ensure that there were no foreign objects in the oysters, she replied that "the cook has to *458 physically hold the oyster and bread it and at that time they could feel if there's anything in there. If it's something large or if it's something—now if it's embedded in the oyster, no, we don't dissect the oyster...." She also stated that the cooks have to grab the oysters to bread them, and if they were to find an object, they would remove it. She did not recall any time when she was told that a cook found an object in an oyster. Moreover, although the cooks do not wash the oysters before they are battered, the cooks do visually inspect the oysters and touch them before applying the batter.

In light of the above-described testimony, we

determine that the defendant did not act unreasonably in selecting, preparing and cooking the food. There was nothing more the defendant restaurant could reasonably have done to eliminate the small possibility that a customer might find a pearl in an oyster and be injured thereby.[7] The law should not impose upon restaurants the responsibility of dissecting every oyster in order to determine whether there is a pearl formed or forming inside each one. We determine, therefore, under the traditional duty risk tort analysis, that the defendant restaurant did not breach its duty to this plaintiff and, thus, is not liable for the plaintiff's injury.

DECREE

For the foregoing reasons, the judgments of the district court and the court of appeal in favor of plaintiff are reversed. Judgment is rendered in favor of the defendants, dismissing plaintiff's suit with prejudice and at his cost.

DISTRICT COURT AND COURT OF APPEAL JUDGMENTS REVERSED; JUDGMENT RENDERED FOR DEFENDANT; SUIT DISMISSED WITH PREJUDICE AT PLAINTIFF'S COST.

[1] Two other areas of substantive law that arguably could apply in this case were the sales and obligation articles on breach of contract and the sales articles on redhibition. See LeBlanc v. La. Coca Cola Bottling Co., 221 La. 919, 60 So.2d 873 (1952); Doyle v. Fuerst & Kraemer, 129 La. 838, 56 So. 906 (1911); Demars v. Natchitoches Coca-Cola Bottling Co., 353 So.2d 433 (La. App. 3rd Cir.1977); Givens v. Baton Rouge Coca-Cola Bottling Co., 182 So.2d 532 (La. App. 1st Cir. 1966); McAvin v. Morrison Cafeteria Co. of La, 85 So.2d 63 (La. App. Orl.1956); Ogden v. Rosedale Inn, 189 So. 162 (La. App.Orl.1939). This Court, however, finds that the duty risk tort analysis in Louisiana negligence law is the proper analysis for this type of case.

[2] Under this Court's standards for granting writs (See

Rule X, Section 1 of the Louisiana Supreme Court Rules), the Court does not normally grant simply to review the facts of a case. In this case, we granted the writ because in the jurisprudence of this Court, the legal issue here was an unresolved one. (See Rule X, Section 1(a)(2) of the Louisiana Supreme Court Rules.) After granting certiorari, this Court has the authority to decide any and all issues in the case. La. Const. art. 5, § 5(C).

[3] The following is a more detailed explanation of the two common law tests to which reference was made earlier in this opinion, the foreign natural test and the reasonable expectation test, which have been utilized by state courts to determine the restaurant's liability, when a plaintiff sustains injuries because of an injurious substance in food he is served in a restaurant. Under either test, courts have no difficulty holding a defendant strictly liable for injuries sustained because of "foreign" injurious substances (such as glass or insects). See LeBlanc v. Louisiana Coca Cola Bottling Co., 221 La. 919, 60 So. 2d 873 (1952). But, if the injurious substance is "natural" to the food product, such as bones or shells, courts, depending on whether they follow the foreign-natural test or the reasonable expectation test, are divided as to whether liability should be imposed. See Langiulli v. Bumble Bee Seafood, Inc., 159 Misc.2d 450, 604 N.Y.S.2d 1020 (N.Y.Sup.1993); Jackson v. Nestle-Beich, Inc., 147 Ill.2d 408, 168 Ill. Dec. 147, 589 N.E.2d 547 (1992); Musso v. Picadilly Cafeterias, Inc., 178 So.2d 421 (La. App. 1st Cir.1965).

Under the foreign-natural test, the outset determination is whether the injurious substance is "foreign" or "natural" to the food. As this test evolved nationally, the cases held that if an injurious substance is natural to the food, the plaintiff is denied recovery in all events. Goodwin v. Country Club, 323 Ill.App. 1, 54 N.E.2d 612 (1944); Brown v. Nebiker, 229 Iowa 1223, 296 N.W. 366 (1941); Mix v. Ingersoll

Candy Co., 6 Cal. 2d 674, 59 P.2d 144 (1936), overruled by Mexicali Rose v. Superior Court, 1 Cal. 4th 617, 4 Cal.Rptr.2d 145, 822 P.2d 1292 (1992). But if the injurious substance is foreign, the restaurant is strictly liable. Louisiana Courts of Appeal chose to follow the foreign-natural test to determine the liability of restaurants, but embellished a bit on the strict common law foreign-natural test, in permitting the plaintiff to recover notwithstanding the fact that the injurious substance is natural to the food if the restaurant is negligent in its failing to discover and remove the injurious natural substance. Melady v. Wendy's of New Orleans, Inc., 95-913 (La. App. 5th Cir. 4/16/96); 673 So.2d 1094; Johnson v. South Pacific Canning Co., 580 So.2d 556 (La. App. 5th Cir.1991); Title v. Pontchartrain Hotel, 449 So.2d 677 (La. App. 4th Cir.1984); Loyacano v. Continental Ins., 283 So.2d 302 (La. App. 4th Cir. 1973); Musso v. Picadilly Cafeterias, Inc., 178 So.2d 421 (La. App. 1st Cir.1965).

In time, the foreign-natural test was widely criticized and rejected by many states in favor of the reasonable expectation test. Under the reasonable expectation test, the query to determine liability is whether a reasonable consumer would anticipate, guard against, or expect to find the injurious substance in the type of food dish served. O'Dell v. DeJean's Packing Co., Inc., 585 P.2d 399 (Okl.Ct.App.1978); Jim Dandy Fast Foods, Inc. v. Miriam Carpenter, 535 S.W.2d 786 (Tex.Civ.App.1976); Matthews v. Campbell Soup Co., 380 F. Supp. 1061 (S.D.Tex.1974); Wood v. Waldorf System, Inc., 79 R.I. 1, 83 A.2d 90 (1951); Zabner v. Howard Johnson's Inc., 201 So. 2d 824 (Fla.Dist.Ct.App.1967). Whether the injurious substance is natural or foreign is irrelevant. Rather, liability will be imposed on the restaurant if the customer had a reasonable expectation that the injurious substance would not be found in the food product. On the other hand, if it can be shown that the customer should reasonably have expected the injurious substance in his food, that customer is barred from recovery.

[4] There are, however, two revised statutes that set forth the limitation of liability for damages that result from donated food. See La. Rev. Stat. Ann. §§ 9:2799, 9:2799.3.

[5] The duty set out by this Court, in the case at hand, is similar to the language used in Musso v. Picadilly Cafeterias, Inc., 178 So.2d 421 (La. App. 1st Cir.1965), to determine whether the restaurant was negligent in permitting the injurious natural substance to remain in the food. The Musso court stated,

> We believe the degree of care incumbent upon the restaurant operator in selecting, preparing and cooking food for customers, including the removal of substances natural to the ingredients or finished product, such as bones from fish or meat and stones or seeds from vegetables or fruit, is the same as that which a reasonably prudent man skilled in the culinary art, would exercise in the selection and preparation of food for his own table.

Musso, 178 So.2d at 427.

[6] These are the determinative factors in the foreign-natural test and the reasonable expectation test, but are only factors to be considered by the court when using the duty risk analysis in negligence law.

[7] In Title v. Pontchartrain Hotel, 449 So.2d 677 (La. App. 4th Cir.1984), the Louisiana Fourth Circuit Court of Appeal was also faced with the issue of whether the defendant was liable for the plaintiff's injuries that resulted from the plaintiff biting onto a fried oyster containing a pearl. The Title court stated that from the evidence at trial (such as visual inspection and individually breading), "there [was not] anything further the defendant's oyster fryers could reasonably do to eliminate the very slim possibility of a pearl remaining imbedded in the oyster. Intense scrutiny and through palpitation of every oyster to be served is simply not

feasible in any restaurant situation." <u>Title</u>, 449 So.2d at 680.

In this situation the reported case is distinguishable from the fact pattern, so the rule should not apply. To distinguish <u>Porteous</u> from Mr. Haley's case, use a similar organization. Start by explaining <u>Porteous</u>, like this:

In <u>Porteous v. St. Ann's Cafe & Deli</u>, 713 So. 2d 454 (La. 1998), the plaintiff, Porteous, was dining at a deli and eating an "oyster po-boy" when he bit down onto a pearl in the sandwich. He broke a tooth and "cracked it all the way down the shaft." After the incident, Porteous underwent dental treatment, including a root canal and crown. He then sued the deli, alleging that it was negligent "because of the lack of adequate food inspection procedures, which resulted in the presence of an injurious substance and his sustaining injury to his tooth." At trial, the deli's manager testified that the cook has to "grab the oysters to bread them, and if they were to find an object, they would remove it." But the cook does not "dissect the oyster" as part of the preparation process.

Based on this evidence, the court held that the restaurant did not breach its duty to Porteous. The deli was not liable because "[t]here was nothing more [they] could reasonably have done . . ." to make sure there were no pearls in the oysters they served. A pearl in an oyster is not entirely rare," the court added, but it is "a naturally occurring phenomenon." Furthermore, the court stated that customers eating oysters "should be aware of—and alert to the possibility—that a pearl may be found within the oyster." Therefore, there was no breach of the duty to act as a "reasonably prudent" chef in preparing the oysters.

Then apply the case precedent by comparing the fact

pattern to the facts of the case, apply the reasoning of the reported case to the fact pattern, and, since the facts are distinguishable, come to the opposite conclusion.

Our client, Bill Haley, was also injured by an "injurious substance" in food he was eating, but the similarities end there. Haley was eating a pulled pork sandwich at the Swine Depot. He took a bite of the sandwich and started coughing. His condition worsened, and he was taken to the emergency room. A doctor there performed an operation and removed a piece of pig bone that was lodged in Haley's throat. The bone was ¾ of an inch long, which is substantially larger than a pearl. Also, Chef Billy Bob, the chef at the Depot, testified in a deposition that, unlike an oyster sandwich, a pulled pork sandwich is made by pulling pork apart into thin strips by hand. Unlike the manager in <u>Porteous</u>, Chef Billy Bob further testified that "a piece of bone such as the piece ingested by Haley normally would be discovered and removed during his preparation of the meat."

The <u>Porteous</u> case is distinguishable from Haley's case. Although a piece of bone in pulled pork may be "a naturally occurring phenomenon" a customer eating pork would not reasonably expect to find a bone in a pulled pork sandwich because of the way it is prepared. Unlike breaded oysters, which are not "dissected," pulled pork is pork that is literally pulled apart by hand. Because the pork is pulled into thin strands, one would expect a chef to find and remove any bones in the meat; and a customer eating a pulled pork sandwich would not reasonably expect to find a bone in the sandwich. For all of these reasons, Chef Billy Bob likely breached his duty to act as a "reasonably prudent" chef in the preparation of pulled pork.

Analogizing and distinguishing a reported case to or

from a fact pattern is at the core of legal analysis. If you apply a vague rule (e.g. in a case involving liability arising out of a parties failure to exercise "reasonable" care) to a fact pattern without analogizing or distinguishing a case example, your professor will likely tell you the analysis is superficial. Get this right and you will be well on your way to creating well drafted legal memoranda.

Law school is not just about learning "black letter law." You have to get your hands dirty. You have to get into the facts of the cases to analyze an issue. What is different about lawyering is it often involves analogical reasoning. And you can't do that type of reasoning without comparing facts.

Applying statutory rules is a little different but also often comes down to analogizing and distinguishing cases.

5. ANALYZING STATUTES AND MARSHALING FACTS

Statutes contain legal rules, without any factual context. For that reason you might think analyzing legal issues governed by statute (i.e. simply inserting the relevant facts into the statutory formula to determine the answer to a legal question) is simpler than analyzing cases by analogizing and distinguishing fact patterns. That is true to some extent. Some statutes are very simple to read and apply.

For example, a statute stating the maximum speed on a highway does not require analogical reasoning to apply. If the speed limit is 60 mph and the defendant was going 70 mph then the defendant violated the statute. You don't need to to go to law school to apply a rule that is as simple as that.

However, lawyers are not typically hired to work with simple statutory rules. And the statutes lawyers are hired to interpret are often not only complex but the language they use is also purposefully vague. As a result it often is necessary to study the cases interpreting the statute to fully understand the rule. In that situation you will also need to analogize or distinguish cases to apply the rule to a specific set of facts.

To this point we have been discussing very simple case rules containing just one element. When I say statutory rules are often more complex, I mean they often contain multiple elements joined in various different ways (e.g. the rule may be conjunctive, disjunctive or conditional) and, again, the elements often incorporate vague terms like "reasonable," "good faith," and "diligent". As a result, analyzing a statute is usually not so simple. In fact, it is often a challenge just to determine what the rule is.

A. Determining a Statutory Rule

When you read a statute you should be looking for the statutory rule or formula. In other words, what are the elements of the statute and how are they connected (e.g., with "and" or "or" or "if" and "then," etc.). For example, suppose you looked up the definition of discrimination in the federal Americans with Disabilities Act (ADA), as we did in the chapter on legal research. Using the index, you would then find the following "general rule":

(a) General rule

No covered entity shall discriminate against a qualified individual on the basis of disability in regard to job application procedures, the hiring, advancement, or discharge of employees, employee compensation, job training, and other terms, conditions, and privileges of employment.

(b) Construction

As used in subsection (a) of this section, the term "discriminate against a qualified individual on the basis of disability" includes—

(1) limiting, segregating, or classifying a job applicant or employee in a way that adversely affects the opportunities or status of such applicant or employee because of the disability of such applicant or employee;

(2) participating in a contractual or other arrangement or relationship that has the effect of subjecting a covered entity's qualified applicant or employee with a disability to the discrimination prohibited by this subchapter (such relationship includes a relationship with an employment or referral agency, labor union, an organization providing fringe benefits to an employee of the covered entity, or an organization providing training and apprenticeship programs);

(3) utilizing standards, criteria, or methods of administration—

(A) that have the effect of discrimination on the basis of disability; or

(B) that perpetuate the discrimination of others who are subject to common administrative control;

(4) excluding or otherwise denying equal jobs or benefits to a qualified individual because of the known disability of an individual with whom the qualified individual is known to have a relationship or association;

(5)

(A) not making reasonable accommodations to the known physical or mental limitations of an otherwise qualified individual with a disability who is an applicant or employee, unless such covered entity can demonstrate that the accommodation would impose an undue hardship on the operation of the business of such covered entity; or

(B) denying employment opportunities to a job applicant or employee who is an otherwise qualified individual with a disability, if such denial is based on the need of such covered entity to make reasonable accommodation to the physical or mental impairments of the employee or applicant;

(6) using qualification standards, employment tests or other selection criteria that screen out or tend to screen out an individual with a disability or a class of individuals with disabilities unless the standard, test or other selection criteria, as used by the covered entity, is shown to be job-related for the position in question and is consistent with business necessity; and

(7) failing to select and administer tests concerning employment in the most effective manner to ensure that, when such test is administered to a job applicant or employee who has a disability that impairs sensory, manual, or speaking skills, such test results accurately reflect the skills, aptitude, or whatever other factor of such applicant or employee that such test purports to measure, rather than reflecting the impaired sensory, manual, or speaking skills of such employee or applicant (except where such skills are the factors that the test purports to measure).

42 U.S.C. § 12112.

Likely, not all of that information applies to your situation. So the first step in determining a statutory rule is to ferret out the language that is relevant to the issue you are dealing with. If it is an employer's failure to make a "reasonable accommodation" for a disabled employee, then you can narrow the language down to this:

Discrimination is "not making reasonable accommodations

to the known physical or mental limitations of an otherwise qualified individual with a disability who is an applicant or employee, unless such covered entity can demonstrate that the accommodation would impose an undue hardship on the operation of the business of such covered entity"

42 U.S.C. § 12112(b)(5)(a).

Step two is very important not to overlook; and that is to find the definitions of any terminology used in the statutory language. If you check the definitions section of the ADA, you will find these relevant terms defined:

The term "qualified individual" means an individual who, with or without reasonable accommodation, can perform the essential functions of the employment position that such individual holds or desires.

42 U.S.C. § 12111(8).

The term "reasonable accommodation" may include—"job restructuring, part-time or modified work schedules, reassignment to a vacant position . . . and other similar accommodations for individuals with disabilities."

42 U.S.C. § 12111(9).

The term "undue hardship" means "an action requiring significant difficulty or expense, when considered in light of the . . . the nature and cost of the accommodation needed . . . [and] the overall financial resources of the . . . covered

> entity . . . ."
>
> 42 U.S.C. § 12111(10).

Once you have these definitions, you need to incorporate them into the statutory language and separate out the elements of the statute, paying particular attention to how the elements are joined together (e.g. noting any connectors used). In other words, you have to determine the statutory formula. For example, this statute is a condition with a single element subject to an exception:

> 1.   If the employee is a "qualified individual" ("an individual who, with or without reasonable accommodation, can perform the essential functions of the employment position that such individual holds or desires," 42 U.S.C. § 12111(8)),
>
> 2.   Then the employer must provide for the employee a "reasonable accommodation" ("job restructuring, part-time or modified work schedules, reassignment to a vacant position . . . and other similar accommodations for individuals with disabilities," 42 U.S.C. § 12111(9)),
>
> 3.   Unless the accommodation would impose an "undue hardship" ("an action requiring significant difficulty or expense, when considered in light of the . . . the nature and cost of the accommodation needed . . . [and] the overall financial resources of the . . . covered entity . . . ," 42 U.S.C. § 12111(10)).

If there are cross-references to other parts of the statute in the section you are analyzing, then you need to incorporate them as well. Also, you should always check to see if there are regulations promulgated under the statute. If there are, check the regulations for additional definitions and other relevant provisions. It turns out the regulations under the ADA include an additional, more detailed definitions of essential functions, reasonable accommodation and undue hardship."

---

(1) In general. The term essential functions means the fundamental job duties of the employment position the individual with a disability holds or desires. The term "essential functions" does not include the marginal functions of the position.

(2) A job function may be considered essential for any of several reasons, including but not limited to the following:

(i) The function may be essential because the reason the position exists is to perform that function;

(ii) The function may be essential because of the limited number of employees available among whom the performance of that job function can be distributed;

Evidence of whether a particular function is essential includes, but is not limited to:

(iii) The amount of time spent on the job performing the function;

(iv) The consequences of not requiring the incumbent to perform the function;

29 C.F.R. § 1630.2(n).

---

(1) The term reasonable accommodation means:

(i) Modifications or adjustments to a job application process that enable a qualified applicant with a disability to be considered for the position such qualified applicant desires; or

(ii) Modifications or adjustments to the work environment, or to the manner or circumstances under which the position held or desired is customarily performed, that enable an individual with a disability who is qualified to perform the essential functions of that position; or

(iii) Modifications or adjustments that enable a covered entity's employee with a disability to enjoy equal benefits and privileges of employment as are enjoyed by its other similarly situated employees without disabilities.

(2) Reasonable accommodation may include but is not limited to:

(i) Making existing facilities used by employees readily accessible to and usable by individuals with disabilities; and

(ii) Job restructuring; part-time or modified work schedules; reassignment to a vacant position; acquisition or modifications of equipment or devices; appropriate adjustment or modifications of examinations, training materials, or policies; the provision of qualified readers or interpreters; and other similar accommodations for individuals with disabilities.

29 C.F.R. § 1630.2(O).

(1) In general. Undue hardship means, with respect to the provision of an accommodation, significant difficulty or expense incurred by a covered entity, when considered in light of the factors set forth in paragraph (p)(2) of this section.

(2) Factors to be considered. In determining whether an accommodation would impose an undue hardship on a covered entity, factors to be considered include:

(i) The nature and net cost of the accommodation needed under this part, taking into consideration the availability of tax credits and deductions, and/or outside funding;

(ii) The overall financial resources of the facility or facilities involved in the provision of the reasonable accommodation, the number of persons employed at such facility, and the effect on expenses and resources;

(iii) The overall financial resources of the covered entity, the overall size of the business of the covered entity with respect to the number of its employees, and the number, type and location of its facilities;

(iv) The type of operation or operations of the covered entity, including the composition, structure and functions of the workforce of such entity, and the geographic separateness and administrative or fiscal relationship of the facility or facilities in question to the covered entity; and

(v) The impact of the accommodation upon the operation of the facility, including the impact on the ability of other employees to perform their duties and the impact on the facility's ability to conduct business.

29 C.F.R. § 1630.2(p).

Thus a complete description of the statutory formula for discrimination under the ADA would look like this:

1.   If the employee is a "qualified individual" ("an individual who, with or without reasonable accommodation, can perform the essential functions of the employ ment position that such individual holds or desires," 42 U.S.C. § 12111(8)),

A job function may be considered essential for any of several reasons, including but not limited to the following:

(i) The function may be essential because the reason the position exists is to perform that function;

(ii) The function may be essential because of the limited number of employees available among whom the performance of that job function can be distributed;

Evidence of whether a particular function is essential includes, but is not limited to:

(iii) The amount of time spent on the job performing

the function;

(iv) The consequences of not requiring the incumbent to perform the function; 29 C.F.R. § 1630.2(n).

2.   Then the employer must provide for the employee a "reasonable accommodation" ("job restructuring, part-time or modified work schedules, reassignment to a vacant position . . . and other similar accommodations for individuals with disabilities," 42 U.S.C. § 12111(9)),

(1) The term reasonable accommodation means:

(i) Modifications or adjustments to a job application process that enable a qualified applicant with a disability to be considered for the position such qualified applicant desires; or

(ii) Modifications or adjustments to the work environment, or to the manner or circumstances under which the position held or desired is customarily performed, that enable an individual with a disability who is qualified to perform the essential functions of that position; or

(iii) Modifications or adjustments that enable a covered entity's employee with a disability to enjoy equal benefits and privileges of employment as are enjoyed by its other similarly situated employees without disabilities.

(2) Reasonable accommodation may include but is not limited to:

(i) Making existing facilities used by employees readily accessible to and usable by individuals with disabilities; and

(ii) Job restructuring; part-time or modified work schedules; reassignment to a vacant position; acquisition or modifications of equipment or devices; appropriate adjustment or modifications of examinations, training materials, or policies; the provision of qualified readers or interpreters; and other similar accommodations for individuals with disabilities. 29 C.F.R. § 1630.2(O).

3.   Unless the accommodation would impose an "undue hardship" ("an action requiring significant difficulty or expense, when considered in light of the . . . the nature and cost of the accommodation needed . . . [and] the overall financial resources of the . . . covered entity . . . ," 42 U.S.C. § 12111(10)).

(1) In general. Undue hardship means, with respect to the provision of an accommodation, significant difficulty or expense incurred by a covered entity, when considered in light of the factors set forth in   paragraph (p)(2) of this section.

(2) Factors to be considered. In determining whether an accommodation would impose an undue hardship on a covered entity, factors to be considered include:

(i) The nature and net cost of the accommodation needed under this part, taking into consideration the availability of tax credits and deductions, and/or outside funding;

(ii) The overall financial resources of the facility or facilities involved in the provision of the reasonable accommodation, the number of persons employed at such facility, and the effect on expenses and resources;

(iii) The overall financial resources of the covered entity, the overall size of the business of the covered entity with respect to the number of its employees, and the number, type and location of its facilities;

(iv) The type of operation or operations of the covered entity, including the composition, structure and functions of the workforce of such entity, and the geographic separateness and administrative or fiscal relationship of the facility or facilities in question to the covered entity; and

(v) The impact of the accommodation upon the operation of the facility, including the impact on the ability of other employees to perform their duties and the impact on the facility's ability to conduct business. 29 C.F.R. § 1630.2(p).

I have mnemonic to help you remember everything you need to do when you are analyzing a statute. The mnemonic is "Every Cool Dude Can Rock," which stands for Elements, Connectors, Definitions, Cross-References and Regulations. When you are analyzing a statute, start by determining the Elements of the statute, pay careful attention to how they are Connected (with and, or, etc.), check for Definitions and Cross-references. If you find them, incorporate the language. And then check for any Regulations promulgated under the statute. Remember to do all five of those things whenever you are analyzing a statute.

B. Marshaling Facts

Once you have correctly stated the rule, you can marshal the relevant facts from the fact pattern to begin the process of determining whether the rule is met. For example, if your case involves an employee who is a professor at a university; and the professor teaches two classes per year and writes a law review article every summer, then those facts would be relevant to the issue of what are the "essential functions of the employment position." If the professor suffers from Covid-19 and is contagious but does not have symptoms; and the professor requests that he be permitted to work from home, then those facts would be relevant to the issue of what would be a "reasonable accommodation" for the employee's disability. If the university is a small institution that generates about $15,000,000 per year in revenues from tuition, and it would cost $10,000 to purchase the computer equipment the professor needs to work from home, then that information would be relevant to the issue of "undue hardship." (On the other hand, if it would cost nothing to accommodate the employee, then there might be no question there is no "undue hardship." In other words, that issue would be a "given," and there would be no need to analyze it.). Here is a chart showing how you would marshal these facts to the various elements of this statutory rule.

Statutory Element	Relevant Facts
Qualified Individual / Essential Job Functions	The employee is a professor at a university who teaches two classes per year and writes a law review article every summer.
Reasonable Accommodation	The professor suffers from Covid-19 and is contagious but does not have symptoms; and the professor requests that he be permitted to work from home.
Undue Hardship	The university is a small institution that generates about $15,000,000 per year in revenues from tuition, and it would cost $10,000 to purchase the computer equipment the

	professor needs to work from home.

Marshaling the facts is the first step. The second step is determining whether the relevant facts are sufficient to meet each of the elements of the statute. For example, is it a "reasonable accommodation" to permit a professor who suffers from Covid 19 to work from home? To answer that question, you will need to do some research, find cases on point, and determine whether the cases are analogous or distinguishable. Working from home may be reasonable for an employee who has one type of job but not an employee who does something different. So you may need to analogize or distinguish multiple cases as part of your analysis. Here is an example of how that might look:

> This will analyze the issue of whether working at home would be a reasonable accommodation under the Americans with Disabilities Act for a university professor who has Covid 19. A "reasonable accommodation" under the ADA includes the following:
>
> *Modifications or adjustments to the work environment, or to the manner or circumstances under which the position held or desired is customarily performed, that enable an individual with a disability who is qualified to perform the essential functions of that position is a modification or adjustment to the employment*
>
> 29 C.F.R. § 1630.2(o)(1)(ii). This "may include but is not limited to . . . part-time or modified work schedules . . . acquisition or modifications of equipment or devices . . ..and other similar accommodations . . . ." § 1630.2(o)(2)(ii). Although working from home is not mentioned, it is clear

that the list of accommodations in the regulation is not exhaustive. Id.

Courts interpreting the ADA in this jurisdiction have stated that working from home is "rarely" a reasonable accommodation, but none of the cases have involved circumstances like those presented here. E.g., Vande Zande v. Wis. Dep't of Admin., 44 F.3d 538, 544-45 (7th Cir. 1995) (paralyzed program assistant not permitted to work from home); Rauen v. U.S. Tobacco Mfg., 319 F.3d 891, 896 (7th Cir. 2003)(secretary with rectal cancer not permitted to work from home). Although I find no cases allowing an employee to work from home, I also find no legitimate reason that would not be a reasonable accommodation for the professor in this case.

The decisions in Vande Zande and Rauen are based primarily on the type of work involved, although the plaintiff's disability is also relevant. Vande Zande was employed as a program assistant where her responsibilities included "preparing public information materials, planning meetings, interpreting regulations, typing, mailing, filing, and copying. In short, her tasks were of a clerical, secretarial, and administrative-assistant character." Vande Zande, 44 F.3d at 544. She was "paralyzed from the waist down as a result of a tumor of the spinal cord. Her paralysis [made] her prone to develop pressure ulcers, treatment of which often require[d] that she stay at home for several weeks." Id. at 543.

Rauen was a software engineer whose primary duties were "monitoring contractors' work . . . answering contractors' questions as they arise, and ensuring that the contractors' work does not interfere with the manufacturing process." Rauen, 319 F.3d at 893. She suffered from rectal cancer, and had to have a portion of her small intestine removed. Id. As a result, she took two liters of IV fluids daily and had to use the bathroom up to fourteen times a day. Id. She had to wear an ostomy appliance that needed to be emptied frequently. Id. Also, her condition caused overwhelming fatigue, forcing her to lie down and rest often, and increasing her chances of falling asleep behind the wheel traveling to and from work. Id. And her doctor recommended that she work from a home office. Id.

Both Vande Zande and Rauen were denied the accommodation of working from home, despite their disabilities, because they had jobs that required them to be in the office.

Most jobs in organizations public or private involve team work under supervision rather than solitary unsupervised work, and team work under supervision generally cannot be performed at home without a substantial reduction in the quality of the employee's performance. This will no doubt change as communications technology advances, but is the situation today. Generally, therefore, an employer is not required to accommodate a disability by allowing the disabled worker to work, by himself, without supervision, at home.

Vande Zande, 44 F.3d at 544-45.

However, Vande Zande was decided twenty-five years ago, before anyone started using the internet, let alone on-line conferencing, e-mail, chat rooms and listservs. Rauen was decided eight years later in 2003, but that was still before people started using programs like Skype, Zoom and Uberconference. Today, a professor can easily communicate with his students and peers using an on line service. Virtually all professors are already supplied with the computer equipment necessary to do so. In fact, on line college courses are offered at many universities.

More importantly, the job of being a professor is very

different than the job of being a program assistant or a software engineer. Vande Zande primarily assisted others and worked as part of a team. Vande Zande, 44 F.3d at 544. A university professor primarily works alone. Rauen had to deal with "problems requiring immediate resolution" that would arise "on the spur of the moment." Rauen, 319 F.3d at 897. The same is not true of a university professor. Students need to be able to contact a professor by phone or by e-mail, but immediate responses are not required. Professors must also provide students with office hours but they can easily be held on line. Also, administrative and committee meetings can be attended remotely. In addition, both Vande Zande and Rauen had jobs that required the supervision of others. However, the work of a professor is mostly unsupervised. Clearly Vande Zande and Rauen are outdated and distinguishable. A court today would likely rule that working at home would be a reasonable accommodation for a university professor who has Covid 19.

Analogizing and distinguishing a reported case to or from a fact pattern is part of case analysis, and it is part of statutory analysis too. There is no escaping analogical reasoning in law; that is why there were so many analogies on the LSAT. The ability to work with analogies, as well as complex statutory rules, are core skills every lawyer needs to have (and every law student needs to practice).

Before we get into the organization of legal analyses, we need to discuss citation. As you analogize or distinguish a case, or marshal the facts and the elements of a statute, you need to tell the reader where your information is coming from. You need to cite to the original sources, and there are specific rules for how to do that. So the next step is to learn those rules.

6. CITATION

Most first year law student are taught legal citation using the over five hundred page "Blue Book" that is published by the editors of the law journals at Harvard University, Yale University, Columbia University and the University of Pennsylvania. I doubt anyone covers the whole book. Still, my impression is that many professors teach far more than most students will ever need to know. As a result, many students graduate their first year of law school having some idea of how to cite a lot of different sources, but they still make obvious mistakes doing the most basic citations lawyers use all the time. In my opinion it would make more sense for you to practice basic citation, than attempt to master the minutiae of the Blue Book.

> *The time that law students and lawyers spend mastering and applying the manifold rules of the Bluebook is time taken away from other lawyerly activities, mainly from thinking about what they are writing. It is so hard to get the citation forms right that the writer or editor who has done so is apt to feel that he has acquitted himself of a difficult task and should be allowed to rest his brain. Less attention can be given writing and rewriting because so much is devoted to forms most of which don't matter worth a straw to the reader. Instead of learning the Uniform*

Commercial Code the student learns the Uniform Citation Code, which is almost as long, and far more arbitrary. It is all part of the surprising juvenescence of the legal profession; students study the laws laid down by other students, and teachers teach the law laid down by their just-graduated students, the judges' law clerks.

Richard A. Posner, "Goodbye to the Bluebook," 53 University of Chicago Law Review 1343, 1348-1349 (1986). (Richard A. Posner was a United States Circuit Judge of the United States Court of Appeals for the Seventh Circuit from 1981 until 2017. He is now a Senior Lecturer at the University of Chicago Law School.)

The idea that the Blue Book represents a uniform standard for citation is also misleading. The truth is there are a lot of different reference books for legal citation. And citation practice varies from the U.S. Supreme Court to the other federal courts, from the federal courts to the state courts, and from one state court to another state court.

For those reasons, this book will just cover the basic rules of how to cite cases and statutes. Those are the things you absolutely need to get right every time. These forms are also common to almost every citation reference available. If you decide to go further, at least you will have a solid foundation to build on. At least you will have mastered what is most important.

A.   How to Cite Cases

To cite a case, start with the name. State the last name of the plaintiff (the first plaintiff, if there is more than one). If the plaintiff is an entity, state the full name but abbreviate generic terms, like "Corp." (The Blue Book has a long list of terms that must be abbreviated when they appear in case names. Blue Book, Table 6. That is an example of the type of minutiae I am not covering in this book.) Write "v." not "vrs." or "vs.". Then state the last name of the first defendant. If the defendant is an entity, state the full name. Italicize the entire case name and insert a comma after the name. (You can always underline instead of italicize. But if you do underline a case name, remember not to underline the comma at the end.)

Jones v. Fillmore,

Then state where the case is located. In other words, state the name of the book the case is published in. The books cases are published in are called case reporters. Even if you found the case on line, and read it on line, you still have to cite to the publisher of the reporter. And you also have to cite the page numbers in the paper version of the reporter. You don't cite cases using a hyperlink or the "URL" for the website you found them in.

Put the volume number for the case reporter, then abbreviate the name of the case reporter. The Supreme Court Reporters are U.S. Reports (U.S.), Lawyer's Edition (L. Ed.) and the Supreme Court Reporter (S. Ct.). U.S. Reports is the official reporter. The Federal Court of Appeals reporter is the Federal Reporter (F., F.2d or F.3d); and the Federal District Court (Trial Court) reporter is the Federal Supplement (F. Supp. or F. Supp. 2d.). Do not space between single letters or letters and ordinals (e.g., F.2d). Memorize those reporters and their abbreviations, as well as the state reporters and abbreviations for the state where you are going to practice.

For example, Florida Supreme Court cases are cited to the state reporter Florida Cases (Fla). or the regional Southern Reporter (So. or So. 2d.). Cases of the Florida District Courts of

Appeal are also cited to the Southern Reporter.

Put the page number for the first page of the case. Insert a comma, then put the number for the page cited (this is called a "pin cite" or "jump cite"). If the pin cite is for multiple pages use commas to separate them (don't use "&" or "and") or a dash "-" for a range of pages (and retain the last two digits but remove prior numbers of the last page).

Jones v. Fillmore, **112 F. Supp. 345, 350-53**

If you are doing your research on line, you will find the name of the case reporter, as well as the volume number and page number for the case, at the beginning of the case, either just before or just after the names of the parties. To find the page the specific language appears on, look for numbers in the opinion preceded by an asterisk. So if you read this: "Smith committed the crime *540 of assault and battery," that means the first part of the sentence is on page 539 in the print version of the reporter, and the second part of the sentence is on page 540. Everything that follows the sentence is also on page 540, all the way up to the place in the opinion where you see "*541."

After you are done referring to the case reporter, identify the court that decided the case and the date. Start with an open parenthesis. For federal cases, abbreviate the circuit or district, as appropriate (e.g., 11th Cir. or M.D. Fla.). No abbreviation is needed if the reporter is for the federal Supreme Court only.

For state cases, abbreviate the name of the state court, unless the reporter only contains decisions for that court. For example, in Florida, if you are citing the Supreme Court in the Florida Cases reporter, you don't need to indicate the court in parenthesis. But if you are citing the Supreme Court in the regional reporter, use the abbreviation "Fla." in parenthesis, before the date, to identify the Supreme Court. If you are citing the District Court in the regional reporter, the Blue Book rule is to use the abbreviation "Fla. ___ Dist. Ct. App." in parenthesis before the date, to identify the District Court (fill in the blank by identifying the district number: 1st, 2d, 3d, 4th, 5th, etc. (superscript should not be used)). (Actual practice in Florida is to use the abbreviation "DCA" for the District Court of Appeals).

Next, put the year the case was decided. Then close parenthesis, and finish with a period, so the end result, for a federal case, looks like this:

Jones v. Fillmore, **112 F. Supp. 345, 350-53 (D. Mass. 1993).**

If you cite the case and page again, use a short form. If there is no intervening cite, use *Id.* If you are underlining, instead of italicizing, remember to underline the period, like this:

Id.

If you cite the case again but the page is different, add the new page, like this: "*Id.* at 351." If there is an intervening cite, and you cite the case again, do it like this: *Jones*, 112 F. Supp. at 351 (identify the case with the name of the plaintiff only, omit the page the case starts on, and omit any parenthetical information).

B.   How to Cite Statutes

To cite a statute, start with the title number for

the code or regulation (the name of the statute is usually omitted). Then abbreviate the name of the un-annotated code or regulation. The United States Code is U.S.C., and the Code of Federal Regulations is C.F.R. Memorize the names of the federal statutes and regulations.

Put a section symbol, or two if citing multiple sections. Then the number of the section and letters for any subsection (with each letter in parenthesis), and finish with a period, like this:

---

12 U.S.C. §122(a).

The Blue Book also requires that the year of the code edition as it appears on the spine of the print volume or the title page be added in parenthesis after the cite. *Blue Book*, Rule B12. But that rule is not followed by the U.S. Supreme Court and many other courts.

In Florida state statutes are abbreviated Fla. Stat. and regulations are Fla. Admin. Code. So the correct Blue Book form is "Fla. Stat. §48". Also, when citing a Florida statute, the year of the code is usually included in parenthesis after the cite, so the full cite would be "Fla. Stat. §48 (1975)." (Actual practice in Florida is a little different; you cite the section first then the statute, like this: "§48, Fla. Stat. (1975).")

If you cite the statute again, use a short form. If there is no intervening cite, use *Id.* If you cite the statute again, but the section is different, do it like this: *Id.* §122(b). or §122(b) (i.e. omit "at"). If there is an intervening cite, and you cite the statute again, restate the section number or restate the full cite, like this: §122(a) or 12 U.S.C. §122(a).

C.   Quotations, Signals and Parentheticals

To quote the language from a case or a statute, follow these four simple rules.

> *(1) If the quote is in the text, use quotation marks. (2) To do a block quote, either because the quote is long or for emphasis, single space the text, then indent and single space the body of the quote, leaving out any quotation marks. Left justify the citation for the quote; and then continue on with the text. (3) To alter text, use brackets [ ]. (4) To omit words in text, use an ellipsis . . . (and add a fourth period if the ellipsis is at the end of a sentence).*

And don't forget to put the citation in the right place (leave a space between the quote and the citation, and left justify the citation so it is part of the paragraph not the bock quote).

If you are not either quoting or paraphrasing language in a case, you should place a signal between your statement and the citation for the case. For example, *"See"* means the authority supports the proposition either implicitly or in the form of dicta. *"Cf."* means the authority supports the proposition by analogy. And *"E.g."* means the authority is one of many that state the proposition. If you are using any of those signals, remember not to put a comma after the signal.

It is also often helpful to include an explanatory parenthetical after a citation. Here are two examples: *See County of Riverside v. McLaugh-lin*, 500 U.S. 44 (1991) (civil suit challenging timing of probable-cause hearing); *see* 18 U.S.C. 3742 (authorizing appeals from final sentences in certain circumstances). A citation with a signal in front and a parenthetical in the rear gives the reader a lot of information in a concise format.

That is, in my opinion, all the citation you really need to know. If you encounter anything else, you will obviously have to look up the correct form. But those are the forms you encounter all the time. Get one of those wrong, and people will notice the mistake. Consistently get these right, and you'll do fine!

D.   Reference Materials

When you do encounter something other than the basic forms I have described, you will need a good reference book. Fortunately, there are a number of them available on line. And they are all free.

The *Indigo Book* is an excellent citation manual that was compiled by a team of students at the New York University School of Law, working under the direction of Professor Christopher Jon Sprigman. It is available to on line for free.

THE INDIGO BOOK

An Open and Compatible Implementation of
A Uniform System of Citation

NOT AFFILIATED WITH OR AUTHORIZED BY
THE BLUEBOOK® A UNIFORM SYSTEM OF CITATION®

If you want something shorter than the *Indigo Book* you may be interested in the 90 page *Maroonbook a/k/a The University of Chicago Manual of Legal Citation*, which is published by the law review at the University of Chicago. The *Maroonbook* is also well done, and it is also available on line for free.

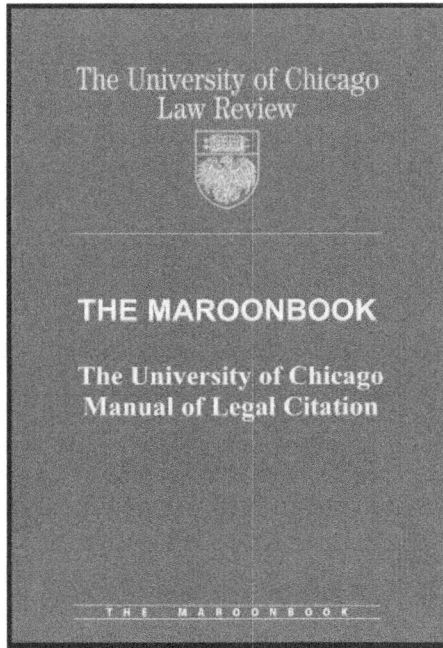

Another excellent resource that is that is much longer is the 500 page *Introduction to Basic Legal Citation* by Cornell Law School Professor Peter Martin. Prof. Martin's text is every bit as comprehensive as the *Blue Book*; and it is available on line for free.

And if you want something even more authoritative the *U.S. Supreme Court Style Guide* is yet another excellent resource that is available on line for free. The *Style Guide* contains the style preferences of the Supreme Court, used by its Reporter of Decisions when preparing the Court's official opinions.

THE
SUPREME COURT'S
STYLE GUIDE

Supreme Court of the United States
Office of the Reporter of Decisions

Edited and Introduction by Jack Metzler

$i\Lambda$
INTERALIAS
Washington, D.C.

If you practice in Florida, you should have a copy of the Uniform Citation System for Florida legal documents in Rule 9.800 of the Florida Rules of Appellate Procedure plus the *Blue Book* and the *Florida Style Manual* for Florida-specific sources, particularly those generated by the Florida Legislature. The *Style Manual* is published by the Florida State University Law Review and is available on line for free.

Additional examples of state specific citation resources include the *Writing Manual* published by the Supreme Court of Ohio and the *Style Manual* written by the Supreme Court of Illinois. If there is no similar manual for your state, you can familiarize yourself with state citation practice (e.g. how state statutes and regulations, state courts and court reporters are commonly abbreviated) by simply reviewing some recent court opinions.

With all those fine resources available at no cost, why

would anyone force students to buy the Blue Book? Harvard, Yale, Columbia and the University of Pennsylvania are the wealthiest universities in the country. *See* U.S. Department of Education, National Center for Education Statistics. (2019). *Digest of Education Statistics, 2017* (NCES 2018-094), Table 333.90. As of the date of this book, Harvard alone had an endowment of almost $40 billion. Yet the Blue Book is also the only citation reference on this list that you have to pay for.

I admit the Blue Book is an excellent resource for law review articles. So, if you want to join the law review at your school, you should probably spend the money. Also, if you want to be a law professor after you graduate, it would not be a bad idea to try and master as much of the Blue Book as you can. Most law professors write law review articles, so you will need to know the rules for citing articles. (Professors who teach skills classes, like me, and professors who actually practice law in student clinics are exceptions to that rule.)

But if your primary interest is in passing the bar, getting a good job, and practicing law well, then just make sure you get the basics of citation down pat. Be aware the rules vary depending upon the context. Have some good reference materials available; and use them the same way you would use a good dictionary. When you encounter something with which you are unfamiliar, open the book and look it up.

Now we can finally talk about how to organize your analysis of a legal issue, and how to write a legal research memorandum.

7. IRAC

The philosopher Socrates is credited with developing the basic organization for deductive reasoning. He called it a "syllogism." Likely you already know about his famous example:

1. All men are mortal. (This the premise.)

2. Socrates is a man. (This is the second premise.)

3. Therefore, Socrates is mortal. (This is the conclusion.)

If you added the issue to the beginning of this form, you would start with "The issue is whether Socrates is mortal." If you then thought of "All men are mortal" as the rule, "Socrates is a man," as an application of the rule to Socrates, and "Therefore, Socrates is mortal," as the conclusion, you would have created what law students call "IRAC," the basic form for legal reasoning, deductive or analogical.

To organize your analysis of a legal issue, whether you are stating it orally or in writing, start by stating what the issue is, and then state the legal rule that applies to that issue. Next apply that rule to the relevant facts, and then come to a conclusion. That is the most basic structure for analyzing a legal issue. Here is an example of an analysis of a simple issue using the IRAC organization:

> Issue   The issue in this case is whether Supermarket Corp. was responsible for maintaining the premises in reasonably safe condition.
>
> Rule   A basic tenet of premises liability in tort law is those who own or control property have a duty to maintain it in safe condition. E.g., Oliveri v. Massachusetts Bay Transp. Authority, 363 Mass. 165, 167 (1973).
>
> Application   Supermarket Corp. was the owner of the property where the accident occurred, and was also in control of the store on the property.
>
> Conclusion   Therefore Supermarket Corp. was responsible for maintaining the premises in reasonably safe condition.

Of course lawyers do not often get paid to analyze issues that are that simple. Usually the rule involves some legal concept that needs to be explained before it can be applied. Also, many of the rules lawyers deal with are purposefully vague, and some must be derived from multiple case opinions. In each of those situations the IRAC model must be expanded upon to accommodate a more complex situation.

A. Use "IREAC" when it is Necessary to Explain the Meaning of a Rule

If the meaning of a rule is not clear and needs to be

explained, you would use a modified version of IRAC called IREAC (Issue, Rule, Explanation, Application and Conclusion) as the structure of your organization. In other words, you would explain the rule before you apply it. If the rule is a common law rule from a case decision, you would explain the rule by citing the case as an example, and then saying what happened in the case, how the court decided the issue and why the court decided the way it did. Here is an example:

Issue	The issue in this case is whether the contract between Client and Contractor is enforceable.
Rule	A basic principle of contract law is that a contract, to be enforceable, must be supported by adequate consideration. E.g., Office Pavilion S. Fla., Inc. v. ASAL Products, Inc., 849 So.2d 367, 370 (Fla. 4th DCA 2003). An exchange of promises may constitute such consideration, but not if one of the promises is illusory. Id.
Explanation	In Office Pavilion one of the parties agreed to sell to the other party "any chairs it chooses to order at the price set forth in the price list." Id. The court held that agreeing to buy as many items as a person "choses to order" is illusory. Id. An agreement like that is not supported by sufficient consideration because accepting it involves no promised performance. Id.
Application	The contract between Client and

contractor is also illusory, since the Client only agreed to hire the Contractor on the days and times the Client decided were appropriate. That is not sufficient consideration to make an agreement binding. Accepting that involves no promised performance.

Conclusion   Therefore the contract between Client and Contractor is not enforceable.

In the previous example I stated the issue in a general way, explained and applied a more specific rule applicable to the facts, and then stated the conclusion in the same general way as the I stated the issue. When you analyze a legal issue, you usually want to start with a broad statement of the issue, then get into the specific rule that is involved in analyzing the broader issue, explain the rule and apply it to the facts, then finish with a broad statement of the conclusion (i.e. a statement that mirrors the original issue).

If the explanation of the rule is simple enough, you can make your analysis more concise by putting your explanation in parenthesis after the case cite. Here is a revision of the previous example organized this way.

Issue   The issue in this case is whether the contract between Client and Contractor is enforceable.

Rule   A basic principle of contract law is that a contract, to be enforceable, must be supported by adequate consideration. E.g., Office Pavilion S. Fla., Inc. v. ASAL Products,

> _Inc._, 849 So.2d 367, 370 (Fla. 4th DCA 2003) (agreement to buy "any chairs [a party] choses to order" held illusory and not supported by sufficient consideration).
>
> <u>Application</u>   The contract between Client and contractor is illusory, since the Client only agreed to hire the Contractor on the days and times the Client decided were appropriate. That is not sufficient consideration to make an agreement binding.
>
> <u>Conclusion</u>   Therefore the contract between Client and Contractor is not enforceable.

B. <u>Use "Ferrari Has Really Cool Race Cars" when it is Necessary to Analogize or Distinguish a Case</u>

The third type of rule is a rule that is purposefully vague. A vague rule must be explained by giving an example of how it is interpreted in a specific context, and it must be applied by comparing that context to the situation involved in a fact pattern. That is the most difficult type of rule to analyze.

An example would be the tort rule that people are responsible to pay for the damages they cause as a result of their failure to exercise "reasonable" care. When you analyze vague rule like that, you not only need to explain the rule by explaining what happened in a case involving the rule, what the court decided and why. You also need to apply the rule differently. You don't just insert the relevant facts of the fact pattern. Instead you compare the facts of the fact pattern to the facts of the case, state whether the facts are analogous or distinguishable. Then either apply the reasoning or say it doesn't apply, and come to the same conclusion as the case, if the facts are analogous, or a different conclusion, if they are distinguishable.

To help organize the analysis of an issue in that situation, remember the mnemonic "**Ferrari Has Really Cool Race Cars**," which stands for Facts, Holding, Reasoning, Comparison, Reasoning and Conclusion. Explain the rule by stating the <u>Facts</u> of a representative case, the <u>Holding</u> of the case and the <u>Reasoning</u> of the court's decision. Then apply the rule by <u>Comparing</u> the facts of the case to the facts of the fact pattern, applying the <u>Reasoning</u> of the case to the fact pattern and coming to a <u>Conclusion</u>.

Here is an example of an analysis of a vague rule using this formula:

<u>Issue</u> The issue in this case is whether evidence of dirty brown wax beans and black strawberries on the floor of a supermarket is enough to show the property owner breached the owner's duty to keep the premises in reasonably safe

condition.

<u>Rule</u>   When business visitor slips and falls on foreign substance "he may prove the negligence of the defendant by proof that . . . the foreign substance was present on the defendant's premises for such a length of time that the defendant should have known about it." <u>E.g.</u>, <u>Oliveri v. Massachusetts Bay Transp. Authority</u>, 363 Mass. 165, 167 (1973); <u>Anjou v. Boston Elevated Ry. Co.</u>, 208 Mass. 273, 274 (1911).

<u>Explanation: Facts</u> **(Ferrari)**   For example, in <u>Anjou</u> the plaintiff slipped and fell on a banana peel. <u>Id.</u> at 273. According to a witness who had examined it, the banana peel "'felt dry, gritty, as if there were dirt upon it,' as if 'trampled over a good deal;' it was 'flattened down, and black in color,' and 'every bit of it was black, there wasn't a particle of yellow." <u>Id.</u> at 274.

<u>Explanation: Holding</u> **(Has)**   Based on that evidence, the court held that "[t]he inference might have been drawn from the appearance and condition of the banana peel that it had been upon the platform a considerable period of time, in such position that it would have been seen and removed by the employees of the defendant if they had been reasonably careful in performing their duty." <u>Id.</u>

<u>Explanation:Reasoning</u> **(Really)**   A banana peel is perishable. It decays over time and turns black. Therefore, if a banana peel looks black and gritty, it is reasonable to infer it's been sitting for a while.

<u>Application: Comparison</u> **(Cool)**   This case is analogous. The customers in both cases slipped and fell on perishable

substances. Wax beans and strawberries, like bananas, are perishable. After the passage of time, beans turn brown and strawberries turn black, just like bananas turn black when they decay.

Application: Reasoning (**Race**)   For the same reason it is reasonable to infer a black banana peel has been on the floor for a substantial length of time, it is also reasonable to infer dirty brown beans and black strawberries have been on the floor for a long time.

Application: Conclusion (**Cars**)   Based on the evidence, the store owner in this case should have known of unsafe condition and either cleaned it up or warned customers of its existence.

Conclusion   Evidence of dirty brown wax beans and black strawberries on the floor of a supermarket is enough to show the property owner breached the owner's duty to keep the premises in reasonably safe condition.

Of course, if you were writing any of these examples in a legal memo you would delete the underlined headings. You don't actually label your sections "Issue," "Rule," "Application," and "Conclusion" in a memo. And you definitely would delete any references to Ferrari having really cool race cars. So your end result would look like this:

The issue in this case is whether evidence of dirty brown wax beans and black strawberries on the floor of a supermarket is enough to show the property owner breached the owner's duty to keep the premises in reasonably safe condition. When business visitor slips and

falls on foreign substance "he may prove the negligence of the defendant by proof that . . . the foreign substance was present on the defendant's premises for such a length of time that the defendant should have known about it." E.g., Oliveri v. Massachusetts Bay Transp. Authority, 363 Mass. 165, 167 (1973); Anjou v. Boston Elevated Ry. Co., 208 Mass. 273, 274(1911).

For example, in Anjou the plaintiff slipped and fell on a banana peel. Id. at 273. According to a witness who had examined it, the banana peel "'felt dry, gritty, as if there were dirt upon it,' as if 'trampled over a good deal;' it was 'flattened down, and black in color,' and 'every bit of it was black, there wasn't a particle of yellow." Id. at 274. Based on that evidence, the court held that "[t]he inference might have been drawn from the appearance and condition of the banana peel that it had been upon the platform a considerable period of time, in such position that it would have been seen and removed by the employees of the defendant if they had been reasonably careful in performing their duty." Id. A banana peel is perishable. It decays over time and turns black. Therefore, if a banana peel looks black and gritty, it is reasonable to infer it's been sitting for a while.

This case is analogous. The customers in both cases slipped and fell on perishable substances. Wax beans and strawberries, like bananas, are perishable. After the passage of time, beans turn brown and strawberries turn black, just like bananas turn black when they decay. For the same reason it is reasonable to infer a black banana peel has been on the floor for a substantial length of time, it is also reasonable to infer dirty brown beans and black strawberries have been on the floor for a long time. Based on the evidence, the store owner in this case should have known of unsafe condition and either cleaned it up or warned customers of its existence. Evidence

> **of dirty brown wax beans and black strawberries on the floor of a supermarket is enough to show the property owner breached the owner's duty to keep the premises in reasonably safe condition.**

Note that the "conclusion" at the end of the "Ferrari has really cool race cars" organization is meant to be more a more specific conclusion to the more specific rule explained and applied. The conclusion at the end of IRAC or IREAC (the "C" in IRAC or IREAC) should be broader, like the broader statement of the issue in the beginning of IRAC (the "I" in IRAC or IREAC).

C. Synthesizing a Rule From Multiple Cases

Sometimes the entire rule for an issue is included in a single case; but other times a complete statement of the rule must be derived from multiple case examples. In other words, you sometimes have to look at two or more cases interpreting pieces of the rule, and then put the pieces together to figure out what the whole rule is. The process of doing that is called "synthesizing a rule" from multiple cases.

Here is an example of synthesizing a rule for the application of equitable estoppel to the defense of the statute of limitations. The cases are General Stencils, Inc. v. Chiappa, Zumpano v. Quinn and Kotlyarsky v. N.Y. Post. Read through the summary of each case to determine the holding, then combine the three holdings to construct a complete statement of the rule.

Zumpano v. Quinn, 6 N.Y.3d 666 (2006).

The plaintiffs in Zumpano sued the defendant priests for sexual abuse that occurred when the plaintiffs were children. The defendants raised the statute of limitations as a defense, and the plaintiffs countered by claiming the defendants were equitably estopped from raising the defense because the defendants were aware of the abuse and remained silent about it. The plaintiffs further alleged that, "for over 40 years, defendants did not report abuse by priests to law enforcement officials; reassigned offending priests without disclosure of their offenses; and, when victims complained, made private payments to them so that the charges would not be publicized."

Based on these facts, the court held that the doctrine of equitable estoppel did not apply. Although the defendants conduct "might be morally questionable in any defendant, let alone a religious institution," it did not constitute fraudulent concealment. "A wrongdoer is not legally obliged to make a public confession, or to alert people who may have claims against it, to get the benefit of a statute of limitations." Because there was no fraudulent concealment, the defendants were not equitably estopped from raising the statute of limitations as a defense to the sexual abuse claims.

General Stencils, Inc. v. Chiappa,
18 N.Y.2d 125 (N.Y. 1966).

In General Stencils, the plaintiff filed an action against a former employee claiming the individual converted over $30,000 out of petty cash funds while in plaintiff's employ as head bookkeeper. The defendant raised the statute of limitations as a defense. In response, the plaintiff further alleged that the defendant fraudulently concealed her defalcations and, as a result, the plaintiff did not become aware of them until well after the defendant's employment ended.

The court agreed stating that equitable estoppel applied because "it is the defendant's affirmative wrongdoing -- a carefully concealed crime here -- which produced the long delay between the accrual of the cause of action and the institution of the legal proceeding." However, the court also stated that the assertion of that defense would not be barred if "it was solely due to the negligence of plaintiff and the acquiescence of its corporate officers that it was unable to discover the conversion until several years had elapsed."

<u>Kotlyarsky v. N.Y. Post</u>, 757 N.Y.S.2d 703 (2003).

<u>Kotylarsky</u> involved a claim for libel based on an article written by an employee of the defendant. The article reported that the plaintiff was under a federal indictment charging him with conspiracy and money laundering. The plaintiff requested a retraction, after advising defendant that the contents of the article were false, and that his reputation had been damaged. At a meeting between the two parties the plaintiff brought court documents from his criminal case, attempting to prove the falsity of the statements in the article. During the course of the meeting, it was either expressly or impliedly promised that a retraction would be published. Nine months later the plaintiff wrote a letter to the defendant requesting a copy of the retraction. The defendant responded that she had left messages with plaintiff's attorney about a possible article, but she did not receive a response, so the requested retraction article was withdrawn. The plaintiff sued and the defendant raised the statute of limitations as a defense. The plaintiff responded by claiming the defendant should be equitably estopped from raising that defense because any delay was the result of his own lack of diligence in failing to timely following up with the plaintiff and failing to respond to her calls.

The court agreed stating that a plaintiff seeking to invoke the doctrines of equitable estoppel or equitable tolling is required to demonstrate "that the failure to timely commence the lawsuit is not attributable to a lack of diligence on his or her part." Because plaintiff waited approximately nine months before writing a letter requesting a copy of the newspaper in which the retraction had been printed, due diligence was not shown, and plaintiff failed to allege sufficient facts to warrant the tolling or estoppel of the limitation period.

If you synthesize the holdings of General Stencils, Inc. v. Chiappa, Zumpano v. Quinn and Kotlyarsky v. N.Y. Post, you will end up with a complete statement of the rule for equitable estoppel of the statute of limitations that is something like this:

> **The doctrine of equitable estoppel applies to toll the statute of limitations if the defendant's wrongdoing caused the delay in filing the case, including if the defendant covered up the claim, General Stencils, Inc. v. Chiappa, 18 N.Y.2d 125 (N.Y. 1966), but not if the defendant simply failed to disclose it, Zumpano v. Quinn, 6 N.Y.3d 666 (2006), or if the delay was attributable to a lack of diligence on plaintiff's part. Kotlyarsky v. N.Y. Post, Kotlyarsky v. N.Y. Post, 757 N.Y.S.2d 703 (2003).**

You would then apply the synthesized rule the same way you would apply any other rule. If the rule is clear, marshal the facts and come to a conclusion. If the rule needs an explanation, add the facts of one or all of the cases to explain it. If the rule is vague, apply it by analogizing or distinguishing the case that is closest factually to the situation involved in the fact pattern. For example, you would use General Stencils, Inc. v. Chiappa, if your case involves something like a cover-up, Zumpano v. Quinn, if the facts describe something similar to a failure to disclose, or Kotlyarsky v. N.Y. Post, if the delay is attributable to something that could be characterized as a lack of diligence on plaintiff's part.

D. Explaining and Applying a Rule with Multiple Cases

Up to this point I have been using legal analysis examples that involve the application of just one case to a fact pattern. However, in practice, it is often necessary to use multiple cases not just to state the rule completely, but also to explain what the rule means and then apply it.

When you are dealing with multiple cases, strict adherence to "Ferrari Has Really Cool Race Cars" is usually inappropriate. Instead it is often more effective to explain the rule with a single sentence (a "one liner") for each case. For example, you can cite a case that contains one element of the rule and state the holding for the case (or just the relevant facts) in parenthesis after the cite.

> **The doctrine of equitable estoppel applies to toll the statute of limitations if, for example, the defendant's wrongdoing caused the delay in filing the case. E.g., General Stencils, Inc. v. Chiappa, 18 N.Y.2d 125 (N.Y. 1966)(defendant committed wrongdoing by covering up the claim).**

Or you can state the holding for the case and then add the reasoning for the holding in parenthesis after the case cite.

> **If the failure to disclose was unintentional it does not constitute wrongdoing sufficient to toll the statute of limitations. E.g., Zumpano v. Quinn, 6 N.Y.3d 666 (2006) (equitable estoppel does not apply if what the defendant did does not constitute fraudulent concealment).**

Here is an example for how to explain a rule synthesized from multiple cases using one liners and then apply the rule to a fact pattern. Under Illinois law the rule for "constructive eviction requires that the landlord have done something of a grave and permanent character with the intention of depriving the tenant of the enjoyment of the premises." E.g., St. Louis North Joint Venture v. P & L Enterprises, 116 F.3d 262 (7th Cir. 1997); Metropolitan Life Ins. Co. v. Nauss, 226 Ill. App. 3d 1014 (4th Dist. 1992); Applegate v. Inland Real Estate Corp., 109 Ill. App. 3d 986 (2nd Dist. 1982). An explanation of the rule using those three cases might look something like this:

> A constructive eviction requires that the landlord have done some "wrongful act" of a "grave and permanent character" with the intention of depriving the tenant of enjoyment of the premises. **E.g., Applegate v. Inland Real Estate Corp.**, 109 Ill. App. 3d 986 (2nd Dist. 1982) (A permanent condition that causes a health hazard, like cockroach infestation that could not be remedied, could support a claim for constructive conviction); **St. Louis North Joint Venture v. P & L Enterprises**, 116 F.3d 262 (7th Cir. 1997)(Temporary inconveniences, like issues with parking and access resulting from renovations to the property, would not support such a claim). Also, if the landlord takes steps to rectify the situation in response to the tenant's complaints, there would likely not be any basis for a finding that the landlord intentionally deprived the tenant of the use of the premises. **E.g., Metropolitan Life Ins. Co. v. Nauss**, 226 Ill. App. 3d 1014 (4th Dist. 1992) (landlord attempted to mitigate the effects of construction by having the work done only at night).

As you can see, I started my explanation by stating the rule, citing a case (Applegate) and then providing examples of the application of the rule by just stating the holdings for

<u>Applegate</u> and another case (<u>St. Louis North Joint Venture</u>) in parenthesis after each cite. Then I included an additional aspect of the rule (steps the landlord takes to rectify the situation), cited another case (<u>Metropolitan Life</u>) and explained that aspect of the rule by including the relevant facts in parenthesis after the cite for that case.

When you are dealing with a rule that takes multiple cases to describe or explain, there may be one case that is closest to the fact pattern. If there is, you could use that case to apply the rule. Otherwise, the application of the rule to the fact pattern will likely also involve multiple cases. In other words, you will have to compare portions of multiple cases to portions of the fact pattern; you will not be able to just explain and apply a single case. Here is an example of an application of the constructive eviction rule stated above that involves multiple cases:

> **The tenant in this case claims he was constructively evicted because of loud music from a neighboring apartment occupied by a student who would be leaving in three months. Since a landlord's action to remedy the situation is evidence the landlord did not intentionally deprive the tenant of his enjoyment of the property, the tenant may argue that his landlord's repeated refusal to do anything to rectify the problem is evidence his landlord did have such intent. Regardless, loud music would likely be considered a temporary inconvenience, and would not be sufficiently "grave" to support a claim for constructive eviction. Although a condition that poses a danger to the tenant's health would serious enough to support a claim for constructive eviction, a mere inconvenience like loud music would not support such a claim. Therefore, a court would likely find that the tenant in this case was not constructively evicted.**

In addition to using alternate structures to explain a rule, it may also be appropriate to modify the IREAC structure to better suit the circumstances. For example, rather than explain all the cases in one paragraph and then apply them in the next, it may make more sense to explain and apply one case, and then explain and apply the next case(s) (*i.e.* use IREAEAC), if doing that makes the analysis clearer.

The rule may be clear or it may need to be explained, and you may need to do an analogy to apply it. The rule may be derived from multiple cases, not just one case; and it may take multiple cases to explain and apply it. Regardless of the situation, some variation of IRAC will work to organize your analysis.

Up until this point, I have been talking about what is often called "small scale organization," which is the use of various structures to organize your paragraphs as you analyze a specific issue. The last step in this process is "large scale organization," which is the organization of multiple issues into a legal memorandum. And that is the topic for the next chapter.

8. OBJECTIVE LEGAL MEMORANDA

U nlike everything we have to discussed to this point, a legal memorandum is a finished product you give to someone else to read. A memorandum is something someone else may rely on in making a legal decision. It may just be the person you gave it to who reads it. Or that person may give it to someone else. It may even be something that gets circulated around a law firm and read by people you don't even know. Because of that, it is very important that a legal memorandum stand on its own two feet. You aren't going to be able to explain and clarify what you said to everyone who reads it. So the writing has to be clear. You need to state the facts your opinions are based on, and it is often appropriate to state what the source of those facts was. Also, the scope of what you were asked to write about must be set forth. And your conclusions must be appropriately limited and qualified.

A legal memorandum is also the end product of everything we have discussed thus far. To draft one well, you need to know how they are typically organized. The structure I will discuss consists of five sections: the issue presented, brief answer, facts, discussion and conclusion. Like everything else, there is more than one way to do it; but that is the most common format. I'll explain each section separately, give you some advice and some pointers, and then provide an example of a memorandum that was drafted using this organization.

A. Organization of a Legal Memorandum

Legal memoranda typically start with a heading, like this:

MEMORANDUM

To: _____

From: _____

Date: _____ __, ____

Subject: Client / Matter

After the heading is the text of the memo (the issue presented, brief answer, facts, discussion and conclusion). I'll organize my discussion of each of those elements the same way I would organize them in a legal memo. Also, for purposes of this discussion, I will use the example of analyzing an issue governed by a statutory rule.

I.   Issue Presented

State the issue as whether a specific legal principle will be applied to particular facts in one way or another. Make sure you are following the instructions in the assignment. Don't just state a legal conclusion; the issue is how the law will be applied to specific facts. Use two or three sentences, if necessary, but be concise.

II.   Brief Answer

Answer the issue in a word (i.e. "Yes." or "No.") or a sentence. And then briefly explain the legal and factual basis for your conclusion in three to five sentences or more, but, again, be concise. Use "likely" or "probably" to qualify your answer, since it is impossible to predict with certainty what a court will do. If there are multiple reasons for your position, just state a few of the more important reasons and leave the rest for the discussion. Also, make sure what is stated here is consistent with what is presented in the discussion (i.e. you don't have one conclusion in the brief answer, and then come to a different conclusion in the discussion).

III.   Facts

It is usually appropriate to start by indicating what the source of the facts is. If your memo is based on what the client told you (or what the senior partner in the firm told you the client told her), you should indicate that at the beginning of the facts section. If you are getting the facts from discovery responses in litigation, then cite to the applicable deposition transcript or answers to interrogatories or other pleading containing that information. That way the reader can look up the specific statements you are referring to, if he desires to do that.

Also, you usually don't want to just copy the facts from the fact pattern. Paraphrase and summarize background facts; and state relevant facts in detail, quoting oral or written statements where appropriate. Use short, clear sentences, and make sure your verb tenses are consistent (I'd recommend describing the facts in the past tense). Tell a story in chronological order, or adopt some other organization for the information you are presenting. Also, make sure your descriptions of the facts are accurate; double check to make sure you haven't misstated any facts.

IV.   Discussion

Start the discussion by stating the issue you have been asked to analyze. If the issue has to do with the interpretation of a statute, put the language of the statute in quotations or do a block quote.

> *Remember to use the block quote form for long quotations or for quotations you want to emphasize. Indent and single space the quoted language; and use brackets for alterations and ellipses for omitted words or phrases.*

Also, make sure you put the citation in the right place (there should be a black space above the citation and it should be left justified and double spaced so it is part of the original paragraph not the block quote).

If your analysis is based on a statute, then separate out the elements of the statute, and use the structure of the statute as the structure for your memo. If the statute has two elements, and the second element has two additional sub-elements, then your memo should have two sections, and the second section should have two additional sub-sections. If one of the issues is a "given" (i.e. there is no dispute as to how the rule applies to that issue), then obviously you don't have to analyze it. You can just dispense with it in the introduction. But otherwise organize the memo around the organization of the statutory rule.

A.   State the First Issue in Your First Subheading

Since you have already stated the first issue in your first subheading, you don't have to repeat the issue in the text. Start off by stating the rule applicable to the issue. If the rule is stated in a lot of cases, resist the temptation to pad the memo with a long chain cite. Instead just use those cases that are close factually to the fact pattern. Then cite the cases using the appropriate forms. Add a signal if appropriate and include a parenthetical highlighting the key facts or a relevant legal principle.

Now that you have stated the issue and the rule, the next step is to marshal the relevant facts, or explain the rule first, then apply the facts, or explain the rule and do a case analogy. If you are explaining a case, don't be superficial with the facts; go into sufficient depth so the reader can understand what happened. But don't spend time reciting irrelevant facts either; just focus in on the information relevant to the issue. Then state the holding and any rationale or reasoning for the court's decision. If you are not quoting the court directly, make sure you are accurately paraphrasing what the court said or decided. And don't forget to include pin cites after each sentence (don't just put one cite at the end of the paragraph), so the reader can see where you got your information from.

If need to compare a case to the fact pattern, start with a good topic sentence, like saying whether you think the case is analogous or distinguishable. Then restate the facts relevant to the first issue in the discussion section. You will have already stated the facts in the fact section, but you still need to restate the relevant facts in the discussion section. And, again, make sure your description of the facts is accurate. Compare the facts of the two cases (e.g. using "like" and "as") to support the position your case is either analogous or distinguishable. Make sure you are not comparing "apples to oranges." Your reasoning has to be consistent with the court's rationale for the case. And finish by stating your conclusion, even if you think it's obvious.

B.   State the Second Sub Issue in Your
Second Subheading

Organize the second sub issue the same way you organized the text under the first sub issue. Use IRAC, IREAC and Ferrari has really cool race cars, as applicable. Here is an outline that includes all three:

1. Start with a broad statement of Issue in the heading or text
2. Then the applicable Rule, cite case(s), use signals, parentheticals
3. Explain the rule with the case that is closest factually to the fact pattern
   a. State the case Facts, include pin cites
   b. State the case Holding, include pin cites
   c. Explain the case Rationale, include pin cites
4. Apply the rule, state whether the case is analogous or distinguishable, if you are comparing the case to a fact pattern
   a. Compare the Facts of the fact pattern to the facts of the case
   b. Apply the Rationale of the case
   c. Come to a specific Conclusion
5. Finish with a broad statement of the Conclusion

You don't always have to address a counterargument. But if there is an obvious one, you should deal with it in your memo. Start by stating what the argument is and how it would be supported. A counterargument may be based on a different case that seems to support a different conclusion, or it may be based on different interpretation of the same case or a different interpretation of the applicable facts. Regardless, if you are going to address a counterargument, you need to effectively refute the argument and reiterate your conclusion. You can't have it both ways; you need to take a position one way or the other and be consistent throughout the memo.

C.   State the Third Sub Issue in Your Third Subheading

Make sure you are not running out of gas when you write the final sections of your memo. Among other things, the last sections may be the most important, so you may need to go into more depth and detail than the other sections. Assuming you have been taking notes, you already have written down everything you need to know to organize the third section. If you haven't been taking notes, go back and write down what I said under the first two subheadings, and then organize the third sub issue the same way you organized the first two.

Also, before you pass the memo in make sure to proofread it for spelling and grammatical errors. Make sure every sentence begins with a capital letter and ends with a period, and every citation sentence ends with a period. Double check citations using an appropriate reference book to make sure they are in the proper form. Also, check the font and paragraph format for each page. I prefer Century or Times New Roman size twelve font; I wouldn't use Courier because it makes it look like you used a typewriter to write the memo. But you should use whatever font your teacher or you're the person you are working for prefers. The tabs for each paragraph and section should line up under each other. There should be one inch margins all around, each page should be numbered, and the text should be double spaced (there is no need to quadruple space between sections). Again, those are just my recommendations. If you are doing the memo for a law professor, or law firm partner, then do it however she wants it done.

V.　Conclusion

Reiterate the brief answer, qualifying it in the same way using "likely" or "probably." Even less information is needed at this point, since the reader has now read your discussion. Don't introduce new issues and information in the conclusion. Just restate the answer as succinctly as possible.

B. Sample Legal Memorandum

Here is an example of a short legal memo drafted using these guidelines. This memo involves a Pennsylvania criminal statute for the crime of stalking, which contains a rule with multiple elements.

MEMORANDUM

To:　　　　**Senior Partner**

From:　　　**Junior Associate**

Date:　　　**September 18, 2019**

Subject:　　**Edwards / Stalking Charge**

I. Issue Presented

Whether our client, Philip Edwards (Edwards) committed the crime of stalking his ex-girlfriend, Mary Rodriguez (Rodriguez), after she terminated a romantic relationship with him, by threatening her, following her home from work, and vandalizing her car.

II. Brief Answer

Yes. Edwards likely committed the crime of stalking by threatening Rodriguez, following her home from work, and vandalizing her car.

III.<u>Statement of Facts</u>

According to a lengthy report submitted by Scranton police on December 1, 2019, Rodriguez terminated a romantic relationship with her boyfriend, Edwards, in June of 2018.

Unhappy with this arrangement, Edwards tried to rekindle the relationship. On one occasion, he brought Rodriguez flowers in a glass vase, which she rejected. He then flew into a rage, smashed the vase on her front step and told her "if I can't have you, no one else can either. I'll make sure of that one way or another."

In August of 2018, Edwards also began calling Rodriguez and delivering love letters to her. Rodriguez mother told Edwards he was upsetting Rodriguez. When he heard that he smiled and said "maybe if I keep going she will eventually come to her senses." And he continued calling her and sending her letters.

In October Edwards behavior escalated further. On two occasions, he followed Rodriguez home from work. On another occasion, Rodriquez came home late one evening to find him asleep on her doorstep. He was drunk and apparently had been lying there for a long time.

Then, in the early morning hours of November 15,

2019 Edwards rang Rodriguez's doorbell. Rodriguez called the police, who arrived to discover that Edwards had keyed "Mary Loves Philip" on the bumper of Rodriguez's car. Edwards was arrested and confessed to the police that he rang the doorbell and vandalized the car. He was charged with committing the crime of stalking.

IV. Discussion

You have asked me to analyze the issue of whether Edwards committed the crime of stalking his ex-girlfriend, Rodriguez.

In Pennsylvania, the offense of stalking is defined as follows:

(a) Offense defined. A person commits the crime of stalking when the person . . .

(1) engages in a course of conduct or repeatedly commits acts toward another person, including following the person without proper authority, under circumstances which demonstrate either an intent to place such other person in reasonable fear of bodily injury or to cause substantial emotional distress to such other person . . . .

18 Pa. Cons. Stat. Ann. § 2709.1(a)(1).

Pennsylvania's stalking statute was enacted to protect victims by providing early intervention since stalking was seen as a precursor to violence. Commonwealth v. Urrutia, 653 A.2d 706, 708 (Pa. Super. Ct. 1995). The crime has two elements, the first is "course of conduct" and the second is intent. 18 Pa. Cons. Stat. Ann. § 2709.1(a)(1). The required intent is either intent to place another in fear of bodily injury or intent to cause substantial emotional distress to another. Id.

In this case there is no question Edwards engaged in a course of conduct by, among other things, following Rodriguez home from work on two occasions. The only issue is whether his actions demonstrated intent to place her in fear of bodily injury or to cause her substantial emotional distress. Among other things, Edwards claims he still loves Rodriguez and his intent was only to somehow rekindle their relationship.

A.   Whether Edwards' Conduct Demonstrated Intent to Cause Rodriquez Fear of Bodily Injury.

Intent to instill fear of bodily injury is demonstrated by threatening a person, berating someone, acting violently or actually assaulting the person. See, e.g., Commonwealth v. Urrutia, 653 A.2d 706 (Pa. Super. Ct. 1995) (ex-boyfriend exhibited violent behavior and threatened to kill victim); Commonwealth v. Johnson, 768 A.2d 1177 (Pa. Super. Ct. 2001) (ex-boyfriend threatened and physically assaulted victim, yelled and made obscene gestures); Commonwealth v. Davis, 737 A.2d 792 (Pa. Super. Ct. 1999) (former husband threatened to break victim's legs, and tried to hit victim with car). Notably, it is irrelevant whether actual or attempted bodily injury is actually caused or whether the defendant offers "innocuous explanations" for what he did. Commonwealth v. Miller, 689 A.2d 238, 240 (Pa. Super. Ct. 1997).

Like the ex-lovers in Urrutia, Johnson and Davis, Edwards threatened his victim by telling her "if I can't have you, no one else can either. I'll make sure of that one way or another." He may claim he was still in love and meant no harm but his innocuous explanations for what he did are irrelevant. The threat is enough to show intent to instill fear of bodily injury. In addition, Edwards acted violently by flying into a rage and smashing a flower vase on Rodriguez door step. Based on the precedent in Urrutia, Johnson and Davis, Edwards behavior likely demonstrated his intent to put Rodriguez in imminent fear of bodily injury.

C.   Whether Edwards' Conduct Demonstrated Intent to Cause Rodriguez Emotional Distress.

Intent to cause substantial emotional distress is shown by repeatedly harassing a person, and continuing that conduct after being made aware that it was causing the person emotional distress. See, e.g., Commonwealth v. Roefaro, 691 A.2d 472 (Pa. Super. Ct. 1997) (defendant 's unabated romantic advances caused victim to move out of state, and he continued his actions after she returned); Commonwealth v. Schierscher, 668 A.2d 164 (Pa. Super. Ct. 1995) (defendant harassed victim by repeatedly calling her office and distributing materials disparaging her even after being told what has was doing was making the victim ill).

Like the defendants in Roefaro and Schierscher, Edwards repeatedly harassed his victim by calling her and sending her letters. More importantly, his conduct continued even after it was made clear to him that his actions were causing her distress. Rodriguez mother told Edwards he was upsetting Rodriguez, but that didn't influence him to stop; it had the opposite effect. He smiled and said "maybe if I keep going she will eventually come to her senses," and he kept going. That incident is enough to demonstrate intent to cause emotional distress. Again, it is irrelevant whether Rodriguez claims his ultimate motives were benign. Continuing to engage in contact after you are made aware of its effect demonstrates intent to cause that effect. Based on <u>Roefaro</u> and <u>Schierscher</u>, Edwards behavior also demonstrated intent to cause emotional distress.

V. <u>Conclusion.</u>

For all of the above reasons, Edwards likely committed the crime of stalking Rodriguez.

Like IRAC, the rules for organizing an office memo are not written in stone. If a modified version of this structure would work better for the issues you are analyzing, then modify the structure accordingly.

The principles that apply to legal memoranda are also applicable to other types of legal writing, like client letters and exam answers. Those additional examples of legal writing are discussed in the next chapter.

9. OTHER EXAMPLES OF LEGAL WRITING

T he basic principles outlined in this book also apply to the letters you write to clients when you are practicing and the answers you write for professors when you are in law school. The primary reason you have to alter the form for clients is because of the audience. You wouldn't communicate with a client the same way you would communicate with another lawyer. The primary reason you have to alter the form for law school is because of the circumstances. You don't have an unlimited amount of time when you write an exam answer. And you are usually required to take the exam without consulting the books you read.

A. Client Letters

Client letters need to be drafted a little differently than other types of legal writing. Basically, what you need to do is translate the substance to make it understandable by someone who didn't go to law school. Instead of saying the court "held," say the court "decided." Instead of saying the decision was "reversed," just say who won. Make sure your conclusions are appropriately qualified. Never say the client's case will or will not be successful. Instead say the client is likely or unlikely to succeed. And also delete case cites and other references intended for lawyers, not laypeople.

Here is an example of a client letter:

CONFIDENTIAL
ATTORNEY CLIENT PRIVILEGE

April 24, 2020

Steve and Mary Jones
101 University Avenue
Gainesville, FL

Re: Habitability Claim

Dear Mr. and Mrs. Jones:

You have asked me to research and analyze the issue of whether the presence of plant extract aromas in your apartment makes the space so unlivable that you would legally be permitted to move out. Unfortunately, a Massachusetts court will likely decide that the presence of plant extract aromas in your apartment does not render the apartment uninhabitable.

When we met you stated that you have been living in a fourth floor apartment in an old building in Boston for the past year. You have a daughter, Jane, who has allergies. One month ago, three law school students moved into the apartment just below. The students are using aromatherapy to help deal with the stress and pressure of law school. They have diffusers located throughout their apartment. The diffusers emit strong aromas from various plant extracts and oils. The fumes from the diffusers are seeping into your apartment, and causing Jane to have difficulty breathing. She wheezes while she is sleeping

---

because of the odors; and her doctor has advised you that the constant presence of the fumes is a danger to Jane's health.

You also stated that you spoke to the students about the aromas seeping into your apartment and explained Jane's problem with allergies but the students refused to stop using the diffusers. You then went to the landlord to complain, However, the landlord said he could not stop the students from doing aromatherapy because the students' lease did not contain any provision that would prohibit them from using aroma diffusers in the apartment. Also, the plant aromas were infiltrating your apartment because the building was heated with steam heat. There were gaps around the pipes that carried the steam up through the building. The gaps were needed to accommodate the expansion of the pipes when they get hot. The fumes traveled up through the gaps around the pipes and into your apartment. The landlord said he would have to install a new heating system for the entire building to eliminate the gaps and make each apartment more air tight.

Based on my research, a condition that the state sanitary code prohibits because it "may endanger or impair the health, or safety and well-being of a person or persons occupying the premises" makes an apartment legally uninhabitable. For example, in the case of *Elliott v. Chaouche*, a tenant with a three year old child claimed that the apartment the tenant occupied was not livable because it contained lead paint in violation of the sanitary code. The code states that lead paint is a condition which "may endanger or materially impair the health or safety, and well-being of an occupant.' As a result, the Court decided that the lead paint made the apartment uninhabitable.

Regrettably, I think your situation is different. Among other things, there is no violation of any sanitary code or the building code in your case. It may be illegal to have lead paint in a residential apartment, but there is nothing illegal about using aromatherapy diffusers in an apartment. In fact, the aromas they produced are claimed to have health benefits. And the gaps around the pipes in your apartment are also not in violation of any statute or regulation. Therefore, the reasoning of the *Elliott* case probably would not apply. The presence of plant extract fumes in your apartment likely does not make it uninhabitable.

In another case, *Lynch v. James,* a tenant with an infant child claimed her apartment was uninhabitable because it did not have "window stops or guards" on the windows. Because that protection was absent, the child fell from their third floor apartment window and sustained serious injuries. However, the court disagreed with the tenant's position, observing that there was nothing in the sanitary code requiring the use of window stops. The court decided that, since the use of stops was "optional with the tenant," the apartment was not uninhabitable without them.

In my judgment, your case is similar to the *Lynch* case. Again, there is no statutory prohibition against doing aromatherapy in residential apartments; and there is no regulatory requirement that a building be free of gaps in the walls and ceilings. As your landlord stated, "the infiltration of fumes is to be expected in older apartments." Because there is no code violation, our position that the apartment is uninhabitable is unlikely to succeed.

A Massachusetts court will likely decide that the presence of plant extract fumes in your apartment does not make your apartment so unlivable that you would legally be permitted to move out.

Sincerely,

Ben L. Fernandez

Since a client letter is, by definition, a privileged communication, it is good idea to mark it as such. If you have a "Confidential" stamp, at least put a stamp on the letter. Better yet, put a statement to that effect in the header or footer so it appears on every page. One of your ethical duties is to take reasonable steps to protect the confidentiality of client communications. That is why I wrote "Confidential: Attorney Client Privilege" at the top of this letter.

If your client is reasonably sophisticated (and interested), you could also send him copies of the case opinions you refer to (or offer to do that). But for most clients a letter like this has more than enough depth. The bottom line here is that a court is unlikely to find a breach of the implied warranty of habitability where no violation of the sanitary code exists. In this case there is no violation, so the client is unlikely to succeed. And just that bottom line may be all the client wants to know. So use your good judgment to vary the level of depth and detail, depending upon what you think would be most beneficial for the client's needs.

B. Exam Answers

The best advice I can give you for how to write an exam answer is to find out what your professor wants. Different professors are looking for different things from you in an exam answer. So find out as much as you can about what the professor wants. Ask for past exams and sample answers. Ask if the professor has a grading checklist she is willing to share. Find out who booked the class last year, take that guy out for lunch, and pick his brain as much as he will let you!

Usually, writing an exam answer in law school is primarily about issue spotting. So the first order of business is to spot the issues. If you know the material, that will not be as difficult as you think. Figure out what the issues are, and then separately address each issue in your answer.

Second is reciting the rule for each issue, which you hopefully remember from the cases you read for class. Even better if you can remember the name of the case and refer to the case by name in the exam answer. If the rule has multiple elements, address each element separately.

The third aspect of answering a law school exam is probably what most separates an "A" exam from a "B" exam, and that is being able to analogize or distinguish the facts in the exam question to or from the facts of the case you read in class, and come to a conclusion. Again, legal reasoning is primarily analogical reasoning. If you just say the issue is proximate cause and, in your opinion, the requirement is not met based on the facts in the prompt, your answer will likely be too superficial. In other words, you saw the issue but you really didn't analyze it.

To organize your answer, use IRAC, or some variation of IRAC, and the Ferrari has really cool race cars mnemonic, as applicable. Apply the principles you learned in this book. Allocate your time and go into as much depth as you can. Don't just state the issue, rule and conclusion. Apply the rule by analogizing and distinguishing facts. That is at the core of legal reasoning, and it is one of the primary things you are expected to learn your first year of law school.

After the exam is over, resist the temptation to discuss the answers with your peers. For one thing, there usually is no right answer to a law school exam question, if it is well put together. What I mean is that you can legitimately answer one way or another. What is important is that you saw the issue, applied the rule and came to a conclusion. Often there is more than one way to do that correctly, so don't get all upset if your classmate came to a completely different conclusion than the one you came to.

The advice I got when I was in law school was that if you thought the exam was difficult and you aren't sure how you did, you probably did well. If you thought the exam was easy and you aced it, you probably bombed. So let those people who are boasting that they aced the exam have their time in the sun. They may be singing a different tune when grades come out. As long as you did your best, learned as much as you could and tried to demonstrate that on the exam, give yourself a break. Don't worry about how you did; let it go and turn your attention to whatever you have to do next.

The last thing I want to do is give you some general advice about writing well. This isn't a book on grammar so I'll keep it short and sweet, and recommend some reading if you need more. Then I'll let you go on your way.

10. IMPROVING YOUR WRITING

If you could be a fly on the wall in a teacher's lounge for legal writing professors you would likely overhear some complaining about the quality of student writing. In my opinion, the primary reason for that is because it is virtually impossible to write well about something you don't completely understand. And that is exactly what law school requires you to do. You are just starting to read cases and understand legal reasoning during your first year of law school. And that is when you are also required to learn how to write legal memoranda.

In addition to that not all law students did a lot of writing as undergraduates. Take me for example. I studied chemistry as an undergraduate. I don't think I did any writing at all in my chemistry classes. Those weren't the only courses I had to take to get a degree from the College of Arts and Sciences. But still, I didn't have to do much writing as an undergraduate. Law school was completely different than my undergraduate experience. Not only were there mountains of things to read, but I had to do a do a lot of writing as well.

Plus legal writing is different than any type of writing

you may have studied as an undergraduate. You can be an English major who did very well in college and still have a lot of trouble with legal writing. There are no points for creativity and imagination in legal writing. The style is very structured. You have to think and write in a very organized way. You have to pay very close attention to the language you read in cases and the language you use to write about them. And it is very important that your writing is clear.

If you have trouble doing all that, there is no need be discouraged. Welcome to the club! A lot of law students have trouble with legal writing. In fact, some of the students with the best grades in other classes don't do well in their legal writing course. Writing is a skill. Learning to do it well is completely different than learning substantive legal principles in classes like torts, contracts and property.

Probably the most important thing to learn for legal writing is clarity and organization. To make your analysis of legal problems clear, your writing has to be very well organized. That is why law students learn IRAC and the sections of a legal memo. To make your writing even more effective, you may want to add subheadings to the sections we covered here. Also, start your paragraphs with good topic sentences and finish with good transitions to whatever is discussed next.

The second most important thing is concision. You need to practice writing concisely. When you are explaining a complex concept, the sentences you use should be short, simple and straightforward, or you will make it even harder to understand than it already is. If your writing is wordy and awkward, it will be impossible to understand what you are saying.

And the third most important thing is accuracy. You

can't get the facts wrong. You can't say a case says something the case doesn't actually say. You can't have typos in your case cites. You have to get those things exactly correct. You have to learn pay close attention to the statutes and cases you read; and you have to pay close attention to what you write about them. "Close enough" is not enough for legal writing.

As luck would have it the rules of grammar and punctuation are designed to accomplish those same goals. So if your grammar isn't that great or if you aren't always sure how to correctly punctuate a sentence, you are going to have trouble writing clearly. Misplacing a modifier or making an indefinite pronoun reference will make your writing ambiguous. Put a comma in the wrong place and you may inadvertently change the meaning of what you have written.

There are computer programs out there that can help you, including Core Grammar for Lawyers, which many law schools offer to their law students. If that is not within reach there are also grammar programs for consumers available on line, including one called Grammarly that you may find helpful.

When I was in law school I read a copy of Strunk & White's *The Elements of Style*, which is probably one of the most well-known books on grammar. I especially liked that book because it was short, concise and easy to digest, like the books I write for law students.

Two of my peers at the University of Florida have also written a similar book especially for lawyers called *Grammar, Punctuation, and Style: A Quick Guide for Lawyers and Other Writers,* Cupples and Temple-Smith (West Academic Publishing July 9, 2013). That is probably the best book I could recommend for a law student looking for additional writing support.

No matter what your background is you shouldn't expect to write like a legal expert the first time you try writing a research memo. Don't get flustered or defensive when your writing professor gives you a lot of feedback on your work. He is just trying to help you; and you have a lot to learn. So try to absorb as much feedback as you can.

Never feel like anything you create is written in stone. You can always do better. Never feel like you know everything there is to know. You can always learn more.

Stay motivated and practice as much as you can.

PART II: PERSUASIVE WRITING

11. CREDIBILITY

Persuasive legal documents are drafted the way that they are for three reasons. The first reason is because they apply the same customs and practices we discussed in the first ten chapters of this book, including starting a memo or brief with a description of the applicable facts, then discussing the applicable law, and finishing with a conclusion, as well as structuring the analyses of specific issues using CREAC (stating the conclusion first, then the rule, explaining the rule and applying it to the facts, and coming to a conclusion). If you haven't mastered those skills yet, you will have to continue to work on them as you learn persuasive drafting.

The second reason is because persuasive legal documents are subject to the rules of civil and appellate procedure, including the requirements for granting the relief requested and the requirements for the form and substance of the documents. In addition, the conduct of attorneys in litigation is governed by the ethical rules for the jurisdiction in which they are practicing.

And the third reason persuasive documents are written the way they are is because they try to compensate for or take advantage of the way people think. To persuade someone to do something you have to consider how that person thinks about you, your client and the information you are providing. Among other things, you have to consider the effects of credibility and bias. I'll discuss credibility in this chapter and bias in the next.

The reason credibility is important is because judges have to rely to varying degrees on the information they receive from counsel, and credibility is a way of determining the reliability of that information. If you argue a motion and the judge rules in your favor from the bench, then he is doing that relying on what you told him. If you lack credibility and he questions the reliability of what you said, it is more likely your motion will be denied. If he takes the matter under advisement and issues a ruling later, he may also take the time and effort required to do his own independent investigation of the law. But, if you lack credibility, he isn't likely to do that either.

Normally a person would rely on your identity to determine your credibility. They would know who you are and what your reputation is. But especially when you are just starting out, the judge will likely not know who you are. Instead, she will make inferences about you based on the way you present yourself in person and in writing. I bet you already know well how to make a good impression in person. I don't think I've ever seen a student show up for a job interview who wasn't properly dressed and conducting herself in a professional manner. To ensure your writing is credible, you need to make sure your memos and briefs are just as presentable.

Credible persuasive writing is writing that is done well. A well written document should earn the court's respect; a poorly written document will likely not be taken seriously. If you cite a case that has been overruled or heavily criticized, your credibility will be harmed. If you consistently cite cases incorrectly, you will look like you don't know what you are doing. So research and citation are important skills for an advocate to master.

Incorrectly structuring a legal argument using CREAC, comparing apples to oranges in a case analogy, or misinterpreting a statutory formula, will also hurt your credibility as an advocate. Legal reasoning is at the heart of persuasive writing. If your reasoning is invalid, your credibility will be lost, and it will likely become impossible to convince the judge of your position. If you don't understand relevance and can't marshal the facts to the elements of a statutory formula, you will likely suffer the same consequences.

The same thing is true of every other aspect of writing a memo or brief. If your document does not conform properly to the rules of procedure, or even if it just has a lot of typos, numbering mistakes or formatting errors, all those things will also hurt your credibility as an advocate. You wouldn't show up to an oral argument with your shirt hanging out of your pants. You need to make sure your writing is polished for the same reason.

Because credibility so important and credibility in writing is achieved by writing well, it is a good idea to start the topic of persuasive writing by reviewing what you learned about writing objective research memoranda. Take some time to review the basic principles of legal writing in the first half of this book, including the chapters on legal research, applying cases, analyzing statutes and basic legal citation. To draft a persuasive document well you have to have first master the basics of research, analysis, CREAC and citation.

In addition to writing well, credibility in writing is also

established by writing persuasively. When you draft a memo or brief, you need to write with conviction, like you believe in what you are saying and you think it is important. You need to take every opportunity you have to persuade the judge of your position. When you state the issue, state it persuasively. As you make each point, make your statements in a way that makes clear the merit of your argument. When you explain and apply cases, do it convincingly. And state your conclusions persuasively as well. If you don't do that, your credibility as an advocate will suffer.

For example, you would never write in a brief something like "My client's position is that the motion should be allowed." You are not there to pass along your client's request. You might qualify your statement that way if you are writing a research memo for a law firm. But when you are drafting a memo or brief for a judge, you are not just analyzing a problem and reporting on the answer. Your job is to convince the judge he must grant the relief your client requests. If you do that sounding like you don't believe in your own case, no judge is going to be willing to waste time listening to your argument.

In addition to writing persuasively, you also need to write purposefully. You need to think about what you are doing, come up with a strategy for persuading the judge to see things your way, and then pursue that strategy in your writing. You can't just blindly apply everything you read here. I will show you a lot of techniques for persuasively stating facts and arguing law. But that does not mean you should use all those techniques all the time. If you overdo it, that will also affect your credibility. So you need to consider the context and how your statements are being received. If what you are doing isn't working, change course. In the end credibility is more important than continuing to follow a rule or some advice that isn't working.

Credibility is not only relevant to the impression made by you and your writing, it is also relevant to the audience you are addressing. Trying to persuade a judge who is biased against you or your client for whatever reason is an extremely difficult thing to do. The reason is because the bias of your audience can have a profound negative effect on your credibility and your client's credibility. So it is also important to think about bias when you advocate on behalf of someone else. And that is the subject we will discuss in the next chapter.

12. BIAS

Everyone has biases, some they are aware of, and some they are not. Some biases are harmless. Others can get in the way of your ability to do your job. And that is particularly true of biases that relate to a person's race, ethnicity, gender, religion or sexual orientation. As an attorney you need to be aware of your own biases because they can hamper your ability to communicate with clients who are different than you, and whose experiences are different than your own. And you also you need to be aware of the biases of your audience, including the judges you are trying to persuade.

You may not think of yourself as biased. Most people don't. But most of us nonetheless have many biases that are unconscious or "implicit".

Implicit bias is formed and trapped in the subconscious by years of teachings, experiences, and other environmental and social influences. It exists beneath the surface. Our implicit biases function as an unfortunate default position for the brain in times of controversy, conflict, and disagreement.

*   *   *

The troubling thing about implicit bias is that it

is insidious, hiding in the recesses of the brain. Implicit bias can be so dormant that we are offended by the very suggestion that it exists within us. Whether in times of harmony or conflict, when we are confronted about our obvious biases, we are quick to deny with the common response that "I have friends" who are members of the group at issue.

*   *   *

Most people are sincerely confident that they do not fall into the category of bigot. At the same time, too many really good people are unaware that they are captive to their subconscious biases, even to a point that it renders them incapable of making meaningful and effective contributions to the dialogue, too often at the most critical moments.

Vincent F. Cornelius, *Understanding Implicit Bias*, 104 ILL. B.J. 10 (2016).

To eliminate implicit bias you must first recognize that it exists and take conscientious measures to surmount it. Julia L. Ernst, *Eliminating Implicit Bias*, 67 GAVEL 16 (2020). Talking about bias helps, as does "maintaining an open posture, making eye contact, and speaking fluidly." Michael B. Hyman, *Reining in Implicit Bias*, 105 ILL. B.J. 26 (2017). Also, "exposing ourselves to individuals who, and situations that, do not align with our subconscious associations" helps us to "construct new mental associations to override those in our subconscious." Sarah Q. Simmons, *Litigators Beware: Implicit Bias*, 59 ADVOCATE 35 (2016).

When you harbor misconceptions about people you may unintentionally make statements to them that they experience as aggressive, invalidating or otherwise offensive. Those types of statements are called "microaggressions," meaning they are "common place daily verbal, behavioral, or environmental indignities, whether intentional or unintentional, that communicate hostile, derogatory, or negative racial . . . slights and insults toward people of color." Derald Wing Sue, *Microaggressions in Everyday Life: Race, Gender and Sexual Orientation* (2010). Examples of microaggressions include statements like "I don't think of you as Black," "You don't look Jewish" and "Where are you from? No, where are you really from?" Catharine Wells, *Microaggressions: What They Are and Why They Matter*, 24 TEX. Hisp. J. L. & POL'y 61 (2017). Being aware of these micromessages and paying more attention to your own messaging is also part of overcoming implicit bias. Bernice B. Donald & Sarah E. Redfield, *Arcing toward Justice: Strategies to Disrupt Implicit Bias and Limit Its Negative Impact*, 35 CRIM. Just. 55 (2020).

Additional examples of microagressions that are unique to the LGBT community include "(1) the use of heterosexist terminology, (2) the endorsement of heteronormative or gender-conforming culture / behaviors, (3) the assumption of universal LGBT experience, (4) exoticization, (5) discomfort/disapproval of LGBT experience, (6) denial of societal heterosexism / transphobia, and (7) assumption of sexual pathology / abnormality." Ronald Wheeler, *About Microaggressions*, 108 LAW LIBR. J. 321 (2016), citing Kevin L. Nadal *et al.*, *Sexual Orientation Microaggressions: Processes and Coping Mechanisms for Lesbian, Gay, and Bisexual Individuals*, 5 J. LGBT ISSUES COUNSELING 21, 30-32 (2011).

To eliminate microaggressions you need to understand that we all live in different worlds. If you have dealt with racism in your life you tend to see it everywhere. If you have never had that experience, then you tend to think it doesn't exist. Recognize those differences and think about how what you are saying might be perceived by someone whose experiences are different than your own. If you don't do that you may unintentionally make statements that reveal your own bias and offend your audience.

That is one reason why many find it uncomfortable to talk about topics like racism, sexism and heterosexism. Rather than confronting their own misconceptions, and acknowledging the differing experiences of others, what a lot of people do is simply choose not to talk about these topics. People don't want to talk about race or gender because they are afraid they will say something wrong. They are afraid they will inadvertently reveal their own biases.

Avoiding the problem may be an effective plan for some people. But that is not a good strategy for a student training to be an advocate for others. You need to deal with implicit bias and microaggressions relating to race, ethnicity, gender, religion and sexual preference because they can impede your ability to communicate with your client, empathize with their claims and effectively persuade judges to grant them the relief they request.

On top of that, if you are going to practice law you can't be afraid of having difficult conversations with people. Interviewing a criminal defendant charged with child molestation is uncomfortable. Asking a husband to describe the car accident that killed his wife is difficult. If you need to confront a liar in open court, you can't be timid and shy away from calling that person out. You have to go on the attack. And when another attorney launches an attack on your client, you have to go on the defense. You have to open your mouth. You can't just avoid talking about the issue.

In addition to dealing with your own biases, you may also need to deal with the biases of others, including a judge you are trying to persuade or an attorney on the other side of your case. We would like to think prejudice has no place in a courtroom but judges have implicit biases too. Rachlinski, Jeffrey J.; Johnson, Sheri; Wistrich, Andrew J.; and Guthrie, Chris, *"Does Unconscious Racial Bias Affect Trial Judges?"* Cornell Law Faculty Publications. Paper 786 (2009). Prosecuting attorneys possess biases and may even use them against your client. Praatika Prasad, *Implicit Racial Biases in Prosecutorial Summations: Proposing an Integrated Response*, 86 FordhamL. Rev. 667 (2018). In fact, some take the view that the presence of bias in the legal profession is pervasive. Emma Bienias, *et al.*, *Implicit Bias in the Legal Profession*, Intellectual Property Owners Association (2017).

If you represent a client in oral argument and the color of your skin, your facial features, your accent or the way you dress reveals your race, ethnicity, gender, religion or sexual preference, and you are speaking to judge who is prejudiced or harbors misconceptions about you based on stereotypes he adheres to, then that judge's biases may have a negative impact on your credibility. The same thing is true for your client. You may not have had to deal with prejudice in your life, but you may represent clients who have.

To overcome bias in judges first realize the person you are interacting with may not be aware of their own biases, and may not have intended to be aggressive, insulting or patronizing. So give the person who made the statements the benefit of the doubt. Infer whatever she said was not conscious or intentional.   And then address the issue in a calm, non-confrontational way. Try not to get emotional or argumentative. If you do that things will likely just escalate. So don't go on the offensive and launch an attack; and resist personalizing the issue. Just address it and move on.

In addition to calling attention to the issue, look for common ground. People are biased against others who are not like them, but they are also biased in favor of others who are like them. That is called "affinity bias." Stella Tsai & Debra Rosen, *Know Thyself: Affinity Bias in the Legal Profession*, 20 Woman Advoc. 23 (2015). The differences can have a negative effect on credibility, but commonality can offset that effect. So one way you can overcome bias is by appealing to common values and interests.

A great example of a trial lawyer dealing with bias and overcoming it by appealing to a commonality is Clarence Darrow's argument to the judge in the Loeb and Leopold case. Darrow was probably the greatest American advocate who has ever lived. And his argument to the judge in that case was successful. The bias he was dealing with was classism (his clients came from a wealthy family) and he overcame it by calling it out and then appealing to the judge's Christian values (mercy, overcoming hatred with love, etc.).

Affinity bias is not the only bias you can use to your advantage. People are also affected by "anchoring bias." They tend to rely mostly on the first piece of information they learn when they make decisions; that initial piece of information tends to have the most impact on the decision they end up making. Bernice B. Donald & Sarah Redfield, *Arcing toward Justice: Can Understanding Implicit Bias Help Change the Path of Criminal Justice*, 34 CRIM. Just. 18, 25 (2019). A good advocate will take advantage of that unconscious bias by always stating her strongest arguments first in a memo or brief. And that is one of the persuasive techniques we will be discussing in the following chapters.

As we discuss the rules of ethics and procedure in the following chapters, keep the issues of credibility and bias in the back of your mind. Because persuasive writing is done in the context of litigation, you always need to make sure you are following the rules. Because the process involves human beings, you need to deal with the issues of credibility and bias as well.

13. ETHICAL RULES FOR ADVOCACY

W hen you write persuasively and argue a motion or appeal before a court, your conduct and the form and substance of what you write are subject to the rules of ethics and the rules of civil and appellate procedure. In this chapter we will take a brief look at the relevant ethical rules. Those are the requirements that attorneys provide competent and diligent representation, not assert frivolous claims or defenses, act with candor toward the tribunal, and treat the opposing party and counsel fairly.

The first rule is that a lawyer must provide competent representation.

A lawyer must provide competent representation to a client. Competent representation requires the legal knowledge, skill, thoroughness, and preparation reasonably necessary for the representation.

Model R. Prof. Conduct 4.1. Note that knowledge and skill are not the only components of competence. Thoroughness and preparation are also required. In the context of litigation, that means fully investigating the facts of your case and thoroughly researching the applicable law. Here is the explanation in the comments to the rule:

> _Competent handling of a particular matter includes inquiry into and analysis of the factual and legal elements of the problem, and use of methods and procedures meeting the standards of competent practitioners. It also includes adequate preparation._ The required attention and preparation are determined in part by what is at stake; major litigation and complex transactions ordinarily require more extensive treatment than matters of lesser complexity and consequence. The lawyer should consult with the client about the degree of thoroughness and the level of preparation required as well as the estimated costs involved under the circumstances.

Model R. Prof. Conduct 4.1 (comments) (emphasis added).

To provide competent representation to a client in connection with civil litigation or an appeal, you must first learn the rules that govern those processes. You can't just look at a memo or brief someone else drafted and try to figure out how to do it from there. Documents submitted in litigation are drafted the way they are because the rules require them to be done that way. That is one of the many respects in which persuasive writing is different than the objective writing we discussed in chapter eight. To achieve competence in drafting a memo or brief, you must first learn the rules of civil and appellate procedure.

The second rule requires that lawyers act with reasonable diligence:

> _A lawyer shall act with reasonable diligence and promptness in representing a client._

Model R. Prof. Conduct 1.3. The comments make clear that diligence requires a lawyer to, among other things, act with "zeal in advocacy upon the client's behalf."

> *[1] <u>A lawyer should pursue a matter on behalf of a client despite opposition, obstruction or personal inconvenience to the lawyer, and take whatever lawful and ethical measures are required to vindicate a client's cause or endeavor. A lawyer must also act with commitment and dedication to the interests of the client and with zeal in advocacy upon the client's behalf.</u> A lawyer is not bound, however, to press for every advantage that might be realized for a client. For example, a lawyer may have authority to exercise professional discretion in determining the means by which a matter should be pursued. See Rule 1.2. The lawyer's duty to act with reasonable diligence does not require the use of offensive tactics or preclude the treating of all persons involved in the legal process with courtesy and respect.*

Model R. Prof. Conduct 1.3 (comments) (emphasis added).

Representing a client with zeal means doing it with enthusiasm and passion. And that zeal must be reflected in your writing. Your job is to do whatever is necessary to achieve the client's goals. You need to take every opportunity in your memos and briefs to persuade the judge of your position. You need to describe the facts persuasively and state your legal argument persuasively as well. In addition to the rules of procedure you must also learn how to write persuasively, so that you will be able to represent your client with competence and diligence (zeal).

There are three more ethical rules you need to be aware of. The first prohibits counsel from making frivolous claims, and is similar to what is in Fed. R. Civ. P. 11(b)(by signing a pleading the attorney certifies that it is not being presented for an improper purpose, the legal claims are supported by law, and the factual statements are supported by the evidence). Here is relevant part of the rule:

> *A lawyer shall not bring or defend a proceeding, or assert or controvert an issue therein, unless there is a basis in law and fact for doing so that is not frivolous, which includes a good faith argument for an extension, modification or reversal of existing law.*

Model R. Prof. Conduct 3.1. There must be a basis in law (or a good faith argument for an extension, modification or reversal of existing law) for the requests you make. And it is no excuse that you didn't take the time to thoroughly investigate the facts or research the applicable legal issues.

The second rule prohibits a lawyer submitting false information to the court.

> *(a) A lawyer shall not knowingly:*
>
> *(1) make a false statement of fact or law to a tribunal or fail to correct a false statement of material fact or law previously made to the tribunal by the lawyer;*
>
> *(2) fail to disclose to the tribunal legal authority in the controlling jurisdiction known to the lawyer to be directly adverse to the position of the client and not disclosed by opposing counsel; or*
>
> *(3) offer evidence that the lawyer knows to be false.*

Model R. Prof. Conduct 3.3. Sections (1) and (3) of the rule are no surprise. You can't lie to the court! That should probably go without saying. But section (2) is a little counter-intuitive.

You wouldn't think it is inconsistent with your obligations to your own client to disclose adverse authority. You would think that is the job of opposing counsel and not something you need be concerned with. Here is what little explanation is given in the comments to the rule:

> *A lawyer is not required to make a disinterested exposition of the law, but must recognize the existence of pertinent legal authorities. Furthermore, as stated in paragraph (a)(2), an advocate has a duty to disclose directly adverse authority in the controlling jurisdiction that has not been disclosed by the opposing party. The underlying concept is that legal argument is a discussion seeking to determine the legal premises properly applicable to the case.*

Model R. Prof. Conduct 3.3 (comment 4). The way you typically meet this requirement in a memo or brief is by addressing an obvious counterargument. If there is adverse authority, you don't just disclose it. You need to refute it as well. You should expect opposing counsel to find the same thing you did and use it against you. So you need to anticipate that and address in your own submissions whatever counterarguments there are.

The third rule states, in pertinent part, that you also cannot obstruct the other party's access to information:

> *A lawyer shall not:*
>
> *(a) unlawfully obstruct another party's access to evidence or unlawfully alter, destroy or conceal a document or other material having potential evidentiary value. A lawyer shall not counsel or assist another person to do any such act;*

Model R. Prof. Conduct 3.4. This rule is really more relevant to discovery. Here is the explanation in the comments:

> *[1] The procedure of the adversary system contemplates that the evidence in a case is to be marshaled competitively by the contending parties. Fair competition in the adversary system is secured by prohibitions against destruction or concealment of evidence, improperly influencing witnesses, obstructive tactics in discovery procedure, and the like.*
>
> *[2] Documents and other items of evidence are often essential to establish a claim or defense. Subject to evidentiary privileges, the right of an opposing party, including the government, to obtain evidence through discovery or subpoena is an important procedural right. The exercise of that right can be frustrated if relevant material is altered, concealed or destroyed. Applicable law in many jurisdictions makes it an offense to destroy material for purpose of impairing its availability in a pending proceeding or one whose commencement can be foreseen. Falsifying evidence is also generally a criminal offense.*

Model R. Prof. Conduct 3.4 (comments 1 & 2). So you can't shred documents! That should probably go without saying too. You can de-emphasize and downplay information in a memo or brief. But you can't go further than that and actually conceal the facts or destroy the documents.

That is a quick overview of the relevant ethical rules. In the next chapter I will outline the rules applicable to civil litigation and appeals, including the requirements for the form and substance of the persuasive memos and briefs we will be drafting.

14. CIVIL AND APPELLATE PROCEDURE

T
he two primary examples of persuasive writing
lawyers produce are a memorandum in support of a
dispositive motion in civil litigation and a brief in
support of an appeal. To understand how to draft both types of
documents you first have to understand the context in which
they are created. You have to become familiar with the rules
that govern civil and appellate procedure. I'll use the federal
rules of civil and appellate procedure as examples for the
discussion of these topics. Every state has its own rules for
civil and appellate procedure, but they tend to be very similar
to the federal rules.

A. Civil Procedure

The first step in beginning a lawsuit is filing a complaint
with the clerk's office of the court. Fed. R. Civ. P. 3. There
are specific rules for the structure and content of a complaint,
as well as other documents filed in litigation. The complaint
must start with a caption containing the court's name, the
names of the parties, a file number, and a designation (title).

Fed. R. Civ. P. 10. The body of the complaint must include a short and plain statement of the grounds for the court's jurisdiction, a short and plain statement of the claim showing that the pleader is entitled to relief, and a demand for the relief sought. Fed. R. Civ. P. 8(a). The attorney of record must also sign at the end of the document and state the attorney's name, address, e-mail address, and telephone number. Fed. R. Civ. P. 11(a).

The second step is to serve the defendant with a summons and a copy of the complaint. Fed. R. Civ. P. 4(c). The defendant then has 21 days to file an answer. Fed. R. Civ. P. 12(a)(1)(A)(i). In the answer, the defendant must state in short and plain terms its defenses to each claim asserted against it; and admit or deny the allegations asserted against it by the plaintiff. Fed. R. Civ. P. 8(b).

The defendant then may file a counterclaim against the plaintiff, if required or appropriate. Fed. R. Civ. P. 13(a)&(b). If there are multiple defendants, they may file cross claims against each other. Fed. R. Civ. P 13 (g). Also, under certain circumstances a defendant may join a third party to the litigation and assert a claim against that third party. Fed. R. Civ. P. 14.

If a pleading fails to state a claim upon which relief can be granted, the party responding to the claim may bring a motion to dismiss. Fed. R. Civ. P. 12(b)(6). Like all other documents filed in litigation, a motion must start with a caption containing the court's name, the names of the parties, a file number, and a designation (title). Fed. R. Civ. P. 10. The body of the motion must state with particularity the grounds for seeking the order, and state the relief sought. Fed. R. Civ. P. 7(b). And the end of the motion must contain the signature of the attorney of record, as well as the attorney's name, address, e-mail address, and telephone number. Fed. R. Civ. P. 11(a).

After the pleading stage each party is required to make certain mandatory disclosures of information and documents to the other party. Fed. R. Civ. P. 26(a). In addition, each party may send the other party up to 25 written questions (interrogatories). Fed. R. Civ. P. 33(a). A party may formally request that the other party produce documents. Fed. R. Civ. P. 34(a). Also, each party may take a deposition upon oral examination of the other party. Fed. R. Civ. P. 30(a).

If there are no genuine disputes as to any material fact and one party is entitled to judgment as a matter of law, that party may file a motion for summary judgment. Fed. R. Civ. P. 56. The same requirements that apply to a motion to dismiss also apply to a motion for summary judgment (the document must start with a caption, state the grounds for the motion and the relief sought, and end with a signature block for the attorney of record). In addition, affidavits submitted in support of motion for summary judgment, must be made "on personal knowledge, set out facts that would be admissible in evidence, and show that the affiant or declarant is competent to testify on the matters stated." Fed. R. Civ. P. (c)(4). In any opposition to the motion, the party asserting that a fact cannot be or is genuinely disputed must support that assertion by citing to discovery responses or showing that the other party cannot produce admissible evidence to support the fact. Fed. R. Civ. P. 56(c)(1).

Litigation is concluded with a trial on the merits and the entry of judgment in favor of one party or the other. The procedures and practices associated with civil trials are beyond the scope of this book, as are the rules of evidence. However, the drafting of an appeal brief is another example of persuasive writing discussed here, so you will also need to become familiar with the appellate process.

B. Appellate Procedure

An appeal is begun by filing a notice of appeal with the appellate court. Fed. R. App. P. 3(a). There are strict timelines for doing that: typically you have 30 days from the date the final judgment was entered. Fed. R. App. P. 4(a)(1).

After the notice is filed, the appellant (the party filing the appeal) has 14 days to order a copy of the trial transcript. Fed. R. App. P. 10(b). And the appellant must also do whatever else is necessary to enable the clerk to assemble and forward the record for the appeal. Fed. R. App. P. 11(a).

Once the record is filed the appellant has 40 days to serve and file an appeal brief. Fed. R. Civ. P. 31(a). I will go through the very detailed rules for the form and content of appeal briefs in chapter nineteen. After the appellant files a brief, the appellee (the party against whom the appeal was taken) has 30 days to file their appeal brief. *Id.*

The next step is often for the attorneys to "participate in one or more conferences to address any matter that may aid in disposing of the proceedings, including simplifying the issues and discussing settlement." Fed. R. App. P. 33.

The process then culminates with oral argument, which consists of both attorneys orally presenting their case to a panel of judges, and responding to whatever questions the judges may have. Fed. R. App. P. 34(a). Oral argument is discussed in more detail in chapter twenty. After the argument, the court renders its judgment and the appeal is concluded. Fed. R. App. P. 36.

These are the contexts within which a memorandum in support of a dispositive motion in civil litigation and a brief in support of an appeal are submitted. Unlike when you write an office memorandum, when you write a memo or brief in litigation you have to make sure your document conforms with the rules of procedure.

Now that we have discussed the general rules for civil and appellate procedure, we can turn to the specific requirements for granting the relief you request (e.g. the requirements for a motion to dismiss or a motion for summary judgment and the standards of review for an appeal). When you draft a persuasive document you have to apply those requirements and standards in addition to the substantive rule you learned to apply when you write an objective research memo.

15. REQUIREMENTS FOR CIVIL MOTIONS AND STANDARDS FOR APPEALS

When you write for litigation you have to apply the requirements for granting the relief you are requesting in addition to the substantive rule you learned to apply in the first ten chapters of this book. The requirements for granting relief will be discuss in this chapter. To more clearly differentiate among the three sets of rules that apply to persuasive documents, I have drafted a chart with an example of what those rules would be if you were drafting a motion to dismiss in a tort case:

Procedural Rules for Document Form and Substance	Rule Establishing Requirements for Granting Relief	Substantive Rule for Cause of Action
A motion must start with a caption. The body must state the grounds and the relief sought. A motion must also end with the attorney's signature and identifying information.	A motion to dismiss must be allowed if the complaint fails to state a claim upon which relief can be granted.	In a tort case a plaintiff must prove duty, breach, causation and damages to recover.

When you write an objective memo analyzing a legal issue you apply the substantive rule to a set of facts, and organize your analysis using CREAC. When you write a persuasive memo or brief, you apply the requirements for granting the relief you request at the same time, and you do it within the CREAC structure. You do that by stating the requirements for granting the relief you request before you begin analyzing the substantive rule, and then reflecting those requirements and demonstrating they are satisfied within your application of the substantive rule.

For example, if you were drafting a memo in support of a motion to dismiss, you might start by stating the requirement that a complaint contain a "short and plain statement of the claim showing that the pleader is entitled to relief." Fed. R. Civ. P. 8(a). In other words, a complaint must contain sufficient factual allegations to "state a claim to relief that is plausible on its face." Bell Atlantic Corp. v. Twombly, 550 U.S. 544, 570 (2007); Ashcroft v. Iqbal, 556 U.S. 662 (2009). That is the requirement for granting the relief you request.

If you were drafting an objective memo, you might start your CREAC by stating "The plaintiff is unlikely to succeed because the defendant did not owe him a duty of care." But if you are drafting a persuasive memo you would instead start by saying "the plaintiff fails to state a claim upon which relief can be granted because the plaintiff doesn't even allege that the defendant owed him a duty of care." That would be the "C" in CREAC.

You would then state the common law rule that a cause of action for a tort consists of the four elements: duty, breach, causation and damages; and you would explain the rule with a analogous case. Ideally, you would cite a case where the court dismissed a complaint for failing to allege each of those four elements. That would be the "R" and "E" in CREAC.

And then you would apply the substantive rule. If you were drafting an objective memo, you would apply the rule to your description of the facts. In a memo in support of a motion to dismiss, you would apply the rule to the allegations of the complaint. And instead of concluding that the plaintiff is unlikely to succeed, you would conclude that the plaintiff fails to state a plausible claim for relief. Therefore, the complaint should be dismissed.

As another example, if you were writing a memo in support of a motion for summary judgment, you would start by stating the requirement that a motion for summary judgment must be granted if there are no genuine issues of material fact and the moving party is entitled to judgment as a matter of law. Fed. R. Civ. P. 56. To decide the motion the court must view the facts in the light most favorable to the non-moving party. Celotex Corp. v. Catrett, 477 U.S. 317, 322 (1986). Facts are material if they "might affect the outcome of the suit under the governing law" and disputes are genuine "if they the evidence is such that a reasonable jury could return a verdict for the nonmoving party." <u>Anderson v. Liberty Lobby, Inc.</u>, 477 U.S. 242 (1986), <u>Celotex Corp. v. Catrett</u>, 477 U.S. 317 (1986), <u>Matsushita Elec. Indus. Co. v. Zenith Radio Corp.</u>, 475 U.S. 574 (1986). That is the requirement for granting the relief you request.

You would then do your CREAC reflecting that requirement and demonstrating it is satisfied within your application of the substantive rule. If the case involved a car accident at a traffic light, you might start by saying the defendant is entitled to judgment as a matter of law because he had the right of way. You would then state the rule that the driver who has a green light has the right of way. You would apply the rule to the facts by saying there is no genuine dispute the light was green when the accident happened (and cite to the deposition transcripts of both parties admitting the defendant had a green light). Then you would conclude by saying the defendant's motion for summary judgment should be allowed.

If you are drafting an appeal brief, the rule establishing the requirements for reviewing a lower court decision is called the standard of review. When an appellate court reviews a trial court decision they give the trial court varying levels of deference. Questions of law are typically reviewed de novo, meaning the appellate court need not defer to the trial court at all; questions of fact are reviewable for clear error, meaning they will be accepted unless clearly erroneous; and matters of discretion will be upheld unless it is shown that the trial court abused its discretion. <u>Pierce v. Underwood</u>, 487 U.S. 552 (1988). So if you are asking the appellate court to overturn factual findings made by a trial court, you should be arguing that they are clearly erroneous. If your argument is that a discretionary decision by a judge should be reversed, then you should be arguing that the judge abused his discretion in making that decision. In other words, you should frame your issue to correspond to the conclusion you want the appellate court to come to.

If there was a trial on the merits, then you would source the facts for your appeal brief from the trial transcript. But if you are appealing the decision to allow a motion to dismiss or a motion for summary judgment, then you would source the facts from the same place they were sourced in the motion. In the latter cases, if you are asking the appellate court to review questions of law decided by the trial court, your brief will look a lot like your original memo. In those situations, you are essentially asking for a do over of what happened in the trial court. You make the same arguments in basically the same way but before a new panel of judges.

I've given you an overview of the process and the requirements for granting a motion or deciding an appeal in your client's favor. When we discuss memos and briefs I'll go into more detail as to what the specific requirements are (there are more of them, especially for appeal briefs). But first I'll give you a brief introduction to persuasive writing, including describing facts persuasively and arguing law persuasively.

16. PERSUASIVE WRITING

Persuasive writing is not about determining how a court will likely apply the law to a set of facts. Persuasive writing is about convincing a court to apply the law one way or another. Persuasive writing is describing facts from your client's perspective, and presenting the law in a way that best supports your request for relief.

A. <u>Describing Facts Persuasively</u>

When you write your memo or brief you need to describe the facts in the light most favorable to your client. One way to do that is to describe facts that benefit your client in more detail, and state unfavorable facts as concisely as possible. As an example, if you represented the defendant in a personal injury case you might describe what happened like this:

> **The plaintiff slipped and fell through a glass door at the entrance to Bob's Pizza Emporium, and, as a result, she had a laceration on her face.**

Describing the plaintiff's injuries in a summary, conclusory way has the effect of deemphasizing what happened to her.

If you represented the plaintiff in the same case you would want to do the opposite. You would want to emphasize the injury by going into detail when you describe what happened to your client, like this:

> **The plaintiff slipped and fell through a glass door at the entrance to Bob's Pizza Emporium, and, as a result, she had <u>an incision across her forehead that was four inches long and more than one-half an inch deep</u>.**

Describing the laceration in detail makes in clear how serious the plaintiff's injury was. And that information better supports the plaintiff's claim for damages.

In describing the facts you would also want to personalize your client and depersonalize the other side. If you represent the plaintiff, you might change the facts to this:

> **<u>Mrs. Jones</u> slipped and fell through a glass door at the entrance to the <u>defendant's place of business</u>, and, as a result, she had an incision across her forehead that was four inches long and more than one-half of an inch deep.**

If you represent the defendant, you might instead refer to your client as "Bob's" or "Bob's Pizza" and Mrs. Jones as the "customer" or the "complainant."

To make your description even more effective you might also make the description a little more graphic and visual.

> **Mrs. Jones slipped and fell through a glass door at the entrance to the defendant's place of business, and, as a result, <u>a piece of glass sliced through the skin on</u>**

**her face and left her with a gash across her forehead
and blood soaking the front of her white blouse.** The
gash was four inches long and more than one-half of an
inch deep.

Saying the glass "sliced through the skin on her face" helps
the reader understand how painful that must have been. And
the image of the plaintiff with a "gash across her forehead
and blood soaking the front of her white blouse" effectively
demonstrates the seriousness of the injury.

To demonstrate more of these techniques, let's switch
to a different example. Suppose the police officer in a police
brutality case described an incident in his police report like
this:

**When the police officer attempted to arrest the
perpetrator he resisted and had to be subdued.**

If you represented the victim in the case, you would
obviously want to describe the incident in more detail, and you
might also use repetition to emphasize the brutality the victim
endured, like this:

**The police officer <u>pushed</u> the victim to the
ground, and then <u>punched</u> him in the face. The victim
tried to protect himself but the officer <u>punched</u> him
again. Even after the victim was in handcuffs, the
officer continued to <u>punch</u> him and <u>pushed</u> his head
into the ground with his knee. In total, the officer
<u>punched</u> the victim five (5) times.**

That example also uses alliteration (repeating the same sound
over and over again for emphasis) to emphasize the officer's
violent actions.

LEGAL WRITING I & II

If you represented the victim you might also develop a theme for the case or a characterization of what happened that is easy to relate to. Here is an example of how you might do that:

> **This was a classic incident of police brutality. The defendant pushed the victim to the ground, and then punched him in the face. The victim tried to protect himself but the <u>rogue cop</u> punched him again. Even after the victim was in handcuffs, the defendant continued to <u>brutalize him</u> by punching him and pushing his head into the ground. <u>In furtherance of this illegal use of force</u>, the defendant punched the victim five (5) times.**

In that example I labeled the police conduct as "brutality" and further defined it as the "illegal use of force," because those are the conclusions I want the audience to come to.

If you represented the police officer in the same case you would want to deemphasize what the officer did and, instead, put the focus on the justification:

> **<u>Because the perpetrator was becoming agitated, raised his voice and started moving towards the officer</u>, the officer pushed the perpetrator away and he fell to the ground. <u>The perpetrator resisted the officer's efforts to subdue him</u> and an altercation ensued. The officer was able to put the perpetrator in handcuffs <u>but he continued to resist</u> and the altercation continued.**

From the officer's perspective this is a case of resisting arrest. If you represented the officer you would want the reader to conclude that the officer was reacting appropriately to the perpetrator's actions. So you would shift the focus to what the perpetrator did, not how the officer reacted.

Another thing you might do, if you represented the officer, would be to describe the absence of facts that aren't part of the fact pattern, if the absence of those facts puts the client in a more favorable light. Here is a revised example to explain what I mean:

> **Because the perpetrator was becoming agitated, raised his voice and started moving towards the officer, the officer pushed the perpetrator away and he fell to the ground. <u>The officer had a firearm but he did not use it. The officer also had a taser and a club, but he did not use either of those things either.</u> The perpetrator resisted the officer's efforts to subdue him and an altercation ensued. The officer was able to put the perpetrator in handcuffs but he continued to resist and the altercation continued.**

By making clear the officer could have elevated the situation but chose not to, you highlight the reasonableness of the officer's actions.

Finally, you could also use passive voice to take the reader's attention away from the officer when describing what happened, like this:

> **Because the perpetrator was becoming agitated, raised his voice and started moving towards the officer, <u>he was pushed</u> away and he fell to the ground. The officer had a firearm but he did not use it. The officer also had a taser and a club, but he did not use that equipment either. The perpetrator resisted the officer's efforts to subdue him and an altercation ensued. <u>The perpetrator was put</u> in handcuffs but he continued to resist and the altercation continued.**

Passive voice removes the officer from the description and even more effectively puts the focus on the perpetrator.

B. <u>Arguing Law Persuasively</u>

The most important thing to remember when arguing law persuasively is to support your arguments with primary, binding authority, and make sure your reasoning for why that authority applies is unassailable. It is not enough for you to say what the defendant did was negligent or unreasonable; you need to give the judge a case that supports that conclusion, and then explain why it is analogous. Credibility is important; without it the judge is unlikely to take very seriously whatever you have to say. The facts are important too; you always want to tell the story of what happened from your client's perspective. But ultimately what moves judges is binding authority. The other side will try to distinguish it; and you will need a better argument for why it is controlling. If you can convince the trial court judge that the appellate court above him would give you whatever you are asking for, then the trial court judge will grant your request. If you can't, then your request will likely be denied.

In addition to supporting your positions with binding authority, also remember to put your strongest arguments first. If there is a weakness to your position, put it in the middle of your discussion, and try to finish by reiterating your strongest point. Here are two versions of the same case, each organized to state the applicable parties position in the strongest manner.

Version 1 (plaintiff's argument)

This is a breach of contract case. The defendant agreed to purchase a piece of industrial equipment

for ten thousand dollars but never paid for the item. He breached his obligations to the plaintiff without justification, and this lawsuit was commenced. Now the defendant's legal team tries to defend what he did by raising the technicality that delivery of the equipment was one day late, therefore the defendant was supposedly relieved of his obligation to do what he agreed to do. However a one day delay was not a material breach and did not justify non-payment. The defendant didn't follow through because he changed his mind, not because delivery was late. There is no legal justification for what the defendant did. He has no excuse for breaching the agreement he signed. As a result the plaintiff's request for relief should be granted.

Version 2 (defendant's argument)

The plaintiff in this case is trying to enforce a contract he himself breached. The plaintiff agreed to deliver a piece of industrial equipment on a specific date. The defendant signed the agreement because he needed to use the equipment the day after the date of delivery for a time sensitive project. When the delivery didn't happen the project fell through and the defendant no longer had any need for the equipment. Instead of taking responsibility for the breach, the plaintiff filed this lawsuit and now claims late delivery is not a material breach because the agreement did not have a "time is of the essence" provision. However, the absence that language does not give plaintiff the right to deliver goods whenever he wants. The plaintiff knew full well what the defendant's intended use of the equipment was. He cannot breach the provisions of an agreement and then insist that the other side still do what they agreed to do. The agreement is

not enforceable because of the plaintiff's own failure. As a result the plaintiff's request for relief should be denied.

As you can see, these two versions of the same case state what happened persuasively, first from the perspective of the plaintiff, and then from the perspective of the defendant. And the primary technique each party uses to better state their position is to put their strongest argument at the beginning of the paragraph. The weakness in each party's position is disclosed and dealt with in the middle of the paragraph. And then each version finishes with a reiteration of the party's strongest argument.

Use this same technique when citing cases supporting your position. List statutes before cases. List binding authority before persuasive authority. List cases that are closest factually before cases that are only marginally applicable. When you are citing multiple authorities for your arguments, list the strongest authority first.

Also, vary the level of detail when you describe authority in your writing. If you have a case that is right on point, get into the specifics of that case and explain why it applies. If you have to distinguish a case that supports the other side's position, do it as briefly as possible. Never dwell on a case you have to distinguish or a counterargument you have to refute.

When you analyze a legal issue, state your conclusion first. Use CRAC or CREAC not IRAC or IREAC. State the point you want to make, then the rule, the explanation and application, and the conclusion. Instead of saying the conclusion twice, first state the specific point you are trying to make; then end with the conclusion you want the court to come to (or the relief you want the court to grant).

For example, if you are writing a memo in support of a motion to dismiss, you might start by making the point that "The plaintiff failed to allege in the complaint that he exhausted his administrative remedy." Then state the rule, explain it and apply it. And then you might end by concluding "The complaint fails to state a claim upon which relief can be granted." Alternatively, you might have stated the point this way: "The complaint fails to state a claim because the plaintiff did not even allege he exhausted his administrative remedy." If you did you might conclude with "The motion to dismiss should be allowed."

When you state the rule, emphasize that aspect of the rule that supports the conclusion you want to come to. If you represent the defendant, as above, you might describe the rule like this: "The law does not permit a party to commence a civil action unless he first exhausts his administrative remedy." But if you represent the plaintiff you might describe the same rule like this: "A party may commence a civil action without first exhausting an administrative remedy if it would be pointless and futile to do so."

When you explain the rule and apply it, emphasize the facts that support your position. If you are arguing the case is analogous, focus the reader's attention on the analogous facts. If you are arguing the case is distinguishable, then emphasize the distinguishable facts. If there are facts that don't support your analogy, state concisely why they are irrelevant. And then reiterate your original point in your conclusion.

Add persuasive headings to give the reader a roadmap for the points you are trying to make. In fact, consider making the "C" in CREAC your heading and then start your paragraph with the rule. For example, if there are three points you want to make, then divide your argument into three sections, and begin each section with a heading stating your point for that section. In a slip and fall case the first heading might be "The Plaintiff was Tresspassing when the Accident Occurred." The second might be "Even if the Plaintiff was owed a Duty of Care, the Defendant did not Breach that Duty." And the third might be "The Plaintiff also has no Damages." Once you have made those three points, state the applicable rule, explain it, apply it and conclude in the paragraphs under each heading.

Finally, emphasize language in a statute or case by quoting it in your memo or brief. If what the court said is right on point, then a quoting the language will be more effective than paraphrasing it. If the quote doesn't fit into your explanation of the case, include it in parenthesis after the citation. If there are other aspects of the case that are helpful to your argument, but raising them doesn't work with the explanation you are writing, do the same thing. Put that information in parenthesis after the case cite.

There are two sides to every story. When you write persuasively you are either telling one story or the other. And you are telling the story on behalf of and from the perspective of one party or the other. Regardless of who you represent, your job is to state your position as strongly as you can. You want the judge to interpret the law in a manner that benefits your client; and you want the judge to see the facts in the light most favorable to your client. Those are the objectives of persuasive writing. Now let's finally turn to the specifics of drafting a memorandum in support of a motion and drafting an appeal brief.

17. MEMORANDA IN SUPPORT OF MOTIONS

A memorandum in support of a motion is written for a judge in litigation to persuade the judge to take some action in the case. A motion is a request that the judge take the desired action. The memorandum states the grounds for the motion, including a legal argument why the motion should be allowed. The organization of a memorandum is similar to what we discussed in Chapter 8. There is usually an introduction, a statement of facts, an argument and a conclusion. I'll use the example of a memorandum in support of a motion to dismiss filed in federal court to explain how each section differs in this context. State practice is usually less formal but follows basically the same rules.

Like all documents filed in litigation, a memorandum in support of a motion starts with a caption containing the name of the court, the name of the first party on each side, the file number and the title. Fed. R. Civ. P. R. 10. That information is customarily formatted to look something like this:

**UNITED STATES DISTRICT COURT
FOR THE NORTHERN DISTRICT OF ILLINOIS**

Jane Doe,

    Plaintiff,

v.   Case No: _____

ABC Corp. and XYZ Corp.,

    Defendants.

_____/

**MEMORANDUM IN SUPPORT OF
DEFENDANT XYZ CORP.'S MOTION TO DISMISS**

The next step is to write an introductory statement citing the applicable procedural rule and identifying the parties and the memorandum. Use this section to create defined terms for the parties; and try to personalize your client and/or depersonalize the other side.

Pursuant to Fed. R. Civ. P. 12(b), the defendant, XYZ Corp. (Shareholder) submits this Memorandum in Support of its Motion to Dismiss Count II of the Complaint filed by the plaintiff, Jane Doe (Employee) against ABC Corp. (Employer).

Next you would write a brief introduction. The introduction should tell the court what type of case this is (e.g. a tort case, a breach of contract case, a statutory violation, etc.), and briefly state the factual basis for the plaintiff's claim (who sued who for what). Then identify the type of motion being filed; and state briefly why the motion should be allowed. If you have more than one argument for an issue, state the strongest argument in the introduction.

INTRODUCTION

This is an employment discrimination case. The Employee claims that Employer fired her because of her disability in violation of the Americans with Disabilities Act (the "ADA"). The Employee named the Employer in her charge before the Equal Employment Opportunity Commission (the "EEOC"), but she did not name the Shareholder, which owns all the stock of the Employer. However, the ADA only authorizes the Employee to bring a civil action "against the respondent named in the [EEOC] charge," 42 U.S.C. § 2000e-5(f)(1). Therefore, this Court should dismiss the claim against Shareholder in Count II of the Complaint.

The next section in a trial memorandum is the statement of facts, and it is different than the statement of facts in a research memorandum. In a trial memorandum, you should put the facts in the light most favorable to your client. Don't be objective; be persuasive. Tell the story of what happened from your client's perspective and in a way that best supports your client's position.

At the end of each sentence in your fact statement you also need to put citations to the record. If you are supporting a motion to dismiss, then you would cite to the specific allegations of the complaint. If you are filing a motion for summary judgment, then you would cite to affidavits, answers to interrogatories and deposition transcripts. Also, if you need to present documents and other information to the court's attention, then you would do so by filing an affidavit authenticating the documents or stating the information, and cite the affidavit in your memorandum. Here is a short example of a fact statement.

II. STATEMENT OF FACTS

The Employee did not name the Shareholder in her EEOC charge. The Employee claimed she suffered from "Chronic Fatigue and Immune Deficiency Syndrome (CFIDS)" and the Employer discriminated "against [her] because of [her] disability by not allowing [her] to work at home." Complaint, Exh. B. She did not even mention the Shareholder, or complain about any activity Shareholder was involved in, anywhere in the charge. Id.

Out of the thirty (30) allegations in the Complaint, there are only three (3) conclusory statements that involve Shareholder. The Employee alleges Shareholder and the Employer "share a unity of ownership and interests such that they are not, in fact, two separate

---

corporate entities." Complaint, Par. 5. She claims "[Shareholder], as the parent corporation and sole shareholder of [the Employer], should have been aware of the EEOC Charge...;" and she also asserts Shareholder "knew or should have known about [the Employer's] unlawful employment practices and failed to take action to prohibit such unlawful practices." Complaint, Par. 11 & 29. Even if these allegations were entitled to an assumption of truth, the Complaint would still fail to state a claim against Shareholder because the Employee failed to name Shareholder as a respondent, and failed to make any of these allegations, when she brought her claim to the EEOC.

After you have introduced the case and stated the factual background, the next step is to make your argument for why the motion should be allowed. This section should start by stating the requirement for granting the relief you are requesting. Here is an example of a brief statement of the requirement for a motion to dismiss.

III. ARGUMENT

A party may move to dismiss a complaint if it "fails to state a claim upon which relief can be granted." Fed.

R. Civ. P. 12(b)(6). In analyzing a motion to dismiss, the court construes the complaint "in the light most favorable to the nonmoving party, accept[ing] well-pleaded facts as true, and draw[ing] all inferences in her favor." Reger Development, LLC v. National City Bank, 592 F.3d 759, 763 (7th Cir. 2010). However, "the tenet that a court must accept as true all of the allegations contained in a complaint is inapplicable to legal conclusions. Threadbare recitals of the elements of a cause of action, supported by mere conclusory statements, do not suffice." Ashcroft v. Iqbal, 556 U.S. 662, ___ (2009) (citing Bell Atl. Corp. v. Twombly, 550 U.S. 544, 555 (2007)), see also, Bissessur v. Indiana University Bd. Of Trustees, 581 F.3d 599 (7th Cir. 2009).

> In keeping with these principles a court considering a motion to dismiss can choose to begin by identifying pleadings that, because they are no more than conclusions, are not entitled to the assumption of truth. While legal conclusions can provide the framework of a complaint, they must be supported by factual allegations. When there are well-pleaded factual allegations, a court should assume their veracity and then determine whether they plausibly give rise to an entitlement to relief.

Ashcroft v. Iqbal, 556 U.S. 662, ___ (2009). All three (3)

> **of the allegations against Shareholder are mere conclusory statements; none of them are entitled to an assumption of truth and, even if they were, they would still fail to state a claim against Shareholder.**

Once you have stated the requirement for relief, you should then turn to the substantive rule, applied to the facts of the case, and the conclusion that your motion should be allowed. In a persuasive document you will organize your arguments using CREAC. In other words, state the conclusion first (or the point you are trying to make), then state the rule, explain it and come to a conclusion reiterating your initial point. Also, weave the standard of review into your argument as much as practicable. And don't hesitate to add equitable support for your position as well (i.e. reasons why the judge should sympathize with your client).

When you make your arguments for each of the issues in the case, you usually have at least three options. One, if there is an analogous case that supports your position, draw an analogy between that case and the facts, apply the reasoning of the case, and argue your case should be decided the same way. That is usually your best option.

Two, if there are no cases on point, just state the rule and marshal the relevant facts to each element of the rule to support your position. In other words, structure your analysis with CRAC instead of CREAC, since you don't have a case example to explain the rule.

Three, if the only case on point goes against your position, then use CREAC but distinguish the facts of the case, explain why the reasoning does not apply, and argue the court should come to the opposite conclusion in your case. In other words, at least address the other side's argument that your motion should be denied.

Here is an example of an argument section for the motion to dismiss.

A. **The Claim Against Shareholder Should be Dismissed Because Shareholder Was Not Named as a Respondent in the EEOC Charge**

ADA claims, like other discrimination claims, must be brought before the EEOC before a civil action may be filed in federal court. 42 U.S.C. § 2000e-5(b). And even then a civil action may only be brought "against the respondent named in the [EEOC] charge." 42 U.S.C. § 2000e-5(f)(1), see e.g., LeBeau v. Libbey-Owens-Ford Co., 484 F.2d 798, 799 (7th Cir. 1973)("Ordinarily, a party not named in an EEOC charge may not be sued under Title VII [of the Civil Rights Act].").

The claims against Shareholder should be dismissed because Shareholder was not named as a respondent in the EEOC charge. A parent company not named in an EEOC charge cannot later be joined in a civil action against its

---

subsidiary. E.g., Schnellbaecher v. Baskin Clothing Co., 887 F.2d 124 (7th Cir. 1989)(affirming dismissal of parent company not named in EEOC charge); Olsen v. Marshall & Ilsley Corp., 267 F.3d 597 (7th Cir. 2001)(affirming grant of summary judgment dismissing parent company not named in EEOC charge).

In Schnellbaecher, employees of a clothing company brought a discrimination claim against their employer; in the EEOC charge, they alleged the employer had not promoted them to more lucrative sales positions because they were women. Schnellbaecher, 887 F.2d at 125. The employees named the employer as a respondent in the charge, and then filed a civil action against the employer and its parent company. Id. The parent company moved to dismiss the charges against it; and the employees opposed the motion, claiming that, even though the parent was not named as a respondent, it still had notice of the charge because the parent company and the employer were represented by the same attorneys. Id. at 126. However, the court rejected that argument, finding that the parent company only had notice of the claims against the employer; it did not have notice of any claim against it. Id.

at 127. Therefore, the claims against the parent company were properly dismissed. Id.

The Employee's allegations in this matter present an even stronger case for dismissal than the allegations in Schnellbaecher. The Employee's claim that Shareholder, "as the parent corporation and sole shareholder of [Employer], should have been aware of the EEOC Charge," Complaint, Par. 11, is conclusory and not entitled to an assumption of truth. Unlike the employees in Schnellbaecher, the Employee here does not allege any factual basis for the conclusion that Shareholder had notice. She does not state, for example, that there was any overlap in the attorneys or any other agents who represented the Employer and Shareholder. As a result, there is no basis for concluding the Shareholder knew about the EEOC charge.

In addition, the EEOC charge in this case, like the EEOC charge in Schnellbaecher, complains of discrimination by the Employer; it does not complain about any conduct or activity by Shareholder. As a result, even if the Employee alleged facts supporting the conclusion that Shareholder knew about the charge, the allegations of the charge would still not be sufficient to put Shareholder on notice of a claim against it. For the same reason that the Shareholder's motion to dismiss in <u>Schnellbaecher</u> was allowed, the motion to dismiss in this case should also be granted.

It would be neither fair nor just to require the Shareholder to defend against these charges without notice of the agency proceedings below, and without any opportunity to defend itself in those proceedings. The Employee was not employed by the Shareholder; she was employed by the Employer. And her claim, if she has one, is against the Employer, not the Shareholder. She cannot add a new claim against a new party at this late stage. As a result, the claim against Shareholder should be dismissed.

When you organize your argument be sure to state your strongest points first. If your argument is composed of multiple sections, use headings as the roadmap for your argument, and state a point in each heading. You may argue in the alternative, as I did in this example. Also, when you list cases or statutes in support of your arguments, state binding primary sources first and list cases that are factually similar to your case first. Include lower court cases, out of state precedents and secondary sources, if any, last. Finally, make sure you refute any obvious counterarguments in your memo, like this:

B.   Shareholder did not Otherwise have Notice or an Opportunity to Conciliate

The Employee may argue that this case is analogous to the only case in this circuit involving circumstances where an unnamed affiliated organization that "has been provided with adequate notice of the charge . . . and . . . has been given the opportunity to participate in conciliation proceedings aimed at voluntary compliance . . ." may be joined in a civil action against its subsidiary. Eggleston v. Chicago Journeymen Plumbers' Local Union No. 130, 657 F.2d 890, 905 (7th Cir.1981).   However, that case is distinguishable.

In Eggleston, five persons brought an EEOC charge against a plumbers union, claiming discrimination in the administration of the apprenticeship program for plumbers. Id. at 893. After the EEOC case, they filed a civil action against the union, and also added a claim against the committee that administered the apprenticeship program. Id. The committee was comprised of ten people, five of whom were also were also officers in the union. Id. at 906. Because of the overlap in personnel, and the claim in the

BEN L. FERNANDEZ

EEOC charge that the program the committee administered was discriminatory, the appeals court found the committee "knew or should have known of the EEOC charge and that their conduct would be subject to EEOC inquiry;" and there was nothing preventing the committee "from attempting to resolve the alleged discrimination in an amicable manner." Id. at 906-907. Therefore, the trial court's decision allowing the committee's motion to dismiss was reversed, and the committee was reinstated as a defendant to the plaintiffs' claim. Id. at 907.

Eggleston clearly is not applicable to these facts. Again, there is no allegation that the same people who worked for the Employer also worked for Shareholder. And there is no claim in the Employee's EEOC charge that would have put Shareholder on notice that their conduct would be subject to EEOC inquiry. The Employee only claimed in the charge that the Employer terminated her because of her disability; she didn't allege in the charge that Shareholder had anything to do with the decision to end her employment. Unlike the situation in Eggleston, there is no basis here for finding that Shareholder had notice of any charge against it. In addition, the Employee does not allege there was "nothing preventing" Shareholder from resolving the Employer's case. In other words, the Employee does not claim Shareholder could have taken action to settle her claim. Therefore, there is also no basis for finding that Shareholder had any opportunity to participate in conciliation proceedings. The exception in Eggleston does not apply; the complaint fails to state a claim against Shareholder and should be dismissed.

Now all you have left to do is state a short conclusion to your memo. At this point, the judge is familiar with your arguments so there is no need to repeat them. Just finish by saying the motion should be allowed, like this:

IV.   CONCLUSION

For all the above reasons, co-defendant, Shareholder's Motion to Dismiss should be allowed.

After the conclusion add your signature as the attorney of record, plus your address, e-mail address and telephone number. Fed. R. Civ. P. R. 11(a). A certificate of service is not required if the memorandum is filed with the court's electronic filing system. Fed. R. Civ. P. 5(1)(B). Otherwise, the procedure is to include a certificate at the end of the memo. Here is a final example:

Shareholder Corp.,

> By its attorney,
>
> _____
> Name, bar no.
> Street address
> City, State, Zip Code
> (xxx) xxx-xxxx
> Attorney@gmail.com
>
> ### Certificate of Service
>
> I certify that on this __ day of _____, 20__, I served this Memorandum in Support of Defendant Shareholder's Motion to Dismiss upon all parties by mailing a copy of same to:
>
> Name, bar no.
> Street address
> City, State, Zip Code
>
> _____
> **Name**

There may be additional requirements for motions and memoranda in the local rules for the court in which those materials are submitted. For example, the Local Rules for the Northern District of Florida require that counsel confer in a good faith effort to resolve the issues before filing a motion that would not determine the outcome of a case or a claim, and then add an additional certificate at the end of the motion that the conference requirement has been met. N.D. Fla. Loc. R. 7.1(B). Motions must be submitted in 14 point type, double spaced, with one inch margins. N.D. Fla. Loc. R. 5.1(C). There is an 8,000 word limit for memoranda, and counsel must certify that the memo complies with the limit. N.D. Fla. Loc. R. 7.1(f). Also, counsel must include their bar number in the signature block at the end of the memo. N.D. Fla. Loc. R. 5.1(D). So always remember to check the local court rules in addition to the rules of civil procedure.

If you are drafting a memorandum in opposition to a motion, the process is the same with two notable exceptions. First, in your statement of facts, you should highlight the facts that are favorable to your client and were not included in the memorandum in support of the motion submitted by the other side. Tell the other side to the story, from your client's perspective. Don't just adopt the moving party's version of what happened. And second, in your argument, in addition to arguing your position, you should also address the arguments the other side made in the original motion. State your position first, then develop the counterarguments required to refute whatever the other side's position is.

Now that we have covered the memoranda appropriate for motion practice in the trial court, let's talk about how to argue a motion before a judge.

18. MOTION SESSION

After the filing of your motion and supporting memorandum, as well as any opposition, the court will either decide the issue "on the papers" or hold a hearing. If a hearing is held, you will need to appear and argue the motion orally in court. The practice for hearings varies from court to court, so you need to find out ahead of time what is expected of you; and, as with all things in the practice of law, be prepared.

Start by reading through the case file and making sure you are intimately familiar with the facts and the law cited in the memoranda submitted to the court. I would also make extra copies of the material you filed in case the court is missing something. And then start to outline the argument you want to make. Don't make a script to read to the judge. Just outline the facts and the cases, so you will have something to guide you once you start talking. I also used to put my name and the name of my client at the top of my outline so I wouldn't forget to introduce myself.

Make sure you know where the court is. Print out a copy of the directions if you need to, and leave yourself plenty of time to get there. You don't want to risk running late and showing up all flustered. I would also call the clerk's office ahead of time and confirm the day and time for your hearing. If this is your first time, you should get there early and scope out the courtroom you are in and how things are organized. Some judges will have you argue from a podium. Others want counsel to stand at counsel's table; and others will have you approach the bench or meet in chambers to state your argument.

I'm sure I don't need to tell you to dress appropriately (i.e. conservatively), and sit quietly while you are waiting for your case to be called. When the judge enters the room, stand up, and remain standing until she sits down. When it is your turn to argue, wait for the judge to signal when you should start talking. Usually she will say something like "I'll hear from plaintiff's counsel on the motion."

When you address the court, start with "may it please the court" and refer to the judge as "your honor." Some people refer to the attorney on the other side as "my brother" or "my sister," but I think that sounds a little cheesy. I prefer to refer to the attorney representing the other side as "counsel," "the defendant's attorney" or "the plaintiff's attorney."

If you are nervous, you are not alone. Most people are

nervous in the beginning, and I was no exception. For me what helped is practicing a lot until I had my argument down pat, getting there early so I didn't arrive stressed out, and becoming familiar with the courtroom and the procedures for the hearing. The more prepared you are, the less anxiety you will have about what you are about to do. Also, if there are other attorneys in the audience, be assured they are likely not listening to your argument. They are just hoping you will hurry up and get it over with so they can take their turn.

Before you get into the substance of your argument, tell the judge who you are (introduce yourself), and state in a summary way what you want, and why the judge should give it to you. In other words, do an introduction, just like you did in your memo. Then start going through your argument, and keep talking until the judge interjects a question. Make sure to get to the point quickly. Judges are busy, just like everyone else, so concision is appreciated.

Usually the judge will interrupt you right away, but there are also times when the judge will just sit back and listen. If the judge doesn't ask questions, go through the facts, argument and conclusion, and then address whatever the other side brought up in their opposition, if you are the moving party. Make sure your voice is loud enough for the judge to hear you, make good eye contact and speak with conviction.

If you do get a question, stop talking, listen carefully to the question and answer it. Don't talk over the judge and don't try to avoid answering a direct question. Doing that will hurt your credibility. If there is an obvious weakness in your argument, figure out ahead of time how to address it. When the judge asks about the weakness, give her the answer you prepared and move on.

All communication should go through the judge. Any documents should be handed to the clerk, who will then hand them to the judge. When the other attorney is talking, don't interrupt him. Let him have his turn, as he let you have yours. After he is finished, if there is something you want to say, ask the judge for an opportunity to respond. If she grants your request, then start talking again. But don't speak directly to the other attorney. Speak to the judge.

Be aware of your body language. Try not to make distracting gestures with your hands. If you chew gum, get the gum out of your mouth. If you like to put your hands in your pockets when you talk, empty your pockets before you stand up.

Be sure to treat everyone with respect. Be professional but don't feel like you have to act like a stereotype. Be genuine instead. If you aren't sure what to do, ask. Better to ask and get it right than to do it wrong and get reprimanded. Also, try not to get overly emotional, and don't personalize your arguments.

Listen carefully to the judge and opposing counsel. Often you can tell what the judge's concerns are by listening to the questions she asks. Also, you will want to address any points the other attorney makes in his argument, especially if they raise issues you didn't have an opportunity to address in your memorandum. So take notes while the other side is making his case, and ask for an opportunity to rebut whatever points he makes.

If you are arguing in opposition to a motion, the process is the same with the same two exceptions that apply if you are writing a memorandum in opposition to a motion. When you address the facts be brief. The judge already heard the facts from the moving party so quickly zero in on whatever information the other attorney failed to disclose. Tell the other side to the story, from your client's perspective. But don't force the judge to suffer through a rehash of what the other attorney has already said.

Second, in addition to arguing your position, you should also address the arguments the other side made orally, including any additional arguments that were not included in the papers. If you are caught off guard and can't effectively address an issue raise for the first time at the hearing, then ask the court for the opportunity to submit a reply memo addressing just that new issue.

After the arguments are over, thank the judge for her time and consideration, even if she decided against you. Sometimes the judge will issue a decision from the bench. If she grants your requested relief, it may be appropriate to stick around for a copy of the decision, or you may have to wait until the judge and the clerk are done with motions for the day, and then obtain the copy from the clerk's office. Otherwise, if the judge takes the matter under advisement, just pack up your briefcase and head back to the office.

If you lose and your motion is denied (or the other side's motion is allowed), don't beat yourself up over it. If you practice litigation long enough you will find out that the process is very unpredictable. Sometimes you win cases you should have lost, and sometimes you lose cases you should have won. Enjoy the victories and don't let the losses get to you. Any litigator who tells you he has never lost is a liar trying to intimidate you. You make your case as best you can, and then accept the decision whatever it is, and move on.

19. APPELLATE BRIEFS

The other type of persuasive document you may encounter if you practice in litigation is an appellate brief, which is similar to a memorandum in support of a motion but more formal. In an appellate brief you have to deal with what happened in the trial below, in addition to the facts of the case. The rules are the rules of appellate procedure, instead of the rules of civil procedure. And there are a lot of specific requirements for the brief. Also there is usually more than one judge you address in oral argument, and the process is timed. So it's a process with a lot of differences, but is still similar to the one we just discussed.

Instead of a caption, an appellate brief starts with a cover page printed on colored paper. The cover of the appellant's brief is blue; the appellee's brief is red (The "appellant" is the party filing the appeal, which can be the plaintiff or the defendant; the "appellee" is the other party); an intervener's or amicus curiae's brief is green; any reply brief is gray; and any supplemental brief is tan. Fed. R. App. Proc. R. 32(a). Also, the cover must contain the following information: "(A) the number of the case centered at the top; (B) the name of the court; (C) the title of the case; (D) the nature of the proceeding (*e.g.*, Appeal, Petition for Review) and the name of the court or agency below; (E) the title of the brief, identifying the party or parties for whom the brief is filed; and (F) the name, office address, and telephone number of counsel representing the party for whom the brief is filed." <u>Id.</u> Here is an example of how that information is typically formatted:

CASE NO. _____

IN THE UNITED STATES COURT OF APPEALS FOR THE SEVENTH CIRCUIT

JANE DOE., Plaintiff/Appellant

v.

XYZ Corp, Defendant/Appellee.

On Appeal From The United States District Court For The Central District Of Illinois

---

Plaintiff / Appellant's Appeal Brief

Name, _____Bar No.: _____
Name of Firm
Street Address

City, State Zip Code

Tel. (xxx) xxx-xxxx

E-Mail: _____@____.com

After the cover page, you must include five introductory sections before you get to the facts, argument and conclusion: (1) a statement regarding oral argument; (2) a table of contents, (3) a table of authorities, (4) a jurisdictional statement and (5) a statement of the issues presented for review. Fed. R. App. Proc. 28. (If your client is a corporation, you must also include a statement that "identifies any parent corporation and any publicly held corporation that owns 10% or more of its stock or states that there is no such corporation." Fed. R. App. Proc. 26.1.) I'll cover these introductory sections first because they are the sections that come in the beginning of an appellate brief, but if I were drafting a brief, I would draft the statement of the case (facts) and argument first, then add these sections – as well as the additional sections that come at the end of a brief – later.

The statement regarding oral argument should just explain why oral argument should be permitted or should not be permitted. Fed. R. App. Proc. 34(a)(1).

STATEMENT REGARDING ORAL ARGUMENT

Pursuant to Fed. R. App. Proc. 34(a)(1), Plaintiff / Appellant Jane Doe ("Doe") states that oral argument should be permitted because oral argument would assist the Court in a determination of the issues.

The table of contents should list each of the sections of

the brief and the page numbers on which they begin. Fed. R. App. Proc. 28.

TABLE OF CONTENTS

STATEMENT REGARDING ORAL ARGUMENT...#

TABLE OF AUTHORITIES.................................#

STATEMENT OF JURISDICTION.............................#

STATEMENT OF THE ISSUES ON APPEAL.................................#

STATEMENT OF THE CASE ....#

SUMMARY OF THE ARGUMENT...........................#

ARGUMENT...#

A.   Standard of Review...............................#

B.   The Claim Against Holding Company Should Not Have Been Dismissed Because Holding Company had Notice of the EEOC Charge and an Opportunity to Conciliate...#

C.   The Claim Against Holding Company Should Not Have Been Dismissed Because Doe Stated a Plausible Claim for Piercing the Corporate Veil.....................#

CONCLUSION...#

CERTICATE OF COMPLIANCE...............................#

CERTIFICATE OF SERVICE.................................#

The table of authorities should list all the case cited, alphabetically arranged, as well as all the statutes and other authorities in the brief, with page numbers for the pages in which they appear. Fed. R. App. Proc. 28.

TABLE OF AUTHORITIES

CASES

Ashcroft v. Iqbal, 556 U.S. 662 (2009).....................#

Benson v. Fannie May Confections Brands, Inc., 944 F.3d 639, 644 (7th Cir. 2019)................................#

Eggleston v. Chicago Journeymen Plumbers' Local Union No. 130, 657 F.2d 890, 905 (7th Cir.1981).......#

Reger Development, LLC v. National City Bank, 592 F.3d 759, 763 (7th Cir. 2010)..............................#

STATUTES

42 U.S.C. § 12117..#

42 U.S.C. § 2000e-5(b)...#

42 U.S.C. § 2000e-5(f)(1)......................................#

The jurisdictional statement should include the basis for the lower (trial) court's subject matter jurisdiction as well as the basis for the court of appeals' jurisdiction. Also, you need to list the filing dates demonstrating the timeliness of the appeal, and a statement that "the appeal is from a final order or judgment that disposes of all parties' claims, or information establishing the court of appeals' jurisdiction on some other basis." Fed. R. App. Proc. 28.

STATEMENT OF JURISDICTION

The District Court had jurisdiction in this case pursuant to 28 U.S.C. § 1331, as this action arises under federal law, and 28 U.S.C. § 1332(a)(1), as this also is a civil action where the matter in controversy exceeds the sum or value of $75,000, exclusive of interest and costs, and is between citizens of different States.

This Court has jurisdiction to decide this appeal under 28 U.S.C. § 1291 because this is appeal is from a final decision of a district court of the United States dated _____ __, ____.

The last introductory section is the statement of the issues presented for review, Fed. R. App. Proc. 28, and that section is actually similar to the statement of the issues in a legal research memorandum, except you need to include the context of what happened at the trial court. So, instead of saying the issue is whether a motion to dismiss should be denied, you would say the issue on appeal is whether the Court erred in dismissing the case.

Also, when you add the facts to the issue, add the facts favorable to your client. In other words, state the issues persuasively. In this example, I am arguing the motion to dismiss should have been denied (unlike the trial memo when I was arguing motion should be allowed). I don't want to frame the issue as "whether the District Court erred in dismissing the claim against Holding Company because it was not named in the original EEOC charge." Not naming the Holding Company is the reason to allow the motion. Instead I want to frame the issue as "whether the District Court erred in dismissing the claim against Holding Company because it had notice of the EEOC charge and an opportunity to conciliate." Having notice and an opportunity to conciliate is a reason to deny the motion, which is what I am arguing should have happened below.

STATEMENT OF THE ISSUE

The issue on appeal is whether the District Court erred in dismissing the claim against Defendant/Appellee XYZ Corp. ("Holding Company") because it had notice of the EEOC charge and an opportunity to conciliate.

After you have finished with those introductory sections, you begin with a concise statement of the case, which is basically a statement of facts, but must also include the procedural history below, as well as the rulings presented for review. Fed. R. App. Proc. 28. Just like you would if you were drafting the facts in a memorandum in support of a motion, state the facts in an appellate brief persuasively.

STATEMENT OF THE CASE

In her EEOC charge, Doe claimed she suffered

---

from "Chronic Fatigue and Immune Deficiency Syndrome (CFIDS)" and ABC Corp. (the "Employer") discriminated "against [her] because of [her] disability by not allowing [her] to work at home." Complaint, Exh. B. Doe named the Employer as a respondent in the charge. In addition, Doe alleges in this case that:

1. Holding Company and the Employer "share a unity of ownership and interests such that they are not, in fact, two separate corporate entities." Complaint, Par. 5;

2. Holding Company, "as the parent corporation and sole shareholder of [the Employer], should have been aware of the EEOC Charge...;" Complaint, Par. 11; and

3. Holding Company "knew or should have known about [Employer's] unlawful employment practices and failed to take action to prohibit such unlawful practices." Complaint, Par. 29.

Doe commenced this action on _____ __, ____. Prior to trial, Holding Company filed a motion to dismiss the claim against it. And the District Court allowed the motion without holding a hearing on _____ __, ____.

Then state "a succinct, clear and accurate" summary of your position, and proceed to make your full argument.

Start with the standard of review, then state the applicable substantive law, organized with point headings and CREAC. State your strongest points first, and state the strongest cases first as well. Cite primary binding authority before secondary and/or persuasive authority. Analogize cases that support your point and distinguish those that don't. If you can, don't hesitate to add policy arguments to further support your position (i.e. argue deciding in your favor is best for social policy). And finish strong with a short conclusion reiterating whatever relief you request. Fed. R. App. Proc. 28.

SUMMARY OF ARGUMENT

The claim against Holding Company should not have been dismissed because, even though Holding Company was not named in the original EEOC charge, it still knew or should have known about the charge and could have conciliated the claim. Alternatively, the Doe stated a plausible claim for piercing the corporate veil; Holding Company and the Employer were effectively one and the same.

ARGUMENT

A.   **Standard of Review**

"A dismissal for failure to state a claim is reviewed under a de novo standard." **Benson v. Fannie May Confections Brands, Inc.**, 944 F.3d 639, 644 (7th Cir. 2019). In analyzing a motion to dismiss, the court construes the complaint "in the light most favorable to the nonmoving party, accept[ing] well-pleaded facts as true, and draw[ing] all inferences in her favor." Reger Development, LLC v. National City Bank, 592 F.3d 759, 763 (7th Cir. 2010).

B.   Holding Company Had Notice of the EEOC
       Charge and an Opportunity to Conciliate

ADA claims, like other discrimination claims, must be brought before the EEOC before a civil action may be filed in federal court. 42 U.S.C. § 2000e-5(b). A civil action may then be brought "against the respondent named in the [EEOC] charge." 42 U.S.C. §2000e-5(f)(1). Also, a parent corporation that "has been provided with adequate notice of the charge . . . and . . . has been given the opportunity to participate in conciliation proceedings aimed at voluntary compliance . . ." may be joined in a civil action against its subsidiary. Eggleston v. Chicago Journeymen Plumbers' Local Union No. 130, 657 F.2d 890, 905 (7th Cir.1981).

In Eggleston, five persons brought an EEOC charge against a plumbers union, claiming discrimination in the administration of the apprenticeship program for plumbers. Id. at 893. After the EEOC case, they filed a civil action against the union, and also added a claim against the committee that administered the apprenticeship program. Id. The committee was comprised of ten people, five of whom were also were also officers in the union. Id. at 906. Because of the overlap in personnel, and the claim in the EEOC charge that the program the committee administered was discriminatory, the appeals court found the committee "knew or should have known of the EEOC charge and that their conduct would be subject to EEOC inquiry;" and there was nothing preventing the committee "from attempting to resolve the alleged discrimination in an amicable manner." Id. at 906-907. Therefore, the trial court's decision allowing the committee's motion to dismiss was reversed, and the committee was reinstated as a defendant to the plaintiffs' claim. Id. at 907.

This case is clearly analogous to Eggleston. Here Doe claims Holding Company and the Employer "share a unity of ownership and interests such that they are not, in fact, two separate corporate entities." Complaint, Par. 5. If Holding Company and Employer are effectively the same company, then the Eggleston test is more than satisfied. As Doe alleged, Holding Company "should have been aware of the EEOC Charge...;" and, as a result, there was nothing preventing Holding Company "from attempting to resolve the alleged discrimination in an amicable manner." Therefore, the complaint stated a claim against Holding Company, and should not have been dismissed.

The ADA embodies the very important public policy of helping people with disabilities retain their employment. And this case presents exactly the situation to which that policy applies. Doe is a disabled employee who wants to keep making a contribution to society despite her disability. If what she alleges is true, Holding Company had a role in the discrimination against her. To dismiss her claim against the Holding Company now because of a procedural technicality would be contrary to public policy. As a result the motion to dismiss should not have been allowed.

C.   Doe Stated a Plausible Claim for Piercing

        the Corporate Veil

A corporate entity may be disregarded where there is such "unity of interest and ownership that the separate personalities of the corporation and [the parent company] no longer exist. . ." and the circumstances are such that

". . . adherence to the fiction of separate corporate existence would sanction a fraud or promote injustice." E.g., Van Dorn Co. v. Future Chem. & Oil Corp., 753 F.2d 565, 569-70 (7th Cir.1985). Again, Doe alleges that the Employer and Holding Company "share a unity of ownership and interests such that they are not, in fact, two separate corporate entities." Complaint, Par. 5. If Doe can prove that allegation at trial; and not piercing the veil would "sanction a fraud or promote injustice," then Doe will be entitled to a judgment against Holding Company. Therefore, a claim for piercing the corporate veil was also plausible based on the allegations of the complaint and, again, the District Court erred by dismissing the claim against Holding Company.

D.   The Allegations of the Complaint Were not

Just Legal Conclusions

In its Motion to Dismiss Holding Company argued that a the Employee's allegations against it were "legal conclusions," and, therefore, the court was not required to accept them as true for the purposes of the motion. See e.g., Ashcroft v. Iqbal, 556 U.S. 662, ___ (2009). However, there is a difference between a legal conclusion and a factual conclusion. For example, one could argue that an allegation that a party knew or should have known of some material fact is conclusory, but that clearly is not the type of allegation the Supreme Court was referring to in <u>Ashcroft</u>. Doe did not allege that the statute authorized the claim against Holding Company or that the Court should pierce the corporate veil. She alleged that Holding Company and the Employer were essentially the same company. Complaint, Par. 5. And she specifically stated that Holding Company "should have been aware of the EEOC Charge…" and "failed to take action to prohibit such unlawful practices." Complaint, Par. 11 & 29. Those are allegations which, if accepted as true, more than justified the claim against Holding Company. As a result, that claim should not have been dismissed.

CONCLUSION

For these reasons, Doe requests this Court reverse the dismissal entered in favor of the Holding Company and reinstate the Holding Company as a defendant to the plaintiffs' claim.

After the conclusion you must include two additional

sections. The first is a certificate that the brief complies with the type-volume limitation in Rule 32(a)(7)(the brief contains no more than 13,000 words, or 6,500 words for a reply brief). Fed. R. App. Proc. 32(g). The second is a certificate of service stating "(i) the date and manner of service; (ii) the names of the persons served; and (iii) their mail or electronic addresses, facsimile numbers, or the addresses of the places of delivery, as appropriate for the manner of service." Fed. R. App. Proc. 25(d). Here is a sample of what those sections look like in practice:

CERTIFICATE OF COMPLIANCE

This is to certify that this brief complies with Federal Rule of Appellate Procedure 32(a)(7), and contains _____ words.

CERTIFICATE OF SERVICE

I certify that I electronically filed the this brief on this ____ day of _____ ____, with the Clerk of Court using the CM/ECF electronic filing system and that a true copy of this brief was served via transmission of Notices of Electronic Filing generated by such system to :

_____.

_____

Name

In addition to these required sections, there are also specific binding and formatting requirements for appellate briefs. The document must be bound in any manner that is "secure, does not obscure the text, and permits the brief to lie reasonably flat when open." Fed. R. App. Proc. 32. The required paper size is 8 ½ by 11 with one inch margins on all four sides. Id. The text must be double spaced (except headings and footnotes) and there is a page limitation of 30 pages for the principal brief and 15 pages for a reply brief. Id.

Also, the court rules may add additional requirements. For example, the 11th Circuit Court of Appeals requires that the cover of the brief be on at least 90# paper. 11th Cir. R. 32-2. Attorneys must file a certificate of interested persons in addition to a corporate disclosure. 11th Cir. R. 26.1. The summary of argument "should not be a mere repetition of the headings under which the argument is arranged." 11th Cir. R. 28-1 (j). Also, there is a specific citation rule requiring compliance with "the latest edition of either the "Bluebook" (A Uniform System of Citation) or the "ALWD Guide" Association of Legal Writing Directors' Guide to Legal Citation)." 11th Cir. R. 28-1(k). Again, you should always check the local rules for the court you are practicing in.

That completes your introduction to persuasive drafting. Now you know what is involved you can begin developing the skills you need to advocate well. Keep learning as much as you can. Practice. And seek perfection in everything you write. Good luck!

20. ORAL ARGUMENT

L ike an appellate brief, oral argument before the court of appeals is also more formal. The primary differences between appellate oral argument and trial court motion hearings are two: appellate argument is timed; and it is usually made to a panel of judges, not just one judge. The primary similarity is what is most important for both types of arguments: being prepared.

In addition to the case file, you need to be familiar with the case docket, which lists everything that happened at the court below and all the relevant dates for each event. Also, if there was a trial on the merits, you need to read the transcript and make sure you are up to speed on everything that happened during the trial of the case.

On the day of the argument, the attorneys are usually required to check in with the Clerk's Office before argument is scheduled to begin. At check-in, the Clerk's Office staff will verify the names of arguing counsel and the argument time allotted. Usually, you have either fifteen minutes or thirty minutes to state your argument to the court. Plus you can typically reserve additional time for rebuttal.

When court is in session, there should be no talking in the audience; and only material relating to the court's business can be read by persons sitting in the courtroom. So don't bring the newspaper or a novel to read while you are waiting. Also, taking photographs is prohibited (no selfies), as is eating or drinking, and using any electronic device, including computers, laptops, tablets, and mobile phones.

As in the trial court, everyone in the courtroom must stand when the judges enter the room, and remain standing until the presiding judge invites everyone to sit. Similarly, when court adjourns, everyone must stand until the judges leave the courtroom.

It is a good idea to get there early and get organized, and maybe get a cup of coffee and relax a little before its time to go into the courtroom. Litigators don't usually get to argue appeals very often so it is that much more important to make sure you are familiar with the environment and the process before you begin.

You also want to give the right impression by dressing and acting appropriately, and expressing yourself clearly and concisely. Even more importantly, you need to speak with conviction about your client's position. If you don't believe in what you're saying, you won't be able to convince anyone of anything. And don't avoid questions. Meet the weaknesses in your case head on and deal with them. Then try to finish on a high note.

When you refer to the judge or counsel on the other side, follow the same practices that apply in a motion hearing. Refer the judges as "your honor." Start by introducing yourself, then stating your argument, and answering succinctly whatever questions they ask. Don't feel like your oral argument has to be organized the same way your appellate brief was organized. Likely, you will want to start by stating the issues, then outlining the relevant facts, introducing your position, and then going point by point through the main arguments for granting the relief you request. But be flexible and do whatever you think will work best under the circumstances.

When the judge asks a question, mark where you left off in your outline, so you can return to that section after the question is answered. Also, if your answer will have multiple parts, jot down a quick outline of what you want to say as the judge is speaking. That way you won't forget one of your points (or your response to one aspect of the question) before you are done giving your answer.

There is usually a digital clock on the podium that provides a countdown of the time remaining for your argument. If the light is green you are within your allotted time. Keep talking. If the light is yellow, you are within your allotted time for rebuttal. Keep talking. But if the light is red, your time is up. Sum up by reiterating what you want and stop talking.

While the other side presents their case, listen carefully and continue to take good notes. It is not unusual for things to come up in oral argument that were not discussed in the briefs.

So take note of anything new and any other points you want to make in your rebuttal, then you will have a short outline to refer to when you stand up again. Keep the rebuttal short and to the point. You won't have much time and the judges will be looking to wrap up. So don't feel like you have to repeat what you already said. Just rebut any points you haven't addressed and conclude your presentation.

After you are done, and you are outside the courtroom, go ahead and take that selfie. Plenty of lawyers practice a long time and never have the opportunity to argue a case before a court of appeals. So give yourself something to remember it by!

APPPENDIX

Sources of Authority Chart, Types of Authority Chart, Research Checklist Chart

Sources of Authority (Local, State, Federal, International)

Local Law	Ordinances and Bylaws		
State Law	Constitution		
	Statutes and Regulations	Florida Statutes	Fla. Stat.
		Florida Administrative Code	Fla. Admin. Code
	Cases	Supreme Court	Fla. or So. 2d
		District Courts	Fla. or So. 2d
		Circuit Courts	
		County Courts	
	Executive Orders		
Federal Law	Constitution		
	Statutes and Regulations	United States Code	U.S.C.
		Code of Federal Regulations	C.F.R.
	Cases	Supreme Court	U.S. Sup. Ct. L. Ed. 2d
		Appeals Courts (Circuit)	F. F.2d F.3d
		District Courts	F. Supp. F. Supp. 2d
	Executive Orders		
International Law	Treaties, Compacts, Agreements		

Types of Authority (Primary, Secondary, Binding, Persuasive)

Federal Court	Federal Issue	Constitution USC and CFR Supreme Court Circuit Courts	Primary	Binding
		Cases of other Circuits, Districts	Primary	Persuasive
		CJS, AmJur, ALR, Law Review, etc.	Secondary	Persuasive
	State Issue	State Statutes and Regs State Supreme Court Cases	Primary	Binding
		Federal Cases	Primary	Persuasive
		CJS, AmJur, ALR, Law Review, etc.	Secondary	Persuasive
State Court	State Issue	State Constitution State Statutes & Regs State Supreme Court State Appeals Courts	Primary	Binding
		Cases of other states	Primary	Persuasive
		CJS, AmJur, ALR, Law Review, etc.	Secondary	Persuasive
	Federal Issue	Federal Cases	Primary	Binding
		State Cases	Primary	Persuasive
		CJS, AmJur, ALR, Law Review, etc.	Secondary	Persuasive

Research Checklist

(Sources to Check when Researching an Issue)

	Table of Contents Beginning of Each Volume	Index Last Volume(s)	Word Search Computer
Annotated Statutes Federal or State Statutes and Regulations	√	√	√
Case Digests Federal Cases or State Cases	√	√	√
Secondary Sources AmJur, CJS, ALR, State Sources	√	√	√

CASE BRIEFING EXERCISE

MEMORANDUM

To: Associate

From: Senior Partner

Subject: _____

Date: _____ __, ____

I represent the defendant in a personal injury case involving a rear end collision. Please brief the issue of whether the defendant in the following cases breached the duty of reasonable care by rear ending the plaintiff's vehicle: Clampitt v. Spencer Sales, 786 So.2d 570 (Fla. 2001) and Epler v. Tarmac, 752 So.2d 592 (Fla. 2000). Copies of the decisions are attached.

CLAMPITT V. SPENCER

786 So.2d 570

Supreme Court of Florida.

Colletta P. CLAMPITT, Petitioner,

v.

D.J. SPENCER SALES, et al., Respondents.

No. SC92603.

May 10, 2001.

Preceding motorist brought negligence action against rear motorist to recover for personal injuries suffered in rear-end collision. The Circuit Court, Levy County, granted summary judgment for preceding motorist on issue of liability, and thereafter entered judgment on jury verdict awarding her damages. Rear motorist appealed. The District Court of Appeal reversed and remanded, **704 So.2d 601**. On application for review, the Supreme Court, Shaw, J., held that sudden stop by preceding motorist was insufficient to rebut presumption of negligence on part of rear motorist.

District Court of Appeal's decision quashed.

Pariente, J., issued opinion concurring in result only.

SHAW, J.

We have for review D.J. *Spencer Sales v. Clampitt*, **704 So.2d 601** (Fla. 1st DCA 1997), based on conflict with **Pierce v. Progressive**

American Insurance Co., 582 So.2d 712 (Fla. 5th DCA 1991). We have jurisdiction. *See* art. V, § 3(b)(3), Fla. Const. We quash *D.J. Spencer Sales.*

I. FACTS

During the morning of August 30, 1993, three vehicles were following one another in the southbound lane of Alternate U.S. 27 south of Bronson, Florida. The lead vehicle, which was driven by Charles Huguley, was a pickup truck hauling a small trailer; the second vehicle, driven by Colletta Clampitt, was an automobile; and the third vehicle, driven by Carl Hetz, was a commercial tractor-trailer rig owned by D.J. Spencer Sales ("Spencer Sales" or "Spencer"). The posted speed limit was fifty-five miles per hour; the weather was clear. The three vehicles were involved in an accident about a mile south of the Bronson 572 city limits and Clampitt was seriously injured. She sued Spencer Sales.[1] Prior to trial, she moved for summary judgment on the issue of fault, contending that Spencer had failed to rebut the presumption of negligence that attaches to the rear driver in a rear-end collision. She submitted Huguley's and Hetz's deposition testimony and Hetz's answers to interrogatories. Spencer submitted no evidence on the issue.

Huguley testified in his deposition as follows: He was traveling south at forty-five to fifty-five miles an hour; he activated his turn signal and began braking one hundred and fifty yards prior to entering the driveway of his place of business; his pickup truck and trailer had turned almost completely off the highway when the trailer was struck from behind by Clampitt's auto. Hetz testified as follows: He was traveling at forty-five to fifty miles per hour; he was following Clampitt's auto by approximately one hundred and twenty feet; although he had an unobstructed view of Huguley's vehicle, he did not know that Huguley was turning until he saw Clampitt's auto strike Huguley's trailer and push the pickup truck and trailer off the road; at that point, he saw Clampitt's auto come to a "dead-stop" on the highway; he slammed on his brakes, left

233

one hundred feet of skid marks, and struck Clampitt's auto; he did not see Huguley's turn signal or brake lights illuminate at any time prior to the accident (although he did testify that the trooper at the scene confirmed that Huguley's turn signals and brake lights were operational); he did not see Clampitt's brake lights illuminate at any time.[2]

The trial court granted summary judgment in favor of Clampitt on the issue of fault. The case proceeded to trial on the issue of damages and the jury returned a verdict of $857,997 for Clampitt.[3] The district court reversed on the summary judgment issue, ruling that the evidence in favor of Spencer Sales was sufficient to overcome the presumption of negligence. This Court granted review based on conflict with **Pierce v. Progressive American Insurance Co., 582 So.2d 712 (Fla. 5th DCA 1991)**, wherein the district court held that an abrupt stop, by itself, is insufficient to overcome the presumption of negligence that attaches to a rear driver.[4]

II. THE APPLICABLE LAW

The rebuttable presumption of negligence that attaches to the rear driver in a rear-end collision in Florida arises out of necessity in cases where the lead driver *573 sues the rear driver. The presumption bears only upon the causal negligence of the rear driver:

> The usefulness of the rule is obvious. A plaintiff ordinarily bears the burden of proof of all four elements of negligence-duty of care, breach of that duty, causation and damages. Yet, obtaining proof of two of those elements, breach and causation, is difficult when a plaintiff driver who has been rear-ended knows that the defendant driver rear-ended him but usually does not know why. Beginning with *McNulty*, therefore, the law presumed that the driver of the rear vehicle was negligent unless that driver provided a substantial and reasonable explanation as to why he was not negligent,

in which case the presumption would vanish and the case could go to the jury on its merits.

Jefferies v. Amery Leasing, Inc., 698 So.2d 368, 370-71 (Fla. 5th DCA 1997) (citations omitted).

This Court in Gulle v. Boggs, 174 So.2d 26 (Fla.1965), endorsed the rebuttable presumption established in McNulty v. Cusack, 104 So.2d 785 (Fla. 2d DCA 1958), and held that the burden is on the defendant to come forward with evidence that "fairly and reasonably tends to show" that the presumption of negligence is misplaced:

> We have stated that the presumption announced in *McNulty*, and subsequently followed, is rebuttable. It is constructed by the law to give particular effect to a certain group of facts in the absence of further evidence. The presumption provides a prima facie case which shifts to the defendant the burden to go forward with evidence to contradict or rebut the fact presumed. When the defendant produces evidence which *fairly and reasonably tends to show* that the real fact is not as presumed, the impact of "the presumption is dissipated". Whether the ultimate fact has been established must then be decided by the jury from all of the evidence before it without the aid of the presumption. At this point the entire matter should be deposited with the trier of facts to reconcile the conflicts and evaluate the credibility of the witnesses and the weight of the evidence.

Gulle v. Boggs, 174 So.2d at 28-29 (emphasis added).

The Court recently revisited this issue in Eppler v. Tarmac America, Inc., 752 So.2d 592 (Fla.2000). There, Eppler was stopped in a line of vehicles at a red light and when the light turned green all the vehicles accelerated and proceeded forward in a routine fashion for several seconds. Eppler then suddenly-without warning and for no apparent reason-slammed on her brakes and was struck from behind by the defendant's cement-mixer truck. The Court held that under those circumstances the presumption of negligence was overcome:

> Based on the foregoing, we agree with the decisions of both the trial and district courts below. Abrupt and arbitrary braking in bumper-to-bumper, accelerating traffic is an irresponsible and dangerous act that *invites* a collision. Cases involving allegations of such an act are properly submitted to the jury, for the crucible of cross-examination is well-suited for gleaning meritorious from non-meritorious claims. In the present case, the trial court properly denied Eppler's motion for a directed verdict.

Eppler, 752 So.2d at 595-96.

III. THE PRESENT CASE

In the present case, the district court ruled that the presumption of negligence was overcome by the following alleged *574 facts: Clampitt "dead-stopped" in front of Hetz; and Clampitt failed to use her brakes prior to colliding with Huguley's trailer.[5] From these facts, the court reasoned that a jury could infer that Clampitt negligently failed to decelerate gradually as Huguley's vehicle pulled off the highway.[6] This was error.

The present case differs from *Eppler* wherein the forward driver allegedly made an abrupt and *arbitrary* stop in bumper-to-bumper accelerating traffic, i.e., a "gotcha" stop. Rather, this case is similar to **Pierce v. Progressive American Insurance Co.,** **582 So.2d 712 (Fla. 5th DCA 1991)**, and other "sudden stop" cases wherein the forward driver merely stopped abruptly. The court in *Pierce* explained that a sudden stop standing alone is insufficient to overcome the presumption of negligence:

> It is not merely an "abrupt stop" by a preceding vehicle (if it is in its proper place on the highway) that rebuts

or dissipates the presumption that the negligence of the rear driver was the sole proximate cause of a rear-end collision. It is a sudden stop by the preceding driver at a time and place where it could not reasonably be expected by the following driver that creates the factual issue.

Pierce, 582 So.2d at 714 (citations omitted). The court in *Pierce* also rejected the notion that the rear driver can benefit from a claim that the forward driver was negligent in rear-ending the vehicle in front of him or her.[7]

*575 In the present case, the accident took place at midmorning on a clear day on a level stretch of two-lane roadway just outside the Bronson city limits. In the area of the accident, the roadway is bordered by a farm supply store and several other commercial establishments, several apartment complexes and a residential development, and the campus of Central Florida Junior College, all of which maintain entrances and exits on the roadway. Hetz testified that, in spite of his vantage point in the cab (from where he had a clear view of both vehicles in front of him), he did not see Huguley activate his turn signal; he did not see Huguley illuminate his brake lights; he did not see Huguley slow down; and he did not see Huguley turn into his driveway. Nor did he see Clampitt slow down or activate her brake lights. At best, according to Hetz's own testimony, Clampitt made a sudden stop on the roadway ahead and Hetz did not see her until the last minute.

It is well settled that a sudden stop, without more, is insufficient to overcome the presumption of negligence. We also know that-in spite of Hetz's testimony otherwise-some of the aforementioned events probably did take place. We know, for instance, that Huguley turned off the highway, that he probably slowed down (from fifty miles per hour) in order to do so, that his brake lights (which were in working order) probably illuminated, and that Clampitt probably slowed down before striking the trailer (she did only slight damage to the trailer). Thus, even interpreting the alleged facts in the light most favorable to Spencer Sales, Hetz appears to have been "asleep at the wheel" of a seventy-six thousand pound vehicle traveling at fifty miles an hour.

Based on this record, Spencer Sales failed to meet the *Gulle* standard: It failed to present evidence that "fairly and reasonably" tends to show that Hetz was not negligent in colliding with Clampitt's auto. The trial court properly granted Clampitt's motion for summary judgment and the district court erred in ruling otherwise.

IV. CONCLUSION

This is a classic "sudden stop" case. Clampitt's auto stopped abruptly on the highway as the result of a collision with Huguley's trailer, and Hetz's tractor-trailer rig was unable to stop in time. Unfortunately, accidents on the roadway ahead are a routine hazard faced by the driving public. Such accidents are encountered far too frequently and are to be reasonably expected. Each driver is charged under the law with remaining alert and following the vehicle in front of him or her at a safe distance.[8]

> In effect the law requires all drivers to push ahead of themselves an imaginary clear stopping distance or assured stopping space or adequate zone within which the driven vehicle can come to a stop. Failure to maintain such a zone is normally the sole proximate cause of injuries and damages resulting from the collision of a vehicle with an object ahead. This is why when a vehicle collides *576 with an object ahead of it, including the rear of a leading vehicle, there is a presumption of negligence on the part of the overtaking or following vehicle.

Lynch v. Tennyson, 443 So.2d 1017, 1020-21 (Fla. 5th DCA 1983) (Cowart, J., dissenting). Each driver must be prepared to stop suddenly (particularly during school and business hours on a roadway that is bordered by multiple business and residential establishments and a school, as in the present case). It is logical to charge the rear driver with this responsibility because he or she is the person who is in control of the following distance.

Based on the foregoing we quash D.J. *Spencer Sales v. Clampitt*, 704 So.2d 601 (Fla. 1st DCA 1997).

It is so ordered.

WELLS, C.J., and HARDING, ANSTEAD, LEWIS and QUINCE, JJ., concur.

PARIENTE, J., concurs in result only with an opinion.

PARIENTE, J., concurring in result only.

I concur in the majority's opinion holding that an abrupt stop by the forward driver is insufficient to overcome the presumption of negligence on the part of the rear driver. *See* majority op. at 575. As the majority notes "accidents are encountered far too frequently and are to be reasonably expected. Each driver is charged under the law with remaining alert and following the vehicle in front of him or her at a safe distance." *Id.* at 575.

As observed by the Fifth District in **Pierce v. Progressive American Insurance Co.**, 582 So.2d 712 (Fla. 5th DCA 1991), which we today approve:

> It is not merely an "abrupt stop" by a preceding vehicle (if it is in its proper place on the highway) that rebuts or dissipates the presumption.... *It is a sudden stop by the preceding driver at a time and place where it could not reasonably be expected* by the following driver that creates the factual issue.

Id. at 714 (citation omitted) (emphasis added). As I explained in my dissenting opinion in **Eppler v. Tarmac America, Inc.**, 752 So.2d 592, 597 (Fla.2000) (Pariente, J., dissenting), an abrupt stop at a busy intersection should impose the same obligation on the rear driver as a sudden stop by the forward driver on a highway as in this case. The reason for the forward driver's stop is not the issue, as this factor relates to the issue of comparative fault. *See id.* Rather, the only issue involved in determining whether the rear driver has overcome the presumption of negligence is whether the stop occurred at a time and place that the rear driver reasonably could have expected. *See id.* As the Third District observed in **Tacher v. Asmus**, 743 So.2d 157, 158 (Fla. 3d DCA 1999), *review dismissed,* 767 So.2d 461 (Fla.2000):

> We conclude that a sudden stop by a preceding driver or drivers approaching or going through a busy intersection should be reasonably expected so as to impose a duty on the drivers which follow them to operate their vehicles at a safe distance. It is not at all unusual for vehicles [proceeding] through busy intersections, for example, to have to suddenly brake for pedestrians, emergency vehicles or other drivers running a red traffic light from a cross-street.

As the majority correctly observes in this case, "[e]ach driver must be prepared to stop suddenly (particulary during school and business hours on a roadway that is bordered by multiple business and residential establishments and a school, as in the present case). It is logical to charge the rear driver with this responsibility because *577 he or she is the person who is in control of the following distance." Majority op. at 576. My only dispute is with the majority's distinction of *Eppler* on the basis that the stop in that case was both "arbitrary" and abrupt. *See* majority op. at 574. Because I disagree that the stop in *Eppler* was not reasonably foreseeable for the reasons stated in my dissenting opinion in that case, I concur in the result only in this case.

Footnotes

1   Clampitt also sued Huguley but the trial court dismissed the claim.

2   Hetz testified as follows:

Q. Okay. From where you were sitting in your rig and from your habits and the way you drive, would you have seen her brake lights, do you believe, had she applied the brakes to her vehicle?

A. Yeah, I would have seen them.

Q. Okay. So you believe she did not hit the brakes then; is that correct?

A. I didn't see them, no.

Q. Okay.

A. Because I don't think-well, no.

Q. Okay. But you didn't see brake lights on Mr. Huguley's vehicle either?

A. No.

Q. Okay.

A. Like I said, I didn't see him-like I said, I didn't know for sure he was turning, I didn't even know he was turning until he was [hit], I mean, he was already in motion.

3   Pursuant to a stipulation of the parties, the court reduced the award to $842,997 due to collateral source benefits already paid to Clampitt.

4   Clampitt raises an additional issue that is outside the scope of the inter-district conflict and was not the basis this Court's granting of discretionary review.

5   The district court below summarized the key evidence on the summary judgment issue:

In this case, appellant Hetz, the driver of the rear vehicle, testified that appellee "dead-stopped" in front of him in an area with a posted speed limit of 55 miles per hour. He also testified that after leaving the Bronson city limits, he remained two truck lengths behind appellee's car. Appellant Hetz then stated that when he saw appellee stop on the highway, he hit his brakes and put down 110 feet of skid marks. He further testified that appellee's brake lights did not come on prior to the collision.

D.J. *Spencer Sales v. Clampitt,* 704 So.2d 601, 603 (Fla. 1st DCA 1997).

6   The district court below concluded as follows:

Viewing the evidence in a light most favorable to appellants, we conclude appellant Hetz's affirmative testimony concerning appellee's "dead-stop" in front of him and her seeming failure to use her brakes prior to impact with the lead vehicle, constitutes sufficient evidence to overcome the presumption of negligence which attaches to the driver of the rear vehicle involved in a collision. Since the lead driver testified that he used his turn indicators to signal his turn into his business, a jury could reasonably infer that appellee was negligent in failing to decelerate gradually as the lead driver slowed and turned in front of her vehicle. In these circumstances, we conclude the trial court erred in granting the motion for partial summary judgment and in removing the question of negligence from the jury.

D.J. *Spencer Sales,* 704 So.2d at 603.

7   See *Pierce,* wherein the district court ruled as follows:

The second argument [i.e., that the negligence of the first three drivers in rear-ending the vehicles in front of them inured to Pierce's benefit] is equally fallacious. The presumption of negligence arising from the collision between Boone and Reaves [i.e., the first and second drivers, respectively] inured only in favor of Boone, and against Reaves. Likewise, any presumption of negligence against Tiroff and in favor of Reaves [i.e., the third and second drivers, respectively] arising from a second collision could not benefit Pierce in regard to the third collision where he struck Tiroff.

....

Other than the fact that Reaves and Tiroff each collided with a preceding car, there is no evidence whatsoever of any negligence by either of them to rebut the presumption of Pierce's negligence in regard to the third collision. The burden to produce that evidence was upon Pierce. Even on this appeal, Pierce has not contended that there was any material evidence of negligence on the part of Tiroff or Reaves other than the fact each ran into a preceding vehicle.

Pierce, 582 So.2d at 714-15 (citation omitted).

8   *See* section 316.0895(1), Florida Statutes (1993), which provides in relevant part:

316.0895 Following too closely.-

(1) The driver of a motor vehicle shall not follow another vehicle more closely than is reasonable and prudent, having due regard for the speed of such vehicles and the traffic upon, and the condition of, the highway.

EPPLER V. TARMAC

752 So.2d 592

Supreme Court of Florida.

Sybil EPPLER, Petitioner,

v.

TARMAC AMERICA, INC., Respondent.

No. SC91066.

Feb. 17, 2000.Rehearing Denied March 21, 2000.

Driver of lead vehicle sued employer of rear driver following rear-end accident. The Circuit Court for Duval County, Henry F. Martin, Jr., J., entered judgment on jury verdict for employer. Lead driver appealed and the District Court of Appeal, Wolf, J., 695 So.2d 775, affirmed and certified question. The Supreme Court, Shaw, J., held that rear driver's testimony was sufficient to overcome presumption of negligence.

Certified question answered.

Pariente, J., filed a dissenting opinion.

SHAW, J.

We have for review *Eppler v. Tarmac America, Inc.*, 695 So.2d 775 (Fla. 1st DCA 1997), wherein the district court certified the following question:

> Does the testimony of the defendant of a sudden unexpected stop immediately after starting forward constitute sufficient evidence to overcome the presumption of negligence which attaches in a rear-end collision?

Id. at 778. We have jurisdiction. Art. V, § 3(b)(4), Fla. Const. We answer in the affirmative as explained below and approve *Eppler.*

In the late afternoon of September 27, 1994, Sybil Eppler's station wagon was stopped in a line of traffic at a stoplight and Lawrence Morris's cement-mixer truck, which was owned by Tarmac America, Inc., was stopped directly behind her. At some point after the light turned green, Eppler's car was struck from behind by Morris's truck, which was moving forward at a low rate of speed. Eppler's car rolled forward and made contact with a car driven by James Richards. Richards' car was undamaged and he later drove off. Eppler also appeared uninjured, and she too drove off. The next day, however, Eppler complained that her neck and back hurt, and she sought treatment from a chiropractor and from a psychiatrist. She sued Tarmac.

Eppler testified at trial that she was struck by Morris's truck before she had started moving forward at the stoplight. Morris, on the other hand, testified that once the light had turned green, all the vehicles in line began accelerating and then Eppler suddenly-without warning and for no reason-slammed on her brakes. At the close of all the evidence, Eppler moved for a directed verdict, and the trial court denied the motion. The jury returned a verdict in favor of Tarmac, finding no negligence on Morris's part.[1] Eppler appealed the denial of her motion for a directed verdict and the district court affirmed, ruling that the evidence presented by Tarmac was sufficient to overcome the presumption of negligence that attaches to the driver of a rear vehicle involved in a rear-end collision:

> In the instant case, the evidence viewed in the light most favorable to the defendant established an unexpected stop immediately after starting to move when the signal light changed. We, therefore, [affirm the trial court's ruling on the motion for a directed verdict].

Eppler *v. Tarmac America, Inc.*, 695 So.2d 775, 778 (Fla. 1st DCA 1997) (on motion for rehearing).

While Eppler agrees that evidence of a sudden unexpected stop by the forward driver is sufficient to overcome the presumption of negligence that attaches to the *594 rear driver, she contends that-viewing the testimony in the light most favorable to Tarmac-her own stop was merely sudden, not unexpected. She claims that the trial court erred in denying her motion for a directed verdict. We disagree.

The rebuttable presumption of negligence that attaches to the rear driver in a rear-end collision in Florida arises out of necessity in cases where the lead driver sues the rear driver. The device bears only upon the causal negligence of the rear driver:

> The usefulness of the rule is obvious. A plaintiff ordinarily bears the burden of proof of all four elements of negligence-duty of care, breach of that duty, causation and damages. Yet, obtaining proof of two of those elements, breach and causation, is difficult when a plaintiff driver who has been rear-ended knows that the defendant driver rear-ended him but usually does not know why. Beginning with *McNulty*, therefore, the law presumed that the driver of the rear vehicle was negligent unless that driver provided a substantial and reasonable explanation as to why he was not negligent, in which case the presumption would vanish and the case could go to the jury on its merits.

Jefferies v. Amery Leasing, Inc., 698 So.2d 368, 370-371 (Fla. 5th DCA 1997) (citations omitted).

This Court in Gulle v. Boggs, 174 So.2d 26 (Fla.1965), endorsed the rebuttable presumption established in McNulty v. Cusack, 104 So.2d 785 (Fla. 2d DCA 1958), and held that the burden is on the defendant to come forward with evidence that "fairly and reasonably tends to show" that the presumption of negligence is misplaced:

> We have stated that the presumption announced in *McNulty*, and subsequently followed, is rebuttable. It is constructed by the law to give particular effect to a certain group of facts in the absence of further evidence. The presumption provides a prima facie case which shifts to the defendant the burden to go forward with evidence to contradict or rebut the fact presumed. When the defendant produces evidence which *fairly and reasonably tends to show* that the real fact is not as presumed, the impact of "the presumption is dissipated". Whether the ultimate fact has been established must then be decided by the jury from all of the evidence before it without the aid of the presumption. At this point the entire matter should be deposited with the trier of facts to reconcile the conflicts and evaluate the credibility of the witnesses and the weight of the evidence.

Gulle, 174 So.2d at 28-29 (emphasis added).

In the present case, Tarmac came forward with evidence showing the following: (1) The Tarmac truck was stopped ten to eleven feet behind Eppler's auto in a line of traffic at a red light;[2] (2) when the light turned green, all the vehicles in the line proceeded forward and were accelerating in a routine fashion;[3] (3) the Tarmac*595 driver, Morris, accelerated slowly with the other vehicles, shifted from first to second gear, and had been in second gear for three or four seconds when Eppler suddenly-without warning and for no reason-slammed on her brakes.[4] Pursuant to the *Gulle* standard, this evidence "fairly and reasonably tends to show" that the presumption of negligence on Morris's part is misplaced, for an abrupt and *arbitrary* stop in such a situation is not reasonably expected. In fact, it is a classic surprise.

The present "arbitrary stop" case thus differs from **Tacher v.**

Asmus, 743 So.2d 157 (Fla. 3d DCA 1999), and other "sudden stop" cases wherein the forward driver merely stopped abruptly.[5] In *Tacher*, three autos collided in a chain reaction at a stoplight. The evidence showed the following: After the light had turned green, all the vehicles were proceeding forward when the auto in front of Tacher (driven by Matthews) suddenly stopped; Tacher was unable to stop in time and his vehicle struck Matthews' auto; Matthews' auto then struck Asmus's vehicle. Matthews and Asmus sued Tacher, and the trial court granted their motion for a directed verdict. The district court affirmed.

The district court in *Tacher* explained that the forward driver's stop should have been reasonably expected:

> We conclude that a sudden stop by a preceding driver or drivers approaching or going through a busy intersection should be reasonably expected so as to impose a duty on the drivers which follow them to operate their vehicles at a safe distance. It is not at all unusual for vehicles [proceeding] through busy intersections, for example, to have to suddenly brake for pedestrians, emergency vehicles or other drivers running a red traffic light from a cross-street. For that reason, we do not believe that the evidence of a preceding vehicles' sudden stop at a busy intersection, in this case, was sufficient to overcome the presumption of negligence on the part of appellant, Tacher.

Tacher, 743 So.2d at 158. Unlike the present case where Morris testified repeatedly that Eppler slammed on her brakes "for no reason," the district court in *Tacher* noted no such misconduct on the part of Matthews or Asmus. *Tacher* is framed as a simple "sudden stop" case.

Based on the foregoing, we agree with the decisions of both the trial and district courts below. Abrupt and arbitrary braking in bumper-to-bumper, accelerating traffic is an irresponsible and dangerous act that *invites* a collision. Cases involving allegations of such an act are properly submitted to the jury, for the crucible of *596 cross-examination is well-suited for gleaning meritorious from non-meritorious claims. In the present case, the trial court properly denied Eppler's motion for a directed verdict.

We answer the certified question in the affirmative and approve *Eppler* on this issue. We distinguish *Tacher* as explained herein.[6]

It is so ordered.

HARDING, C.J., and WELLS and ANSTEAD, JJ., concur.

PARIENTE, J., dissents with an opinion.

PARIENTE, J., dissenting.

I respectfully dissent. The question certified by the First District and answered by the majority is whether a defendant's testimony of a "sudden unexpected stop" immediately after starting forward constitutes sufficient evidence to overcome the presumption of negligence. A sudden stop, however, is not necessarily an unexpected or unanticipated stop; that is, one that could not reasonably be anticipated by the rear driver under the circumstances. As observed by the Fifth District:

> It is not merely an "abrupt stop" by a preceding vehicle (if it is in its proper place on the highway) that rebuts or dissipates the presumption.... It is a sudden stop by the preceding driver *at a time and place where it could not reasonably be expected* by the following driver that creates the factual issue.

Pierce v. Progressive Am. Ins. Co., 582 So.2d 712, 714 (Fla. 5th DCA 1991) (emphasis supplied). As explained by Judge Green in her recent opinion in Tacher v. Asmus, 743 So.2d 157 (Fla. 3rd DCA 1999):

> Where, as in this case, it is claimed that the rear-end collision was precipitated by a sudden stop by the

preceding driver, most districts (including our own) have found that the presumption cannot be rebutted if the stop happened at a place and time where it was reasonably expected. *See* Pierce v. Progressive Am. Ins. Co., 582 So.2d 712, 714 (Fla. 5th DCA 1991); *see also* Kao v. Lauredo, 617 So.2d 775, 777 (Fla. 3d DCA 1993); Tozier v. Jarvis, 469 So.2d 884, 888 (Fla. 4th DCA 1985); *but compare* Eppler *v. Tarmac Am., Inc.,* 695 So.2d 775 (Fla. 1st DCA 1997) (the defendants testimony of a sudden and unexpected stop of the preceding driver at an intersection was sufficient to overcome the presumption of negligence and create jury issue of fault).

Id. at 158.

The Third District recognized the conflict between the district courts of appeal as it expressly certified direct conflict with *Eppler* in its opinion:

We conclude that *a sudden stop by a preceding driver or drivers approaching or going through a busy intersection should be reasonably expected so as to impose a duty on the drivers which follow them to operate their vehicles at a safe distance.* It is not at all unusual for vehicles [proceeding] through busy intersections, for example, to have to suddenly brake for pedestrians, emergency vehicles or other drivers running a red traffic light from a cross-street. For that reason, we do not believe that the evidence of a preceding vehicles' sudden stop at a busy intersection, in this case, was sufficient to overcome the presumption of negligence on the part of appellant, Tacher.

We therefore affirm the directed verdict entered on the issue of liability in this case. Further, as we recognize that our holding in this case is in direct conflict with the first district's *Eppler* decision, we certify direct conflict.

*597 Tacher, 743 So.2d at 158 (emphasis supplied).

Likewise, the concern in the present case should be whether the forward driver's sudden stop should have been reasonably expected or anticipated by the rear driver. The majority opinion does little to assist the district courts of appeal in resolving the conflict among them concerning application of the presumption of negligence in a rear-end collision when there is a sudden stop by the forward driver at a busy intersection. Instead of resolving the conflict among the districts, the majority attempts to distinguish *Tacher* from *Eppler* and neither approves nor disapproves of **Kao v. Lauredo, 617 So.2d 775 (Fla. 3rd DCA 1993)**, and **Pierce, 582 So.2d at 712**. In my opinion, the holdings of *Kao* and *Pierce* are contrary to the result reached by the majority in this case but are consistent with the Third District's opinion in *Tacher.*

Further, the additional facts supplied by the majority opinion appear nowhere in the First District's *Eppler* opinion. In *Eppler,* the First District summarized the testimony at trial as follows:

> At trial, both appellant [the plaintiff] and the Tarmac truck driver [the defendant] agreed that appellant had stopped due to a red light, but their testimony differed as to the cause of the accident once the traffic light changed to green. Appellant testified that she was hit by the Tarmac truck before she started forward; however, the Tarmac driver testified that appellant started forward and then stopped suddenly in front of him which caused him to rear-end her vehicle and push it into the vehicle ahead of her. The only other witness to the collision, the driver of the lead vehicle struck by appellant, testified only that he had not started moving forward after the light change when appellant struck him from behind.

Eppler, 695 So.2d at 776. Similarly, in *Tacher,* the Third District explained the facts as follows:

> Tacher was the operator of the third car stopped behind Matthews' vehicle at a distance of three to five feet. After

> the light turned green, Tacher testified that he observed both the Asmus vehicle and the Matthews vehicle begin to move forward. At that point, Tacher stated that he began to move forward traveling at approximately three to five miles per hour. Suddenly, he saw the Matthews vehicle abruptly stop.

Tacher, 743 So.2d at 157.

More importantly, to the extent the majority attempts to distinguish *Eppler* from *Tacher,* the distinction is one without a difference as to the critical issue of the rear driver's negligence. The majority claims that the two cases can be distinguished by asserting that the plaintiff in *Eppler* "slammed on her brakes 'for no reason,' " whereas in *Tacher,* the court "noted no such misconduct ... [rather] *Tacher* is framed as a simple 'sudden stop' case." Majority op. at 595. This distinction, however, is misplaced because the focus of the Third District's opinion in *Tacher* was that "the stop happened at a place and time where it was reasonably expected." Tacher, 743 So.2d at 158.

The majority's concern over the possibility of misconduct on the part of the forward driver should be directed toward the issue of the forward driver's comparative negligence, where, as in this case, that forward driver is the plaintiff. Even if the trial court were to enter a directed verdict as to the rear driver's negligence, this decision would not end the liability equation as to the forward driver's negligence. I would address the majority's concern with fault on the part of the forward driver by holding that if the forward driver stopped suddenly at a busy intersection for no justifiable reason, the forward driver could also be found negligent.

In other words, while a sudden stop alone does not defeat a directed verdict on the issue of the rear driver's negligence, a sudden stop that occurs because the forward *598 driver failed to exercise reasonable care (i.e. stopped for no apparent reason) could also be the basis for a claim of comparative negligence where the forward driver is the plaintiff. Indeed, after this Court first adopted the presumption of negligence in rear-end collisions, the principle of comparative negligence replaced the all-or-nothing contributory negligence doctrine. *See* **Hoffman v. Jones, 280 So.2d 431, 438 (Fla.1973).**[7] Comparative negligence allows a jury to apportion liability between a negligent plaintiff and a negligent defendant. *See id.*

Although addressing a case where the rear driver was the plaintiff, Judge Griffin's explanation in **Jefferies v. Amery Leasing, Inc., 698 So.2d 368, 371 (Fla. 5th DCA 1997)**, is pertinent to the fact that the negligence of the forward driver is a question distinct from the negligence of the rear driver who fails to stop:

> At the time when this rear-end collision rule was developed, Florida was still a contributory negligence state. Thus, if the presumption were not overcome, the following driver's claim would be barred. Under contributory negligence, a negligent plaintiff could not recover against a negligent defendant.
>
> ... Today, when a rear driver sues a lead driver for damages from a rear-end collision, and the lead driver answers with an affirmative defense of comparative negligence, *the rule will, at most, establish as a matter of law that the driver of the rear car is liable for some portion of the overall damages. There is no logic in blindly applying the rear-end collision rule to determine the rear driver automatically to be the sole source of negligence in all rear-end collisions.* If it is sufficiently demonstrated that the lead driver was negligent as well, the jury should pass upon the question of shared liability and apportionment of damages.

Id. at 371 (emphasis supplied) (citations omitted); *see* **Johnson v. Deep S. Crane Rentals, Inc., 634 So.2d 1113, 1114 (Fla. 1st DCA 1994).** I agree. There is no reason that the rear driver should be barred from also establishing that the forward driver's own negligence was a legal cause of a portion of the damages suffered.

As to the defendant's negligence, "If the defendant had a *justifiable reason* for not observing traffic rules, then it was his duty to go forward with the evidence to show that he was not negligent...." McNulty v. Cusack, 104 So.2d 785, 788 (Fla. 2nd DCA 1958) (emphasis supplied). However, if evidence establishes a reasonable explanation for the rear driver's failure to stop in a timely manner, from which a jury could infer that the rear driver was exercising reasonable care under the circumstances, a motion for directed verdict on the rear driver's negligence should not be granted.

As the majority explains, the rebuttable presumption of negligence places the burden on the defendant to produce evidence that "fairly and reasonably tends to show" that the defendant was not negligent. Gulle v. Boggs, 174 So.2d 26, 29 (Fla.1965). As explained in *Gulle,* "When the [rear driver] produces evidence which *fairly and reasonably* tends to show that the real fact [of the rear driver's negligence] is not as presumed, then the impact of 'the presumption is dissipated.' " 174 So.2d at 29. For example, in Yellow Cab Co. v. Betsey, 696 So.2d 769, 771 (Fla. 2d DCA 1996), evidence of the slow moving traffic on a heavily congested bridge, combined with the rear driver's explanation that the collision was caused by his avoidance of another emergency situation, was sufficient to rebut the presumption of negligence and defeat a directed verdict. In Sistrunk v. *599 Douglas,* 468 So.2d 1059, 1060 (Fla. 1st DCA 1985), testimony that the rear driver was avoiding another road emergency that prevented him from braking in time to avoid the collision when the forward driver unexpectedly decelerated was sufficient to create a jury question on whether the rear driver was acting reasonably. Likewise, in Holden v. Dye, 224 So.2d 350, 351 (Fla. 1st DCA 1969), the presumption of negligence was found to be rebutted when the defendant testified that the plaintiff pulled out sharply from a parking spot in front of the defendant, and that the defendant could not avoid hitting the plaintiff despite applying his brakes and skidding.

The issue of whether the defendant's explanation is sufficient to rebut the presumption of negligence should be evaluated under the standard governing directed verdicts. In other words, once the rear driver provides an explanation for the collision, a directed verdict should only be granted if the party opposing the directed verdict could not prevail under any reasonable view of the evidence. *See* **Bruce Constr. Corp. v. State Exch. Bank,** 102 So.2d 288, 291 (Fla.1958); Scott v. Otis Elevator Co., 680 So.2d 462, 462 (Fla. 1st DCA 1996). On a motion for directed verdict, the non-moving party is entitled to all reasonable inferences from the facts that would support his or her claim. *See* **Bruce Constr. Corp.,** 102 So.2d at 291; Stringer v. Katzell, 674 So.2d 193, 195 (Fla. 4th DCA 1996), *review denied,* 698 So.2d 1225 (Fla.1997).

This is particularly true in negligence actions. *See* **Conda v. Plain,** 222 So.2d 417, 418 (Fla.1969). Negligence is the failure to use reasonable care under the circumstances. *See* Fla. Std. Jury Instr. (Civ.) 4.1. Thus, to defeat a directed verdict on negligence,[8] the rear driver is "required only to produce evidence from which his exercise of reasonable care under the circumstances could properly be inferred by the jury." Sistrunk, 468 So.2d at 1060-61; *accord* § 90.302(1), Fla. Stat. (1999) (requiring only "credible evidence" to rebut an evidentiary presumption). Once the presumption of negligence is rebutted, the presumption vanishes and the case is sent "to the jury on the basis of all the evidence submitted, together with justifiable inferences-not presumptions-to be drawn therefrom." Gulle, 174 So.2d at 29.[9]

The undisputed circumstances of this case show that when the light turned green, the plaintiff was in the proper lane of traffic stopped at a traffic light behind three other vehicles. The plaintiff testified that she was stopped at the traffic light when she was rear-ended by the defendant's truck. The defendant driver, however, stated that the plaintiff had started moving forward after the light turned green, and then suddenly "slam[med] on the brakes," just like the forward driver in *Tacher.* Taking the testimony and the reasonable inferences in the light most favorable to the defendant, we must assume that the plaintiff had started moving forward and then stopped before the collision.

*600 The sole evidence that the plaintiff's vehicle started and then stopped after a traffic light turned from red to green at a busy intersection does not provide a basis to infer that the driver of the Tarmac vehicle should not have been able to anticipate the stop and avoid the rear-end collision. As Judge Green noted, "It is not at all unusual for vehicles [proceeding] through busy intersections ... to have to suddenly brake...." Tacher, 743 So.2d at 158.

While the Tarmac driver's testimony may establish that the plaintiff stopped suddenly, there is no evidence from which a jury could properly conclude that his vehicle was being operated with the degree of care required by the traffic regulations[10] to control the vehicle so as to avoid colliding with the forward vehicle. Thus, in *Eppler,* as in *Tacher, Kao,* and *Pierce,* the forward driver's stop, even if abrupt, should have been reasonably anticipated as a matter of law.

If testimony that the rear driver did not know why the forward driver had abruptly or suddenly stopped at an intersection were sufficient to rebut the presumption of negligence, then the rear driver's failure to observe the cause of the stop would always be sufficient to dissipate the presumption. This would inappropriately shift the focus to the forward driver's conduct and away from the conduct of the rear driver for failing to stop under circumstances.

I would point out, however, one other wrinkle in the facts

in this case. In addition to the arguments it advances in support of the First District's decision, the defendant also asserts that even if its driver had been negligent, the trial court's failure to grant a directed verdict on *liability* was not erroneous.[11] Also, because there was still a factual dispute as to whether the defendant was a legal cause of the plaintiff's damages, this would have been a further reason for not granting a directed verdict on liability.[12] Indeed, although the defendant claims that the plaintiff's damages were either pre-existing or caused by a subsequent accident, when the trial court denied the plaintiff's motion for directed verdict on liability at the close of the case, it did so on the basis of the "conflicting evidence about the sudden stop." There was no discussion whatsoever about causation or about the plaintiff's comparative negligence. In affirming and certifying the question for review, the district court did not address these arguments raised by the defendant. *See* Eppler, 695 So.2d at 776 n. 1. Accordingly, while I disagree with the reasoning of the First District in *Eppler* as to the issue of the defendant's negligence, I would remand this case to the First District for consideration of the effect of the causation question on the propriety of a directed verdict as to liability in this case.

Footnotes

1   The jury responded "No" to the following question on the verdict form: "Was there negligence on the part of Defendant Tarmac America, Inc. which was a legal cause of damage to plaintiff Sybil Eppler?"

2   On direct examination of Morris, the following transpired:

Q. How far were you back from her....

A. Yes, at the light I was back approximately 10, 11 feet from her.

3

On cross-examination of Morris by Eppler's lawyer, the

following transpired:

Q. How many cars were in front of Mrs. Eppler's vehicle?

A. I would estimate three cars.

Q. You don't know for sure, though?

A. No, but I estimated it was four in front of me, so she was right in front of me.

Q. Okay. It was Mrs. Eppler's car, and then three more in front of her?

A. Yes, sir.

Q. Now, when the light turned green, do you recall what occurred with regard to the three vehicles in front of Mrs. Eppler's car?

A. Traffic started off, just the way they always do.

Q. Do you have a vivid recollection in your mind as to whether or not the vehicle in front of Mrs. Eppler started off?

A. Yes, as far as I'm concerned, it did.

Q. Okay.

A. All the traffic was moving.

Q. So it's your testimony that the vehicle immediately in front of Mrs. Eppler's vehicle started off?

A. Yes, sir.

4   On cross-examination of Morris, the following transpired:

Q. So it's your testimony that the vehicle immediately in front of Mrs. Eppler's vehicle started off?

A. Yes, sir.

Q. All right. And then Mrs. Eppler just slammed on brakes *without any reason;* is that right?

A. That's what I thought.

....

Q. Now, I got to make sure I understand you now. You took off in first gear, you shifted into second gear, and had you given it any gas in second gear?

A. Somewhat, yes.

Q. And then Mrs. Eppler slammed on brakes *for no apparent reason*, and then you hit the brake; is that right?

A. That's right.

(Emphasis added.)

5   *See, e.g.,* Pierce v. Progressive Am. Ins. Co., 582 So.2d 712, 714 (Fla. 5th DCA 1991) ("As a matter of law, it is not a substantial and reasonable explanation by Pierce to merely say that the vehicles ahead of him ... stopped abruptly."); *see also* Kao v. Lauredo, 617 So.2d 775, 777 (Fla. 3d DCA 1993) ("[T]he defendant testified that he was driving in a careful manner, but that plaintiff stopped in an abrupt manner.... The defendant's version of the collision is not sufficient to rebut or dissipate the presumption that his negligence was the sole proximate cause of the accident.").

The district court in *Tacher* certified conflict with *Eppler; Tacher* is not currently before this Court.

7   After the advent of comparative negligence, an unrebutted presumption of negligence no longer means that the negligence of the rear driver must be the "sole proximate cause" of a rear collision. Thus, I would disapprove of language in cases such as Kao v. Lauredo, 617 So.2d 775, 777 (Fla. 3rd DCA 1993), and Pierce v. Progressive American Insurance. Co., 582 So.2d 712, 714 (Fla. 5th DCA 1991), stating otherwise.

8   A directed verdict on liability includes both the issues of negligence and legal cause. *See, e.g.,* Fla. Std. Jury. Inst. (Civ.) 3.1(d). This instruction is titled, "Directed verdict on liability," and provides:

The court has determined and now instructs you, as a matter of law, that (defendant) was negligent and that such negligence was a legal cause of [loss] [injury] [or] [damage] to (claimant). (Claimant) is therefore entitled to recover from (defendant) for such [loss] [injury] [or] [damage] as is shown by the greater weight of the evidence to have thus been caused.

Id. (brackets and parentheses in original). When a trial court has directed a verdict on the defendant's negligence, the issues for the jury to resolve are causation and damages. *See* Fla. Std. Jury Instr. (Civ.) 3.1(c).

9   This is in contrast to other states that provide that the jury may be instructed on the rebuttable presumption of the rear driver's negligence. *See, e.g.,* **Bettner v. Boring,** 764 P.2d 829, 832 (Colo.1988); **Beausoleil v. Vollucci,** 711 A.2d 643, 644 (R.I.1998).

10   The traffic regulations require that the "driver of a motor vehicle shall not follow another vehicle more closely than is reasonable and prudent, having due regard for the speed of such vehicles and the traffic upon, and the condition of, the highway." § 316.0895(1), Fla. Stat. (1997).

11   Because there was a question of the plaintiff's comparative negligence, the directed verdict should only have been on negligence and not as to liability. *See* Note on use of Fla. Std. Jury Inst. (Civ.) 3.1(d) (instruction on directed verdict on liability "should be given only when the sole issue to be determined by the jury is the matter of damages").

12   *See supra* note 8.

SAMPLE CASE BRIEFS

MEMORANDUM

To: Senior Partner

From: Associate

Subject: _____

Date: _____ __, ____

As you requested, I am attaching briefs of the issue of whether the defendant in the following cases breached the duty of reasonable care by rear ending the plaintiff's vehicle: Clampitt v. Spencer Sales, 786 So.2d 570 (Fla. 2001) and Epler v. Tarmac, 752 So.2d 592 (Fla. 2000).

CLAMPITT V. SPENCER BRIEF

<u>Facts</u>

Three vehicles were traveling on a highway in Florida. The speed limit was fifty-five miles per hour; the weather was clear. The first vehicle was towing a trailer. That vehicle slowed and had turned almost completely off the highway when it was struck from behind by the second vehicle. The third vehicle was traveling at forty-five to fifty miles per hour and following the second vehicle by approximately one hundred and twenty feet. The driver of the third vehicle did not see the first vehicle turning until he saw the second vehicle strike the first vehicle. He then saw the second vehicle come to a "dead-stop" on the highway. He slammed on his brakes, left one hundred feet of skid marks, and struck the second vehicle.

<u>Issue</u>

Whether the defendant breached the duty of reasonable care

by rear ending the plaintiff's vehicle.

Rule

The law presumes that the driver of the rear vehicle in a rear end collision is negligent unless that driver provided a substantial and reasonable explanation as to why he was not negligent. A sudden stop by the driver of the leading vehicle at a "time and place where it could not reasonably be expected" by the driver of the following vehicle rebuts the presumption.

Holding

An accident in the roadway ahead is to be reasonably expected and, therefore, not a substantial and reasonable explanation as to why the driver of the rear vehicle was not negligent in causing a rear-end collision. Therefore, the law presumes that the defendant was negligent in rear-ending the plaintiff.

Rationale

Accidents on the road ahead are a "routine hazard faced by the driving public" and are to "be reasonably expected."

EPPLER V. TARMAC BRIEF

Facts

Three vehicles were stopped in a line of traffic at a stoplight. Once the light had turned green, all the vehicles in line began accelerating in a routine fashion. The third vehicle accelerated slowly with the other vehicles, shifted from first to second gear, and had been in second gear for three or four seconds when the second vehicle "suddenly-without warning and for no reason-slammed on her brakes." Then the third vehicle struck the second vehicle from behind.

Issue

Whether the defendant breached the duty of reasonable care by rear ending the plaintiff's vehicle.

Rule

The law presumes that the driver of the rear vehicle in a

rear end collision is negligent unless that driver provided a substantial and reasonable explanation as to why he was not negligent. A sudden stop by the driver of the leading vehicle at a "time and place where it could not reasonably be expected" by the driver of the following vehicle rebuts the presumption.

Holding

An abrupt and arbitrary stop after a traffic light turns green is not reasonably expected. In fact, it is a classic surprise. Therefore, the presumption of negligence does not apply.

Rationale

"Abrupt and arbitrary braking in bumper-to-bumper, accelerating traffic is an irresponsible and dangerous act that invites a collision." It is not something that should be reasonably expected.

CASE ANALOGY EXERCISE

MEMORANDUM

To: Associate

From: Senior Partner

Subject: _____

Date: _____ __, ____

_____

We represent UF undergraduate student Buford Rawlings in connection with sexual harassment and a criminal charges brought against him by fellow student Cam Lewis. I need your help with a legal memorandum I am working on for the criminal case only.

The criminal charge is based on an incident that occurred six months ago outside the Smathers Library around noon. Lewis is pledging at a fraternity on campus. Rawlings is a brother in the fraternity. Rawlings recently found out Lewis is a transgender student. Although the other brothers are open to Lewis becoming a member of the fraternity, Rawlings does not feel Lewis should be allowed to join.

As part of the hazing that goes along with pledging, Rawlings has been harassing Lewis whenever they meet on campus. On one occasion, Rawlings apparently "pantsed" Lewis in the middle of the courtyard in front of the library. Lewis was standing with a group of peers discussing a class they had just attended. Rawlings came up behind Lewis and pulled Lewis' shorts down below the knees. Lewis was shocked and humiliated. In fact, the emotional repercussions were so bad Lewis has since dropped out of school. Lewis just filed a claim against Rawlings for sexual harassment that another associate in the firm is working on. And Lewis also went to the police and filed a criminal complaint for battery.

Rawlings admits to pantsing Lewis but claims he intended no harm and the whole thing was just a "joke." As to the allegations of battery, Rawlings claims he never touched Lewis. The shorts Lewis was wearing were loose fitting work shorts; Rawlings pulled them down by pulling a tool loop that protruded on one side of the shorts.

My understanding of the law is that it doesn't matter

that Rawlings did not actually touch Lewis' body (he only touched the shorts Lewis was wearing). The case of Malczewski v. State of Florida, 444 So.2d 1096 (Fla. DCA 1984) (attached) appears to be on point. Please do an analogy of the case to this fact pattern. I want to use the analogy in the discussion of this issue in my legal memorandum.

MALCZEWSKI V. FLORIDA

444 So.2d 1096 (1984)

Albert MALCZEWSKI, Appellant,
v.
STATE of Florida, Appellee.

No. 83-1555.

District Court of Appeal of Florida, Second District.

January 25, 1984.

BOARDMAN, Acting Chief Judge.

Albert Malczewski appeals a conviction and sentence for aggravated battery imposed upon him after the denial of his motion to dismiss a count of an amended information which charged him with aggravated battery. We affirm.

The amended aggravated battery count which Malczewski sought to dismiss pursuant to Florida Rule of Criminal Procedure 3.190(c)(4) alleged that on March 16, 1983, Malczewski, "by use of a deadly weapon, to-wit [sic]: a knife, did knowingly and intentionally touch or strike Dwain Reeder against his will by stabbing the money bag Dwain Reeder was clutching to his chest, thereby placing Dwain Reeder in fear."

As grounds for dismissal of this amended count, which he labeled as "confusing and contradictory," Malczewski outlined the following material, undisputed facts:

  1. That on March 16, 1983, Dwain Reeder, an employee of

Publix Supermarkets was walking to a bank accompanied by one Tony Gregoris for the purpose of making a deposit at said bank.

2. Mr. Reeder was carrying a money bag which contained bundles of checks and currency in it.

3. While walking to the bank, Mr. Reeder was accosted by an armed individual who demanded Mr. Reeder relinquish possession of the money bag.

4. Mr. Reeder held said money bag next to his chest and at first did not drop it or relinquish possession of it.

5. The armed individual thereupon struck [sic] an object, believed by Mr. Reeder to be a knife, into said money bag, but not coming into contact with Mr. Reeder himself.

6. Mr. Reeder's body never came into direct contact with the object he believed to be a knife, nor did he suffer any physical injury from said object.

The state filed a traverse under Florida Rule of Criminal Procedure 3.190(d) which admitted the allegations contained in paragraphs 1 through 6 of Malczewski's motion to dismiss. However, the traverse added the following facts which the state believed necessary for a fair determination of the issue:

a. The victim was carrying the night money bag from the Publix Store to a nearby bank for deposit.

b. In the bag was $4,650.00 in cash and over $6,000.00 in checks.

c. The Defendant approached from the rear, pulled out a pistol and pointed it at both victim Reeder and victim's assistant... . The Defendant pointed the pistol at both of them and clicked it twice. Both victims believed the gun was real and deadly and were in great fear for their lives.

d. The Defendant ordered the victim to "drop the bag". Instead, the victim clutched the bag to his chest. The Defendant then pulled out a knife and lunged at the victim

Reeder. The Defendant stabbed the bag, which was held against Reeder's chest. The knife blade went through the bag, puncturing several of the checks and deposit slips which were inside. The victim used the bag for 1098*1098 protection and only the bag prevented the knife from entering victim's chest.

The applicable 1981 Florida Statutes provide in relevant part as follows: "784.03 Battery. — (1) A person commits battery if he: (a) Actually and intentionally touches or strikes another person against the will of the other; ... . 784.045 Aggravated battery. — (1) A person commits aggravated battery who, in committing battery: ... (b) Uses a deadly weapon."

The trial court entered an order denying Malczewski's motion to dismiss the amended aggravated battery count. Malczewski thereafter pled nolo contendere as to the amended count, expressly reserving his right to appeal the denial of his motion to dismiss. The court subsequently rendered an order adjudicating him guilty of aggravated battery and sentencing him thereon to a ten-year term of imprisonment.

Malczewski contends that the stabbing of the money bag carried by Dwain Reeder did not constitute an aggravated battery because there was never any actual contact between the knife which he wielded and Reeder. He contends further that in order for a battery to occur the victim or plaintiff must suffer an actual harmful or unconsented contact which is caused by the criminal defendant or tort-feasor. Goswick v. State, 143 So.2d 817 (Fla. 1962); Chorak v. Naughton, 409 So.2d 35 (Fla. 2d DCA 1981); Rodriguez v. State, 263 So.2d 267 (Fla. 3d DCA 1972). The state responds that the accusatory pleading establishes a harmful or offensive contact, stressing that it is a general proposition of criminal law that a battery may be against something carried by the victim. See 6A C.J.S. Assault & Battery § 70; Respublica v. DeLongchamps, 1 U.S. (Dall.) 111, 1 L.Ed. 59 (1784). The state contends and we agree that under the facts of this case the victim was subjected against his will to an intentional touching by Malczewski. See Grant v. State, 363 So.2d 1063 (Fla. 1978).

The issue before us is whether the language of Florida's battery statute, section 784.03(1)(a), particularly the words, "[a]ctually ... touches or strikes another person," encompasses the conduct engaged in by Malczewski. None of the Florida cases cited by either party is directly on point.

Turning to hornbook law, Dean William Prosser wrote:

> The protection [afforded a plaintiff by an action for the tort of battery] extends to any part of the body, or to anything which is attached to it and practically identified with it. Thus contact with the plaintiff's clothing, or with a cane, a paper, *or any other object held in his hand,* will be sufficient.... *His interest in the integrity of his person includes all those things which are in contact or connected with it.*

W. Prosser, *Law of Torts* § 9 at 34 (4th ed. 1971). (Emphasis added.)

Commentators have stated that the above common law rule with respect to the tort of battery applies as well to the crime of battery. In 6 Am.Jur.**2d** *Assault and Battery* § 37 at 38, it is stated:

> The rules that to be held liable for a battery the offender need not directly affect the unlawful contact with the person of the victim, and that a battery need not be committed directly against the person of the victim, but may be committed against anything **so** intimately connected with the person of the victim as in law to be regarded as a part of that person, *are applicable in criminal prosecutions for battery,* as are the principles that there may be a battery in the legal sense of the term even though no physical harm resulted therefrom... .

(Footnotes omitted and emphasis added.) Similarly, in 6A C.J.S. *Assault and Battery,* § 70 at 440-41, cited by the state, it is said: "It is essential to the [criminal] offense of battery ... that there be a touching of the person of the prosecutor, *or something* **so** *intimately associated with, or attached to, his person as to be regarded as a part thereof... . The contact may have been ... with something carried by him."* (Footnotes omitted and emphasis added.)

1099*1099 The eighteenth century criminal case cited by the state, *Respublica v. DeLongchamps,* lends support to the logical and reasonable proposition of criminal law that there need not be an actual touching of the victim's person in order for a battery to occur, but only a touching of something intimately connected with the victim's body. *See also* Stokes v. State, 233 Ind. 10, 115 N.E.**2d** 442 (1953).

In *Respublica v. DeLongchamps,* which is almost directly on point, the defendant struck the victim's cane. In affirming his conviction for assault and battery, the Supreme Court of Pennsylvania said that the assault and battery

> is, perhaps, one of that kind, in which the insult is more to be considered, than the actual damage; for, though no great bodily pain is suffered by a blow on the palm of the hand, or the skirt of the coat, yet these are clearly within the legal definition of assault and battery... . *[T]herefore, anything attached to the person, partakes of its inviolability... .*

1 U.S. (Dall.) at 114, 1 L.Ed. at 61. (Emphasis added.)

In *Stokes,* the defendant fired a gun at the victim. The bullet perforated the victim's necktie and creased his shirt. In upholding the battery conviction, the Indiana Supreme Court held, quoting from one of its earlier cases, Kirland v. State, 43 Ind. 146 (1873), that "`[o]ne's wearing apparel is **so** intimately connected with the person, as in law to be regarded, in case of a battery, as a part of the person.'" 115 N.E.**2d** at 443.

Several out-of-state cases have suggested the same result as *DeLongchamps* and *Stokes* by way of dicta. *See* Huffman v. State, 200 Tenn. 487, 292 S.W.**2d** 738 (1956); State v. Sudderth, 184 N.C. 753, 114 S.E. 828 (1922); Reese v. State, 3 Tenn. Cr.App. 97, 457 S.W.**2d** 877 (1970).

Considering the above-quoted authorities and case law on the subject of the crime of battery, we hold that the word "person" in our state's battery statute, section 784.03(1)(a), means person or anything intimately connected with the person. Applying this definition of "person" to the facts of this case, we submit that it would be an overly restrictive construction of section 784.03(1)(a) to decide that the money bag which Reeder clutched to his chest to protect himself from a serious injury or death, when Malczewski "actually" stabbed it with a knife during his attack, was not a part of Reeder's "person" as contemplated by the statute.

Accordingly, we affirm Malczewski's conviction and sentence for aggravated battery.

AFFIRMED.

GRIMES and LEHAN, JJ., concur.

SAMPLE CASE
ANALOGY

MEMORANDUM

To: Senior Partner

From: Associate

Subject: _____

Date: _____ __, ____

You asked me to write a case analogy for the Rawlings memorandum you are working on. Rawlings apparently "pantsed" fellow student Cam Lewis in the middle of the courtyard in front of the library. You indicated that Lewis was standing in a group of peers discussing a class they had just attended. Rawlings came up behind Lewis and pulled Lewis' shorts down below the knees. Lewis was shocked and humiliated, and actually dropped out of school because of

275

what happened. Lewis just filed a civil claim against Rawlings for sexual harassment and a criminal complaint for assault. Your memorandum is just for the criminal assault case.

The case you wanted me to analogize is <u>Malczewski v. State of Florida</u>, 444 So.2d 1096 (Fla. DCA 1984). Comparing that case to the fact pattern, I drafted the following case analogy:

In <u>Malczewski v. State of Florida</u>, 444 So.2d 1096 (Fla. DCA 1984), the victim "was carrying a money bag which contained bundles of checks and currency in it." <u>Id.</u> at 1096. On his way to deposit the money at the bank, he "was accosted by an armed individual who demanded [he] relinquish possession of the money bag." <u>Id.</u> The victim "held [the] money bag next to his chest' and the defendant stabbed him with a knife. <u>Id.</u> The knife penetrated the bag but did not "[come] into contact with [the victim] himself." <u>Id.</u> at 1096-1097. The defendant was charged with aggravated battery which involves "intentionally touch[ing] or strik[ing] another person against the will of the other" with a dangerous weapon. <u>Id.</u> at 1097. Based on these facts, the court held that the money bag the victim held to his chest was part of his "person" for the purposes of the law, so the defendant intentionally touched his "person" by touching the bag. <u>Id.</u> at 1099. As is the case with the tort of battery, a person's "interest in the integrity of his person includes all those things which are in contact or connected with it." <u>Id.</u>

    <u>Malczewski</u> is analogous to the case involving the Rawlings. In both cases, the defendant is charged with battery for intentionally touching something intimately connected with the victim. In Rawlings' case, Rawling camp up behind Lewis, and pulled on a tool loop protruding from Lewis' shorts. In <u>Malczewski</u>, the defendant stabbed a bag full of money the victim was clutching to his chest. In both cases it is irrelevant that the defendant did not actually touch the victim. The victim's interest in the integrity of his person includes all things in contact or connected with his person. Just like the money bag, the shorts Lewis was wearing were part of the victim's person for the purposes of the law. Like the defendant in <u>Malczewski,</u> Rawlings actually and intentionally touched Lewis' person by pulling on the tool loop attached to Lewis' shorts. Therefore, Rawlings likely committed the crime of battery by "pantsing" Lewis.

IRAC EXERCISE

MEMORANDUM

To: Associate

From: Senior Partner

Subject: _____

Date: _____ __, ____

Your assistance is requested in connection with a matter involving a senior partner at this firm. The partner, Frederick Washington, is a member of the litigation department. Because of extenuating circumstances, he failed to timely file an answer to a complaint on behalf of one of the firm's clients, and now a default judgment has entered.

As you may recall, Washington left the firm a short time ago for personal reasons, and he was away from the office for six months. He had been taking oxycontin for a recurring back problem he has, and he became addicted to the medication. He self-admitted at a local rehabilitation center and has resolved the issue. Since he has been back, he has been consistently performing at the high level that is expected of every lawyer at this firm.

As you know, the usual procedure is to arrange for coverage of pending cases prior to taking any extended leave. Unfortunately, Washington left under exigent circumstances because of his condition. He was in crisis and had to move quickly. And he was not of his right mind when he left. As a result certain matters Washington had responsibility for "fell through the cracks."

What we would like you to do is determine under what circumstances Washington could obtain a new trial for the case, and, specifically, whether this situation would qualify under the "conscious indifference" standard applicable here in Texas. We are not looking for you to do a full blown legal research memorandum. We only want your analysis of the issue in the usual IRAC format.

Please use the following cases to analyze this issue: Young v. Kirsch, 814 S.W.2d 77 (Tex. App. (Tex. App. 1991); State Farm Life Ins. Co. v. Mosharaf, 794 S.W.2d 578 (Tex. App. 1990); Southland Paint Co. v. Thousand Oaks Racket Club, 724

S.W.2d 809 (Tex. App. 1986). Copies of the cases are attached.

Your discretion is handling this matter is also appreciated.

YOUNG V. KIRSCH

814 S.W.2d 77 (1991)

James B. YOUNG, Appellant,

v.

Raymond R. KIRSCH, Appellee.

No. 04-90-00533-CV.

Court of Appeals of Texas, San Antonio.

June 12, 1991.

CHAPA, Justice.

This court, sitting en banc on its own motion, considers the appeal of appellant, James B. Young, from a default judgment rendered in favor of appellee, Raymond R. Kirsch, and the trial court's denial of a motion for new trial. TEX.R.APP.P. 79.

The issues before this court are whether the trial court erred:

1) in denying the motion for new trial;

2) in granting the default judgment when the evidence was legally and factually insufficient to support the default judgment;

3) in rendering the default judgment where the appellee's petition "did not support the judgment"; and,

4) in rendering the default judgment where appellee's petition "did not properly allege Defendant's residence."

On November 20, 1987, Young and Kirsch were involved in an auto accident in San Antonio, Texas. Plaintiff Kirsch's property damage claim was paid, and the claim file was eventually closed. On November 16, 1989, Kirsch filed a lawsuit against

Young for personal injury damages. Young was eventually served with suit papers in Boca Raton, Florida on January 24, 1990. Young forwarded these suit papers to his insurance carrier's office in Houston, Texas by regular mail upon his agent's instructions. No answer was filed prior to the default judgment being rendered. Default judgment was taken on May 23, 1990. Young filed a motion for new trial, along with affidavits which set forth facts allegedly entitling him to a new trial. *Craddock v. Sunshine Bus Lines,* 134 Tex. 388, 133 S.W.2d 124, 126 (1939). Although no controverting affidavits were filed by the appellee, depositions, as well as live testimony, were presented to the court at a hearing held on appellant's motion for new trial.[1] Appellant's motion was denied, and judgment was rendered for appellee Kirsch in the amount of $350,000.

Initially, appellant contends that the trial court erred in overruling Young's motion for new trial.

In *Craddock,* the Texas Supreme Court established the guiding rule to be applied in determining whether a new trial should be granted:

> A default judgment should be set aside and a new trial ordered in any case in which the failure of the defendant to answer before judgment was not intentional, or the result of conscious indifference on his part, but was due to a mistake or an accident; provided the motion for a new trial sets up a meritorious defense and is filed at a time when the granting thereof will occasion no delay or otherwise work an injury to the plaintiff.

Craddock, 133 S.W.2d at 126.

The appellant argues that the default judgment should have been set aside and a new trial granted because his failure to file an answer was due to accident or mistake and not conscious indifference; further, appellant contends that he demonstrated a meritorious defense and established that the granting of a new trial would occasion no delay and injury. Notwithstanding appellant's assertions, the question of whether the trial court erred in denying a motion for new trial is "directed to the sound discretion of the trial court." *Craddock,* 133 S.W.2d at 126. "[T]he court's ruling on such will not be disturbed on appeal in the absence of a showing of an abuse of *80 that discretion." *Cliff v. Huggins,* 724 S.W.2d 778, 778 (Tex.1987).

However, the trial court's discretion is more limited with regard to the meritorious defense prong of *Craddock. Craddock,* 133 S.W.2d at 126. When the movant "has thus set forth such meritorious defense, supported by such affidavits or other evidence as prima facie to entitle him to a new trial, such new trial should not be denied upon any consideration of counter affidavits or contradictory testimony offered in resistance to such motion." *Cragin v. Henderson County Oil Dev. Co.,* 280 S.W. 554, 555 (Tex.Com.App.1926, holding approved). Likewise, "[w]here factual allegations in a movant's affidavits are not controverted, a conscious indifference question must be determined in the same manner as a claim of meritorious defense" and "[i]t is sufficient that the movant's motion and affidavits set forth facts which, if true, would negate intentional or consciously indifferent conduct." *Strackbein v. Preuritt,* 671 S.W.2d 37, 38-39 (Tex.1984).[2]

Appellant misplaces his reliance on *Strackbein* for the proposition that appellee's failure to present controverting affidavits in response to appellant's motion for new trial and supporting affidavits requires the trial court to grant a new trial, regardless of any other evidence which may have been presented at the hearing. Although appellant concedes the Texas Supreme Court did not specifically state that *only affidavits* could be considered by the court, appellant, nevertheless, insists that this is the proper interpretation of *Strackbein.* We disagree.

In *Strackbein,* the *only* evidence before the trial court was the affidavits presented in support of the motion for new trial, which, if true, negated intentional or consciously indifferent conduct and set up a meritorious defense. *Strackbein*, 671 S.W.2d at 39. The supreme court expressly stated that "a conscious indifference question must be determined in the same manner as a claim of meritorious defense" "[w]here factual allegations in a movant's affidavits [as to conscious indifference] are not controverted"; "the trial judge, in considering the motion for new trial, [can] look only to the record before him at that time which include[s] [the movant's] motion for new trial and the affidavits submitted therewith." *Id.* at 38. As recognized by the appellant, the court did not *require* that the movant's affidavits be controverted *only* by counter affidavits, or that the trial court ignore any other evidence. Indeed, appellate courts have used the term "affidavits or *other evidence*" repeatedly when addressing the issue of setting aside a default judgment on the basis of conscious indifference, which must necessarily include documents, depositions, and testimony. *Ivy v. Carrell*, 407 S.W.2d 212, 214 (Tex.1966) (emphasis added); *Cragin*, 280 S.W. at 555; *Russell v. Northeast Bank*, 527 S.W.2d 783, 788 (Tex.Civ.App. — Houston [1st Dist.] 1975, writ ref'd n.r.e.). Accordingly, our decision must rest on whether the trial judge abused his discretion in denying appellant's motion for new trial in view of "the record before him at that time" which in this case not only included appellant's affidavits, but also depositions and testimony presented by the appellee controverting appellant's affidavits as to the issue of conscious indifference. *Strackbein*, 671 S.W.2d at 38.

In a supplemental brief, appellant cites this court's opinion in *Peoples Sav. & Loan Ass'n v. Barber*, 733 S.W.2d 679, 681 (Tex. App. — San Antonio 1987, writ dism'd by agr.), which appellant says supports his contention that this court should not consider any evidence adduced at the evidentiary hearing other than the affidavits or counter affidavits filed. However, the supreme court granted writ in *Peoples Sav. & Loan Ass'n* on the following point:

> The Court of Appeals erred in reversing the trial court's proper denial of Respondents' Motion for New Trial, because, evidence, which was properly considered, controverted Respondents' *81 allegation that their failure to answer was the result of accident or mistake, which evidence supports the trial court's finding of fact that Respondents' failure to answer was intentional or the result of conscious indifference.

31 Tex.Sup.Ct.J. 9 (October 10, 1987). But by agreement of the parties, the writ was dismissed.

We hereby disapprove of the language in *Peoples Sav. & Loan Ass'n*, or any other prior opinion by this court, which suggests that evidence adduced at a hearing to set aside a default judgment, other than affidavits or counter affidavits, may not be considered by the trial court, in determining whether the failure to answer was intentional or the result of conscious indifference, or by the appellate court, in determining whether the trial court abused its discretion.

As such, we find that the evidence properly before the trial court at the hearing on the motion for new trial reflects the following: suit was filed by Kirsch on November 16, 1989; Young was served with citation on or about January 24, 1990; although an answer was due on February 20, 1990, no answer was filed; Young failed to take any action at all until February 26, 1990, thirty three days after he was served, at which time Young contacted his insurance carrier in San Antonio and notified it of the lawsuit; Kirsch, through his counsel, phoned Young on at least four different occasions, notifying Young that no answer had been filed; between April 17, 1990, when Young phoned his insurance company for the second and last time, and the time the default judgment was entered, Young took no other action; and, on May 23, 1990, four months after Young was originally served, the default judgment was entered. Additionally, there was testimony that Young had previously been employed for twenty years as a stockbroker and manager, and that while so employed, he had been sued on several occasions.

Appellant contends that his actions do not amount to conscious indifference. Conscious indifference has been defined as "the failure to take some action which would seem indicated to a person of reasonable sensibilities under the same or similar circumstances". *Sunrizon Homes, Inc. v. Fuller,* 747 S.W.2d 530, 532 (Tex.App. — San Antonio 1988, writ denied); *Johnson v. Edmonds,* 712 S.W.2d 651, 652 (Tex.App. — Fort Worth 1986, no writ); *see also Liberty Mut. Fire Ins. Co. v. Ybarra,* 751 S.W.2d 615, 618 (Tex.App. — El Paso 1988, no writ); *Holberg v. Short,* 731 S.W.2d 584, 586 (Tex. App. — Houston [14th Dist.] 1987, no writ). Another court has defined conscious indifference to mean that the defendant "was clearly aware of the situation and acted contrary to what such awareness dictated." *Guardsman Life Ins. Co. v. Andrade,* 745 S.W.2d 404, 405 (Tex.App — Houston [1st Dist.] 1987, writ denied). In *Ivy v. Carrell,* 407 S.W.2d 212, 213 (Tex.1966), the Texas Supreme Court disapproved a finding of conscious indifference based on a new trial movant's failure to show that the movant's default was "not due to his fault or negligence". Instead, the supreme court reiterated the rule espoused by the court in *Craddock,* which requires the setting aside of a default judgment upon finding that "the failure of the defendant to answer before judgment was not intentional, or the result of conscious indifference on his part, but was due to a mistake or an accident...." *Craddock,* 133 S.W.2d at 126. Thus, conscious indifference must amount to more than mere negligence to satisfy the *Craddock* rule.

In the present case, we fail to see how the trial judge abused his discretion in denying the motion for new trial. This is especially true in view of the constant phone calls from the appellee reminding the appellant of his responsibility to take some action, the fact that the appellant testified he had some prior familiarity with the legal system, and the length of time which lapsed before the default judgment was finally entered. We hold the trial court's finding was based on more than mere negligence and amounted to conscious indifference.

Moreover, in the absence of findings of fact and conclusions of law, we must *82 affirm the judgment on any legal theory that finds support in the evidence. *Strackbein,* 671 S.W.2d at 38. Accordingly, we hold that the appellant has failed in his burden of showing that the trial court abused its discretion in denying the motion for new trial. The point is, therefore, rejected.

Appellant next argues that the evidence was legally and factually insufficient to support the default judgment.

In considering a "no evidence" or legal sufficiency point, we consider only the evidence favorable to the decision of the trier of fact and disregard all evidence and inferences to the contrary. *Davis v. City of San Antonio,* 752 S.W.2d 518, 522 (Tex.1988); *Garza v. Alviar,* 395 S.W.2d 821, 824 (Tex. 1965).

In considering a factual sufficiency point, we may not substitute our judgment for that of the jury, but must assess all the evidence and reverse for a new trial only if the challenged finding is so against the great weight and preponderance of the evidence as to be manifestly unjust, shocks the conscience, or clearly demonstrates bias. *Pool v. Ford Motor Co.,* 715 S.W.2d 629, 635 (Tex.1986); *Cain v. Bain,* 709 S.W.2d 175, 176 (Tex.1986) (great weight and preponderance); *In re King's Estate,* 150 Tex. 662, 244 S.W.2d 660, 661 (1951). "In considering an `insufficient evidence' point, we must remain cognizant of the fact that it is for the jury, as the trier of fact, to judge the credibility of the witnesses, to assign the weight to be given their testimony, and to resolve any conflicts or inconsistencies in the testimony." *Texas Employers' Ins. Ass'n v.*

Jackson, 719 S.W.2d 245, 249-50 (Tex.App. — El Paso 1986, writ ref'd n.r.e.), citing *Commonwealth Lloyd's Ins. Co. v. Thomas*, 678 S.W.2d 278, 289 (Tex.App. — Fort Worth 1984, writ ref'd n.r.e.).

The record further reflects that Dr. Kirsch, a 54 year old dentist, was sitting stationary in his vehicle at the corner of Broadway and Loop 410 when he was struck from the rear by a vehicle driven by Mr. Young. At the time of obtaining the judgment in May of 1990, Dr. Kirsch testified that he had not had a full night of sleep in the two and a half years since the accident, that he had given up all of his previously extensive athletic endeavors, that the pain relievers given to him by his physician created side effects which were equal to or worse than his neck and back problems, that his physician had told him that the only possible alternative would be steroid injections for temporary relief and that the only potential permanent resolution would be a laminectomy and a discectomy. Other evidence before the trial court was that these surgical procedures could cost as much as $25,000 and that Dr. Kirsch would be off work from his private dental practice for approximately three months at a loss of gross income of approximately $15,000 per month, as well as a significant loss of patients who would choose to go to other dentists. Dr. Kirsch also testified that he had been in constant pain for the two and a half years since the accident. Accordingly, the evidence is amply sufficient to support the default judgment that the rear end collision was caused by the negligence of Mr. Young and that Dr. Kirsch suffered significant damages to his professional practice, his enjoyment of life, and the physical structure of his body. Although a different factfinder might have arrived at a higher or lower figure, the $350,000 does not appear excessive in light of the evidence presented. The point is rejected.

Appellant also contends that the appellee's original petition does not support the default judgment. Specifically, appellant contends that the petition is fatally defective because it "failed to specify the amount of damages [appellee] was claiming" and "merely pleaded for damages in excess of the minimum jurisdiction of the court."

Appellant relies primarily on *White Motor Co. v. Loden,* 373 S.W.2d 863 (Tex.Civ. App. — Dallas 1963, no writ). However, *White Motor Co.* was decided prior to the 1978 amendment to TEX.R.CIV.P. 47, and held that the plaintiff's petition was fatally defective because not only did it fail to *83 specify the amount of damages claimed, but it was "apparently [an] undertaking to plead a products liability tort action in abbreviated form" which did not, in the court's opinion, "give fair notice to the opponent of their claim against it." *Id.* at 866. The holding can be distinguished easily from the case before this court.

First, in 1978, and subsequent to the *White Motor Co.* decision, TEX.R.CIV.P. 47 was amended to read:

> An original pleading which sets forth a claim for relief, whether an original petition, counterclaim, cross-claim, or third party claim, shall contain ...
>
> (b) in all claims for unliquidated damages only the statement that the damages sought are within the jurisdictional limits of the court....

Second, appellant does not contend that appellee's petition is defective in any other manner, or that he had not otherwise received fair notice of the claim; further, the record clearly reflects that the petition gave sufficient notice to the appellant of the claim, and that it supports the default judgment. The point is, therefore, rejected.

Finally, appellant asserts that appellee's petition "did not properly allege Defendant's residence."

It has been held that "[s]ince enactment of Rule 101, T.R.C.P., citation is directed to the individual rather than to a particular county, so the failure to allege residency in a particular county is not a fatal defect." *Stark v. Nationwide Financial Corp.*, 610 S.W.2d 193, 194 (Tex.Civ.App. — Houston [1st Dist] 1980, no writ).[3] Moreover, since the accident was alleged to have occurred in Bexar County, the defendant's residence is irrelevant. The point is rejected.

The judgment is affirmed.

NOTES

[1] While the record contains a statement of facts of the hearing on the motion to set aside the judgment, there are no findings of fact or conclusions of law.

[2] Moreover, the court in *Strackbein* emphasized that "[i]n reviewing the judgment of the trial court where there are no findings of fact and conclusions of law requested or filed, the judgment must be upheld on any legal theory that finds support in the evidence." *Id.* at 38.

[3] TEX.R.CIV.P. 101 was repealed by order of July 15, 1987; however, the substance of this rule, now found in TEX.R.CIV.P. 99, merely requires that the citation "be directed to the defendant."

STATE FARM V. MOSHARAF

794 S.W.2d 578 (1990)

STATE FARM LIFE INSURANCE COMPANY, Appellant,

v.

Ferial MOSHARAF and Narjes Vahdati, Appellees.

No. 01-89-00344-CV.

Court of Appeals of Texas, Houston (1st Dist.).

August 2, 1990.

Rehearing Denied August 30, 1990.

Before MIRABAL, WARREN and DUGGAN, JJ.

DUGGAN, Justice.

This is an appeal from a default judgment rendered against appellant, State Farm Life Insurance Company. Appellant's first point of error complains that the trial court's refusal to grant a new trial was an abuse of discretion. Because we sustain the first point of error, we do not reach the remaining points, but reverse and remand.

Appellees, Ferial Mosharaf and Narjes Vahdati, filed suit on July 27, 1988, against Sykes Roofing & Contracting Company ("Sykes Roofing") and appellant, alleging property damage, emotional distress, and medical expenses incurred as a result of a fire at their Houston apartment unit in the Northwood Apartment complex, owned by appellant. Appellees alleged that appellant hired Sykes Roofing to repair their apartment building's roof, and that a roofer's torch ignited roofing materials on the building and "burned it completely."

On September 28, 1988, appellant's registered agent for service, Bruce Romig, was served in Austin, Texas, by certified mail, return receipt requested, with citation and a copy of appellees' original petition. No answer was filed. On November 1, 1988, the trial court entered an interlocutory default judgment in favor of appellees, with a hearing on damages to be held at a later date. On December 12, 1988, the trial court granted appellees' motion to dismiss Sykes Roofing without prejudice, and entered a final judgment in favor of appellees. The judgment awarded: (1) $298,159 in actual damages and $1,192,636 in exemplary damages to appellee Mosharaf; (2) $804,700 in actual damages and $3,218,800 in exemplary damages to appellee Vahdati; and (3) pre-and post-judgment interest.

On January 13, 1989, appellant filed a motion for new trial and to set aside default judgment. Appellant's motion, accompanied by affidavits from employees of appellant and its affiliated companies, set *581 out facts relied upon to prove that appellant's failure to answer was the result of an accident and mistake, and not conscious indifference.

Appellant's motion and affidavits asserted the following: Bruce Romig was a State Farm Mutual Automobile Insurance Company ("State Farm Auto") regional vice-president for the Texas region, was appellant's registered agent for service of process, and was served on September 28, 1988. That same day, Romig forwarded the citation and petition to Tommy Stinson, a State Farm Auto divisional claims superintendent, also in Austin. Under Stinson's supervision, the lawsuit was entered that day on State Farm Auto's "lawsuit log" used to keep track of incoming lawsuits; the next day, September 29, 1988, the petition was sent by interoffice mail to Charles Owens, State Farm Fire and Casualty Insurance Company's divisional claims superintendent, in Houston.

Owens received the petition in Houston on September 29, 1988, as evidenced by the acknowledgment receipt he signed and returned, which Stinson received on October 5, 1988. On October 6, 1988, Owen telecopied the petition to William J. Hess, State Farm Auto's senior assistant investment counsel, at State Farm's corporate office in Bloomington, Illinois; Hess received it that day.

By an interoffice routing slip, Hess directed the petition to Cynthia Weaver, a real estate administrator employed by State Farm Auto in its investment real estate department. Weaver is responsible for the operations of appellant's Northwood apartment complex. A copy of Hess's routing slip was attached as an exhibit to appellant's motion, and showed Weaver's name and Hess's notation, "Please make sure or [sic] liability carrier is aware of this. B.H."

Somewhere in the routing process between Hess and Weaver, the routing slip and petition were inadvertently filed before Weaver received them. Weaver never saw Hess' instruction or received a copy of the citation and petition, and did not learn of the lawsuit until she received the notice of the final default judgment on December 28, 1988, 12 days after the judgment was signed.

Appellant's motion also set forth the defense that Sykes Roofing's negligence was the sole cause of appellees' losses, and asserted that a new trial in the cause would neither occasion delay nor cause prejudice to appellees.

Appellees filed a controverting plea, but presented no evidence that directly controverted the facts alleged and shown by appellant; the trial court overruled appellant's motion. Appellant filed a motion to reconsider and a motion to supplement the record on motion for new trial, accompanied by affidavits which further detailed the activities of various State Farm entities and appellant's reasons for not answering the original petition. Appellees objected that appellant's motions were untimely under Tex.R.Civ.P. 329b(b), citing *L.B. Foster Co. v. Glacier Energy, Inc.,* 714 S.W.2d 48, 49 (Tex.App.-San Antonio 1986, writ ref'd n.r.e.). The trial court declined to consider these filings and overruled the motion to reconsider; this appeal followed. We likewise decline to consider appellant's motions and affidavits that were not before the trial court at the time of the hearing on appellant's motion for new trial. *L.B. Foster,* 714 S.W.2d at 49.

The *Craddock* Test

Appellant's first point of error alleges that the trial court abused its discretion in overruling appellant's motion for new trial and to set aside the default judgment. The standard for granting a motion for new trial and setting aside a default judgment was established in *Craddock v. Sunshine Bus Lines, Inc.:*

> A default judgment should be set aside and a new trial ordered in any case in which the failure of the defendant to answer before judgment was not intentional, or the result of conscious indifference on his part, but was due to mistake or accident; provided the motion sets up a meritorious defense and is filed at a time when the granting thereof will occasion *582 no delay or otherwise work an injury to the plaintiff.

134 Tex. 388, 393, 133 S.W.2d 124, 126 (Tex.Comm'n App.1939, opinion adopted).

A motion for new trial is addressed to the trial court's discretion, which will not be disturbed on appeal absent a showing of abuse of discretion. *Strackbein v. Prewitt,* 671 S.W.2d 37, 38 (Tex.1984). However, the trial court's discretion is not unbridled. *Craddock,* 134 Tex. at 388, 133 S.W.2d at 126. Because appellant's evidence at the motion for new trial hearing was undisputed, the issue on appeal is whether the trial court's exercise of discretion was erroneous as a matter of law. *Strackbein,* 671 S.W.2d at 39.

The trial court must test the motion for new trial and accompanying affidavits against the *Craddock* requirements, and grant a new trial if those requirements are met. *Strackbein,* 671 S.W.2d at 39.

Conscious Indifference

The first prong of the *Craddock* test requires the determination of whether appellant's failure to answer was due to mistake or accident, or was the result of conscious indifference. *Craddock* and its progeny establish no criteria for applying this test, but "it is clear that courts have applied this prong liberally, and that each case depends on its own facts." *Gotcher v. Barnett,* 757 S.W.2d 398, 401 (Tex.App.- Houston [14th Dist.] 1988, no writ).

Mistakes virtually identical to those of appellant in the present case, all resulting in a failure to answer, have repeatedly been excused under *Craddock* as not being the result of conscious indifference or of bad faith. *See Craddock,* 134 Tex. at 393, 133 S.W.2d at 126 (insurance company, faced with numerous claims because of a flood, inadvertently placed defendant's citation with mail not requiring immediate attention); *Southland Paint Co. v. Thousand Oaks Racket Club,* 724 S.W.2d 809, 811 (Tex.App.-San Antonio 1986, writ ref'd n.r.e.) (late answer filed due to staff shortage at defendant's insurance broker's office); *Evans v. Woodward,* 669 S.W.2d 154, 155 (Tex.App.-Dallas 1984, no writ) (answer not filed due to confusion in attorney's office); *Drake v. McGalin,* 626 S.W.2d 786, 788 (Tex.Civ.App.-Beaumont 1981, no writ) (answer prepared by secretary presumably lost by volunteer exchange student who was assisting defendant's attorney as an "office boy"); *Dallas Heating Co. v. Pardee,* 561 S.W.2d 16, 19 (Tex.Civ.App.-Dallas 1977, writ ref'd n.r.e.) (suit papers inadvertently misplaced in defendant's office); *Leonard v. Leonard,* 512 S.W.2d 771, 773 (Tex.Civ.App.- Corpus Christi 1974, writ dism'd) (attorney misplaced file); *Continental Airlines, Inc. v. Carter,* 499 S.W.2d 673, 674 (Tex.Civ. App.-El

Paso 1973, no writ) (secretary misplaced file); *Republic Bankers Life Ins. Co. v. Dixon,* 469 S.W.2d 646, 647 (Tex.Civ.App.-Tyler 1971, no writ) (attorney forgot to prepare answer when his secretary placed the file with his general files, rather than returning it to his desk for immediate action); *Reynolds v. Looney,* 389 S.W.2d 100, 101 (Tex.Civ.App.- Eastland 1965, writ ref'd n.r.e.) (citation mislaid in insurance company's office).

Appellees contend that appellant nevertheless failed to meet its burden of proof to establish that it did not act with conscious indifference, citing *Grissom v. Watson,* 704 S.W.2d 325, 327 (Tex.1986). There, quoting from *Harris v. LeBow,* 363 S.W.2d 184, 186 (Tex.Civ.App.-Dallas 1962, writ ref'd n.r. e.), the supreme court stated: "A party who has been duly served with citation to appear and defend a cause asserted against him may not relieve himself of the burden of the judgment rendered unless he thoroughly demonstrates that he and his agent were free of negligence or conscious indifference." Appellees urge that Cynthia Weaver and appellant's affiants were not employees of appellant, but of affiliated State Farm companies; that appellant could not explain *how* the filing mistake occurred; and that appellant thereby failed to disprove its own negligence and that of its various agents.

We adopt the reasoning and conclusion of *Ferguson & Co. v. Roll,* where Justice Stewart carefully analyzed *Grissom v. Watson* and the court of civil appeals opinion *583 it relies on, *Harris v. LeBow* (as well as that opinion's cited authorities), and concluded:

> that this line of cases should properly be interpreted as holding that when a defendant's excuse is his reliance on a third party to file his answer ... he must prove that the third party's failure was due to accident or mistake and not intentional or the result of conscious indifference. We do not read these cases as establishing a rule that a defendant must show he and/or his agent were free from negligence.

Roll, 776 S.W.2d 692, 696-97 (Tex.App.- Dallas 1989, no writ). The court in *Roll* cited two sources as support: (1) the supreme court decision in *Cliff v. Huggins,* 724 S.W.2d 778, 779 (Tex.1987), that "makes no mention of a free of negligence standard with regard to the three-prong *Craddock* test;" and (2) "the in-depth analysis given this topic in the law review article of Pohl and Hittner, *Judgment by Default in Texas,* 37 SW.L.J. 421, 443, in which the authors unequivocally state that, under the *Craddock* test, ` The defendant's negligence will not preclude the setting aside of a judgment by default. In fact, the defendant's burden of demonstrating the accidental or mistaken nature of his failure to answer *may often result in an admission of negligence.'" Id.* at 697 (emphasis added).

The applicable test is not whether appellant was negligent in failing to answer. *Ivy v. Carrell,* 407 S.W.2d 212, 213 (Tex.1966); *Gotcher,* 757 S.W.2d at 402. Rather, the controlling factor is the "absence of a purposeful or bad faith failure to answer ... [and] even a slight excuse will suffice...." *Gotcher,* 757 S.W.2d at 401.

Appellees argue that appellant failed to "take some action which would seem indicated to a person of reasonable sensibilities under the same circumstances," citing *Johnson v. Edmonds,* 712 S.W.2d 651, 652-53 (Tex.App.-Fort Worth 1986, no writ). In *Johnson,* the defendant failed to answer because he allegedly did not understand the nature of the citation served upon him; he simply read the "papers" and filed them. The *Johnson* court held that inaction resulting from alleged ignorance amounted to evidence of conscious indifference. The equating of conscious indifference with non-action because of ignorance in *Johnson* is distinguishable from the facts before us. Here, no evidence suggests that the failure to answer resulted from a lack of understanding of the citation and petition.

Appellees further rely on *First Nat'l Bank v. Peterson,* 709 S.W.2d 276 (Tex. App.-Houston [14th Dist.] 1986, writ ref'd n.r.e.), which is likewise distinguishable. In *Peterson,* as in *Johnson,* the defendant took no action after receiving a writ of garnishment. *Id.* at 278-79. Both cases, *Johnson* and *Peterson,* involved inaction by the defendant after service, and are distinguishable from cases where a defendant took actions that resulted in accidental loss or misplacement of suit papers after service. *Roll,* 776 S.W.2d at 697-98.

To determine if appellant acted with intentional disregard or conscious indifference in not answering the suit, we must look to the knowledge and acts of appellant's employees and agents. *Strackbein,* 671 S.W.2d at 39; *Roll,* 776 S.W.2d at 697. Appellant's motion for new trial is supported by the affidavits of Romig, Stinson, Owens, and Hess, and establishes that nine days passed from the service of the citation and petition on Romig, on September 28, 1988, until Hess received and routed them on October 6, 1988, to Cynthia Weaver, whose duty it was to forward them to appellant's insurance carrier. Eighteen days remained within which appellant's answer could have been timely filed, had the petition not been misfiled.

At the motion for new trial hearing, Cynthia Weaver testified that she is a real estate administrator in State Farm Auto's investment department; that the department "handles property owned by any of the State Farm Insurance companies for investment purposes;" that she is responsible for asset management on the Northwood Apartments in Houston; that she "knew we had had a fire at Northwood and that [she] had a loss report in the file;" that appellant maintains a separate insurance *584 file for each property, and "any claim that we would have would go into that file." She testified that Craig Watson of the Risk Management Department called her on December 28, 1988, when a default notice was received, and asked if she had ever seen a petition concerning the Northwood fire; that she replied in the negative and said she would go look in the file and see if she could find anything. She went to the Northwood file and found appellees' petition and Hess' routing slip there, where "normal pieces of correspondence" would be, but not lawsuits, for which separate files would be set up. Weaver testified that in the normal course of business, her secretary would have picked up the routing slip and petition from a central location, date-stamped it, and put it in her basket where she would have seen it. She testified that she does not know how the petition got into the file or who put it there, that no one ever called her on the phone or talked to her about it before Watson's call, and that she first saw it on December 29, 1988. She testified that if she had received the routing slip and petition, she "would have done exactly what Bill [Hess] told me [on the routing slip] to do. I would have made sure our liability carrier received it, which I would have done through our Risk Management Department...."

Appellees did not offer testimony to controvert appellant's above testimony or affidavits at the motion for new trial hearing, but instead relied on their motion in opposition and affidavits, and argued that the facts appellant showed were insufficient to prove a lack of conscious indifference.

Where factual allegations in a movant's motion and affidavits are not controverted, the movant is entitled to have the default judgment set aside if the facts set forth negate intentional or consciously indifferent conduct. *Strackbein*, 671 S.W.2d at 38-39; *Dallas Heating Co.*, 561 S.W.2d at 19-20; *see also Ivy*, 407 S.W.2d at 214. In *Strackbein*, a fact situation similar to ours, the uncontroverted affidavits showed that suit papers were inadvertently misplaced in the defendant's office, rather than mailed to his attorney. The supreme court held that this explanation constituted evidence that the defendant's failure to answer the citation was not the result of an intentional act or conscious indifference. *Strackbein*, 671 S.W.2d at 39.

We hold that while appellant's proof may indeed have shown negligence on the part of its agents, and did fail to explain *how* the filing mistake occurred, appellant nonetheless met its burden to prove that it did not timely answer the suit due to accident or mistake, and proved that its failure to answer was unintentional and not the result of conscious indifference.

Meritorious Defense

Appellant urges that it established a meritorious defense, in accordance with the second requirement of the *Craddock* test,[1] which requires that a defendant set up a meritorious defense, not that it prove one. "The motion must *allege* facts which in law would constitute a defense to the cause of action asserted by the plaintiff, and must be supported by affidavits or other evidence proving prima facie that the defendant has such meritorious defense." *Ivy*, 407 S.W.2d at 214 (emphasis added). When a defendant meets this burden, a trial court cannot deny a motion for new trial based solely on consideration of counteraffidavits or contradictory testimony. *Guaranty Bank v. Thompson*, 632 S.W.2d 338, 340 (Tex.1982); *Harlen v. Pfeffer*, 693 S.W.2d 543, 546 (Tex.App.-San Antonio 1985, no writ); *Farley v. Clark Equip. Co.*, 484 S.W.2d 142, 147 (Tex.Civ.App.-Amarillo 1972, writ ref'd n.r.e.). However, the sufficiency of the facts may be challenged. *See Dallas Heating Co.*, 561 S.W.2d at 20.

A meritorious defense is one that, if ultimately proved, will cause a different result when the case is tried again. *The Moving Co. v. Whitten*, 717 S.W.2d *585 117, 120 (Tex.App.-Houston [14th Dist.] 1986, writ ref'd n.r.e.); *Harlen*, 693 S.W.2d at 546. However, a meritorious defense is not limited to one that, if proved, would lead to an entirely opposite result. It is sufficient if at least a portion of the judgment would not be sustained on retrial. *See, e.g., HST Gathering Co. v. Motor Serv., Inc.*, 683 S.W.2d 743, 745 (Tex. App. —Corpus Christi 1984, no writ) (defendant set up a prima facie defense as "to some, if not all, of the monies" awarded in the judgment); *Folsom Investments, Inc. v. Troutz*, 632 S.W.2d 872, 875 (Tex. App.- Fort Worth 1982, writ ref'd n.r.e.) (defendant set up a meritorious defense as to a lesser amount of damages; opposite result of total nonliability need not be proved).

Appellees claim that appellant's affidavit which asserted that a meritorious defense existed was merely conclusory and does not set forth specific facts to establish a prima facie defense of "sole cause." However, appellees' own live pleading alleged that Sykes Roofing negligently started the fire by leaving its roofing torch on the roof. In its motion for new trial, appellant alleged that the dismissed co-defendant, Sykes Roofing, was negligent in starting the fire, and that such negligence was the "sole cause" of the fire at the Northwood complex. Sole cause and a co-defendant's negligence are valid defenses in Texas. *See generally Ahlschlager v. Remington Arms Co.,* 750 S.W.2d 832, 833-36 (Tex. App.-Houston [14th Dist.] 1988, writ denied) (discussing the current state of Texas law on "sole cause").

To support its defense of sole cause, appellant presented the affidavit of Jan Taylor, a claims adjuster for The Travelers Insurance Company, the liability carrier of Sykes Roofing. Taylor investigated the fire at the Northwood complex, and concluded that it was started by Sykes Roofing. When Taylor demanded reimbursement from Sykes Roofing for damages, Sykes Roofing's liability carrier paid State Farm approximately $31,000.[2] Appellant alleged and presented a prima facie defense that the conduct of a third party was the sole cause of the accident. *See Ahlschlager,* 750 S.W.2d at 835. Appellants successfully raised a meritorious defense so as to satisfy *Craddock.*

No Delay or Injury

The third prong of *Craddock* requires the appellant to demonstrate that at the time of the filing of the motion for new trial, its granting would not occasion a delay or otherwise work an injury to the appellees. *Craddock,* 134 Tex. at 393, 133 S.W.2d at 126. The two key questions in determining whether delay or injury will occur to the plaintiffs are: (1) whether the defendant offers to reimburse the plaintiffs for the costs in obtaining their default judgment; and (2) whether the defendant is ready, willing, and able to go to trial. *Angelo v. Champion Restaurant Equip. Co.,* 713 S.W.2d 96, 98 (Tex.1986). In its motion for new trial, and at the evidentiary hearing on the motion, appellant agreed to reimburse appellees for reasonable costs, attorneys' fees, and any other reasonable expenses incurred in obtaining the default judgment and in responding to the motion for new trial. Additionally, appellant agreed to proceed to trial immediately. In making these offers, appellant satisfied *Craddock's* "no delay or injury" prong for a case where nothing in the record showed that a new trial would work an injury to the plaintiffs. *Cliff v. Huggins,* 724 S.W.2d 778, 779 (Tex.1987).

Once appellant tendered prima facie evidence that the granting of a new trial would not delay or otherwise injure appellees, the burden of going forward with proof of injury then shifted to appellees. *Cliff,* 724 S.W.2d at 779; *Burns v.* *586 *Burns,* 568 S.W.2d 669, 672 (Tex.Civ.App. —Fort Worth 1978, writ ref'd n.r.e.). Appellees were required to come forward with evidence to show that they would be in a "worse condition in the event of a new trial than that in which [they] would have been had answer to [their] suit been timely filed." *Burns,* 568 S.W.2d at 672.

By three affidavits attached to their opposition to appellant's motion for new trial, appellees sought to prove that the granting of appellant's motion would "work an injury" to them. The three affidavits, from one of appellees' attorneys, from appellee Mosharaf, and from Dr. Sajadi, appellee Vahdati's psychiatrist, asserted: (1) appellee Vahdati could suffer severe emotional damage if she was required to testify in another proceeding; and (2) appellee Mosharaf would be delayed in fulfilling her desire to relocate to California, where she wants to go and take her mother, appellee Vahdati, "to get our lives back together."

Only Dr. Sajadi's affidavit presented competent medical

evidence that Vahdati would be harmed by testifying at a retrial. However, appellees did not show that appellee Vahdati would have to testify in a retrial. The bulk of appellees' proof at the damages hearing consisted either of documentary evidence or the testimony of persons other than Vahdati, including appellee Mosharaf, Masoud Mosharaf, the brother and son of the two appellees, and Dr. Sajadi. Vahdati's limited testimony was cumulative to that of other witnesses. In short, Vahdati's testimony would be unnecessary to prove either a cause of action or damages as to either plaintiff at a retrial.

Accordingly, appellees' affidavits were insufficient to controvert appellant's prima facie showing that the granting of the motion for new trial would not "otherwise work an injury" upon appellees.

The amount of reasonable expenses that appellant must pay as a condition of new trial will be determined at an appropriate hearing for that purpose by the trial court, "which should consider not only travel expenses ... but also attorney's fees, and loss of earnings caused by trial attendance, expenses of witnesses, and any other expenses of plaintiff[s] arising from defendant's default." *United Beef Producers, Inc. v. Lookingbill,* 532 S.W.2d 958, 959 (Tex.1976) (footnote omitted).

We hold that appellant has successfully met all three of the *Craddock* criteria for setting aside a default judgment, and that the trial court abused its discretion in overruling appellant's motion for new trial.

Appellant's first point of error is sustained.

The judgment of the trial court is reversed, and the cause is remanded to the trial court.

NOTES

[1] Appellant contends that the recent cases of *Peralta v. Heights Medical Center, Inc.,* 485 U.S. 80, 108 S. Ct. 896, 99 L. Ed. 2d 75 (1988), and *Lopez v. Lopez,* 757 S.W.2d 721 (Tex.1988), establish that it is not required to establish a meritorious

defense. Nevertheless, appellant proceeds to argue that it has met *Craddock's* requirements.

[2] Plaintiffs attempted to controvert appellant's meritorious defense with the affidavit of Phillip Munsen, the Travelers' claims examiner in charge of the claim made against Sykes Roofing. Munsen's affidavit stated that Travelers settled appellant's claim with no knowledge of appellant's negligence, and that the settlement was not an admission of liability on the part of Sykes Roofing. The trial court cannot deny the motion upon consideration of counteraffidavits or contradictory testimony. *Guaranty Bank*, 632 S.W.2d at 340; *Harlen*, 693 S.W.2d at 546; *Farley*, 484 S.W.2d at 147.

SOUTHLAND V. THOUSAND OAKS

724 S.W.2d 809 (1986)

SOUTHLAND PAINT COMPANY, INC., Appellant,

v.

THOUSAND OAKS RACKET CLUB, A DIVISION OF
COUNTRY CLUB CONDOMINIUMS, LTD., et al., Appellees.

No. 04-84-00456-CV.

Court of Appeals of Texas, San Antonio.

January 31, 1986.
Rehearing Denied March 9, 1987.

Before CADENA, C.J., and REEVES and TIJERINA, JJ.

TIJERINA, Justice.

This is an appeal from a default judgment. Appellees brought suit against appellant and Handy Dan Hardware, Inc.; appellant failed to appear and file an answer. The trial court's interlocutory judgment recites that citation was served according to law, properly returned, and filed with the clerk where it remained for the required time. The default judgment entered on July 31, 1984, awarded a total of $5,174,960.74. The motion for a new trial was denied; however, on motion for rehearing a remittitur on the damages and attorney's fees was ordered reducing the default judgment to $3,849,278.50.

The essential facts established that appellees purchased a linseed oil product manufactured by appellant from a Handy

Dan Hardware Store. The product was used to clean floors; the linseed oil soaked rags were left on a table where they later ignited as a result of spontaneous combustion, causing the damages asserted. Appellees' suit alleged that appellant negligently failed to provide a label which warned of the spontaneous combustibility of the product and which gave instructions for the disposal of the rags used.

*810 Appellant initially complains that the trial court did not have jurisdiction to enter the default judgment because appellees failed to prove by affirmative evidence that C.T. Corporation System was the registered agent for service of process on appellant. Plaintiff's First Amended Original Petition alleged that defendant was a Delaware corporation duly licensed to do business under the law of the State of Texas and that its designated agent for service of process was C.T. Corporation System, 3200 Republic National Bank Building, Dallas, Texas, 75201. The constable's return certifies that service of process was executed by delivering the citation and a copy of Plaintiff's First Amended Original Petition to Southland Paint Company, Inc., through its registered agent for service, C.T. Corporation System, by delivery to its registered agent for service, Mary Lou Boring. Appellant argues that its status as a foreign corporation required a showing by affirmative evidence the agency of the person served, apart from the allegations in the pleadings and the statement contained in the constable's return, citing *Anglo Mexicana De Seguros, S.A. v. Elizondo,* 405 S.W.2d 722 (Tex.Civ.App.-Corpus Christi 1966, writ ref'd n.r.e.).

There is authority for the proposition that a citation return showing service on a defendant by serving his agent is sufficient, without proof of such agency, to warrant a default judgment. *Employer's Reinsurance Corp. v. Brock,* 74 S.W.2d 435, 438 (Tex.Civ.App.-Eastland 1934, writ dism'd). Moreover, the affidavit of Robert S. Kersch attached to appellant's motion for new trial acknowledged that C.T. Corporation System was appellant's agent for service of process and was instructed to send all legal notices addressed to Southland Paint Company to De Soto, Inc. in Des Plaines, Illinois. Kersch is corporate secretary for De Soto, Inc., the legal entity that acquired the liabilities of appellant. Similarly, the affidavits of Stephen J. Couto, the claims manager for Emmett and Chandler, the insurance broker for Southland Paint Company, Thomas Karol, President of H.M.K. Industries, and their attorney, Dale Akonou, did not dispute that C.T. Corporation System was their agent for service of process and acknowledged receipt of service of citation. The party seeking to have the default judgment set aside has the burden of proving that the person served was not its agent. *Employer's Reinsurance Corp. v. Brock, supra* at 438; *see also* TEX.REV.CIV.STAT.ANN. art. 2031b, § 3 (Vernon 1964). In this case, appellant had a designated agent in Texas and there is no dispute that the agent was the person actually served with the citation. Appellant's first point of error is overruled.

Secondly, appellant contends that the trial court erroneously denied the motion for a new trial. Specifically, they allege that the default judgment should be vacated under the rule of *Craddock v. Sunshine Bus Lines,* 134 Tex. 388, 133 S.W.2d 124, 126 (1939):

> A default judgment should be set aside and a new trial ordered in any case in which the failure of the defendant to answer before judgment was not intentional, or the result of conscious indifference on his part, but was due to a mistake or an accident; provided the motion for new trial sets up a meritorious defense; and is filed at a time when the granting thereof will occasion no delay or otherwise work an injury to the plaintiff. This is a just rule. It prevents an injustice to the defendant without working an injustice on the plaintiff. Such a rule has the sanction of equity.

The Supreme Court has reaffirmed the *Craddock* rule in

Strackbein v. Prewitt, 671 S.W.2d 37, 39 (Tex.1984) saying: "That law requires the trial court to test the motion for new trial and the accompanying affidavits against the requirements of *Craddock.* If the motion and affidavits meet those requirements, a new trial should be granted." In this case there is no dispute that the motion was timely filed and alleged the three requirements of *Craddock.* Moreover, the supporting affidavits contained statements that the failure to answer was not intentional or the result of conscious indifference.

*811 The record shows that the De Soto, Inc., purchased the name and assets of appellant. De Soto, Inc. received the citation from its agent, C.T. Corporation System, and immediately forwarded it to H.M.K., Inc. The citation was then mailed to De Soto's New York attorneys, who forwarded it to Emmett and Chandler, appellant's insurance broker. The offices of Emmett and Chandler did not mail the citation to Liberty Mutual Company until seven days after the answer was due. The affidavits indicate that the delay in mailing the citation to Liberty Mutual for answer was occasioned by shortness of staff in the word processing and claims departments, due to vacation schedules. In *National Rigging, Inc. v. City of San Antonio,* 657 S.W.2d 171, 173 (Tex.App.-San Antonio 1983, writ ref'd n.r.e.) this court stated:

> We recognize that the excuse for failure to file an answer for National Rigging given by the president of Mashburn and National Rigging, as well as insurance representatives and their attorney, is `certainly very slight' but does indicate no intention by him or the insurance carrier or their attorney to suffer judgment to go by default.

The affidavit of Stephen J. Couto, based on personal knowledge, recites that the failure to file an answer was not the result of conscious indifference. Appellant also established a meritorious defense. We conclude that the granting of a new trial would not cause a delay or injure appellees. Accordingly, we sustain point of error two. We further find it unnecessary to review the other assignment of error in view of our disposition of point of error two.

The judgment is reversed and the cause remanded.

CADENA, Chief Justice, dissenting.

The judgment should be affirmed because appellant failed to prove that the failure to answer was not the result of conscious indifference but was due to a mistake or accident.

The record reflects that the trial court held an evidentiary hearing on appellant's motion for new trial. Appellee had filed a response to the motion and had specifically denied appellant's allegations that the failure to answer was not the result of conscious indifference. At the hearing appellant presented no testimony, although appellee presented evidence that the procedures followed by Emmett and Chandler in this case reflected a conscious indifference. Under these circumstances, the affidavit of Couto, relied on by the majority opinion,

> is not evidence, as distinguished from the situation where no evidentiary hearing is afforded.... [W]hen a hearing is held on a motion to set aside a default judgment and to grant a new trial, the movant has the burden of proving by a preponderance of the evidence that his failure to answer was not intentional or due to conscious indifference, but rather was due to accident or mistake.

Reedy Co., Inc. v. Garnsey, 608 S.W.2d 755, 757 (Tex.1980).

Since appellant presented no testimony, the trial court did not err in refusing to set aside the default judgment and grant a new trial.

SAMPLE IRAC

MEMORANDUM

To: Senior Partner

From: Associate

Subject: _____

Date: _____ __, ____

You have asked me to determine whether we could obtain a new trial for case in which a default judgment has entered against our client. The general rule for removing a default judgment is as follows:

> A default judgment should be set aside and a new trial ordered in any case in which the failure of the defendant to answer before judgment was not intentional, or the result of conscious indifference on his part, but was due to mistake or accident; provided the motion sets up a meritorious defense and is filed at a time when the granting thereof will occasion no delay or otherwise work an injury to the plaintiff.

<u>Young v. Kirsch</u>, 814 S.W.2d 77 (Tex. App. 1991) <u>citing</u> <u>Craddock v. Sunshine Bus Lines</u>, 133 S.W.2d 124, 126 (Tex. 1939). This memo will analyze the issue of "conscious indifference." I am assuming our motion will be filed at a time when granting it will cause no delay or otherwise harm the plaintiff, and that the client has a meritorious defense to the underlying claim.

To act with "conscious indifference" is to act "purposefully" or in "bad faith." <u>State Farm Life Ins. Co. v. Mosharaf</u>, 794 S.W.2d 578 (Tex. App. 1990) (holding that a misfiling, the cause of which could not be explained, was not conscious indifference). The person must act with intent "to suffer judgment to go by default." <u>Southland Paint Co. v. Thousand Oaks Racket Club</u>, 724 S.W.2d 809 (Tex. App. 1986) (holding that a delay in mailing due to "shortness of staff" and "vacation schedules" was not conscious indifference). The controlling factor is the "absence of a purposeful or bad faith failure to answer ... [and] even a slight excuse will suffice...." <u>State Farm</u>, 794 S.W.2d at 583. Further, courts have applied this test liberally <u>Id.</u>

This case is analogous to <u>State Farm</u> and <u>Southland</u>

Paint. Like the responsible parties in those cases, the attorney here was not aware that an answer was due. He did not act purposefully or in bad faith; he missed the deadline due to an accident. He was in the hospital at the time the answer was due. Perhaps he should have done more to compensate for what happened, just like the parties in State Farm and Southland Paint, but that is not the test that applies here. Any excuse – however slight – is enough to preclude a finding that the mistake was purposeful or intentional. As a result, the precedents in State Farm and Southland Paint applied liberally to the facts of this case support the conclusion that this is not a case of conscious indifference.

The other side may argue that this case similar to the Young case because both the plaintiff in Young and the attorney here were familiar with the legal system and presumably knew that had to file an answer within some required time period. Young, 814 S.W.2d at 81. However, it is not knowledge of the legal requirement that supports and inference the individual acted purposefully or intentionally, it is knowledge of the deadline to serve an answer to the complaint that is key. Unlike the plaintiff in Young, the attorney here was not aware an answer was due. As a result,

<u>Young</u> is distinguishable. In this case, a court would likely allow our request for a new trial.

LEGAL MEMORANDUM EXERCISE

MEMORANDUM

To:	Associate
From:	Senior Partner
Subject:	_____
Date:	_____ __, ___

      I need your help with another personal injury case. Our client is Bob Smith; he was involved in a car accident last year and has been sued by the driver of the other car. Apparently, an individual named Fred Jones was traveling east in the left-hand lane of Atlantic Boulevard, a four-lane divided highway, in Jacksonville. He attempted a left turn at a break in the grass median designed for turning, and had to stop to wait for oncoming traffic. While he was stopped, the car he was towing extended into the left lane of Atlantic Boulevard approximately three feet. A car driven by another individual named Mary Miller braked and stopped to avoid the towed car protruding into the left lane.

Meanwhile, our client, Bob Smith, was also traveling East on Atlantic Boulevard. He was in the right hand land and came upon a beer truck that was moving slowly. Smith checked his rear view mirror, accelerated and moved into the left lane to pass the truck. He saw Miller's vehicle but didn't realize it wasn't moving. When he did he braked hard but could not stop in time. As a result, Smith struck Miller's vehicle from behind.

Smith was not injured in the accident but Miller suffered numerous personal injuries, including two broken ribs and a laceration to her forehead. Apparently, the ribs were broken by the force of the seatbelt against her chest. And Miller's head hit the windshield, causing the laceration to her forehead. Miller's car did have airbags but they failed to operate properly and did not inflate. Her car was also totaled as a result of the accident.

Miller has brought a civil action against Smith for personal injury damages. In Florida, a presumption of negligence attaches to the driver of the rear vehicle in a rear-end collision. However, there are exceptions to that rule, and Smith may be able to use one in his defense. I have found two cases I believe would govern on this issue: Clampitt v. D.J. Spencer Sales, 786 So.2d 570 (Fla. 2001) and Eppler v. Tarmac America, Inc., 752 So.2d 592 (Fla. 2000)). What I need you to do is read the cases, analyze the likelihood of Smith's defense succeeding in court, and draft a research memorandum presenting you findings.

SAMPLE LEGAL MEMORANDUM

MEMORANDUM

To: Senior Partner

From: Associate

Subject: _____

Date: _____ __, ____

Issue Presented

Whether Smith is likely at fault for rear-ending Miller's car, which had stopped in the road to avoid another stopped vehicle attempting to make a left hand turn.

Brief Answer

Yes, Smith is likely at fault. People making left hand turns is to be reasonably expected and, therefore, not a substantial and reasonable explanation as to why the driver of the rear vehicle was not negligent in causing a rear-end collision.

Facts

Our client, Bob Smith, was involved in an auto accident last year. Apparently, an individual named Fred Jones was traveling east in the left-hand lane of Atlantic Boulevard, towing a car behind his vehicle. He attempted a left turn at a break in the median, and stopped to wait for oncoming traffic. The car he was towing extended into the left lane of approximately three feet. A car driven by another individual named Mary Miller was traveling behind. She braked and stopped to avoid the towed car protruding into the left lane.

Meanwhile, our client, Bob Smith, was also traveling East on Atlantic Boulevard. He was in the right hand land and went to pass a truck that was moving slowly in that lane. Smith checked his rear view mirror, accelerated and moved into the left lane. When he realized Miller's vehicle had stopped, he braked hard but could not stop in time. As a result, Smith struck Miller's vehicle from behind.

Discussion

The issue here is whether Smith breached the duty of reasonable care by rear-ending Miller's car. The law presumes that the driver of the rear vehicle is negligent unless that driver provides a substantial and reasonable explanation as to why he was not negligent, in which case the presumption will vanish. E.g., Clampitt v. D.J. Spencer Sales, 786 So.2d 570, 573 (Fla. 2001)(an accident in the roadway ahead is to be reasonably expected and is not enough to rebut the presumption of negligence.), Eppler v. Tarmac America, Inc., 752 So.2d 592 (Fla. 2000)(an abrupt and arbitrary stop after a traffic light turns green is not to be reasonably expected and is sufficient to rebut the presumption).

In Clampitt, three vehicles were following one another in the southbound lane of Alternate U.S. 27 south of Bronson, Florida. Clampitt, 786 So.2d at 571. The lead vehicle, which was driven by Charles Huguley, was a pickup truck hauling a small trailer; the second vehicle, driven by Colletta Clampitt, was an automobile; and the third vehicle, driven by Carl Hetz, was a commercial tractor-trailer rig owned by D.J. Spencer Sales. Id.

Huguley was traveling south at forty-five to fifty-five miles an hour; he activated his turn signal and began braking one hundred and fifty yards prior to entering the driveway of his place of business; his pickup truck and trailer had turned almost completely off the highway when the trailer was struck from behind by Clampitt's auto. Id. at 572. Hetz saw Clampitt's auto come to a "dead-stop" on the highway; he slammed on his brakes, left one hundred feet of skid marks, and struck Clampitt's auto. Id. He did not see Huguley's turn signal or brake lights illuminate at any time prior to the accident. Id.

Based on this evidence, the court held that an accident in the roadway ahead is to be reasonably expected and, therefore, not a substantial and reasonable explanation as to why the driver of the rear vehicle was not negligent in causing a rear-end collision. Id. at 575. Unfortunately, accidents on the roadway ahead are a routine hazard faced by the driving public. Id. As a result, every driver is charged under the law with remaining alert and following the vehicle in front of him or her at a safe distance. Id.

The Smith case is analogous. Both cases involve a rear end collision with another vehicle stopped in the roadway. In Clampitt, the vehicle had stopped because of an accident; in the Smith case the reason for the stop was another vehicle turning left. However, people making left hand turns on the roadway ahead, like accidents in the roadway ahead, are routine hazards faced by the driving public. Turning vehicles and accidents are encountered frequently and are to be reasonably expected. In either case, drivers are charged under the law with remaining alert and following the vehicle in front of him or her at a safe distance. Therefore, neither circumstance provides a substantial and reasonable explanation as to why the driver of the rear vehicle was not negligent in causing a rear-end collision.

Conclusion

Smith is likely at fault for rear-ending Miller's car, which had stopped in the road to avoid another stopped vehicle attempting to make a left hand turn.

ABOUT THE AUTHOR

Ben L. Fernandez

Prof. Fernandez teaches Legal Drafting and Legal Writing at the University of Florida Levin College of Law. He had previously taught Legal Methods, Legal Research and Objective Writing, Lawyering Process for Litigation Practice, and Transactional Drafting at Florida Coastal School of Law. Also, he worked as an adjunct professor teaching Legal Writing at Northeastern University School of Law in Boston, and Business Law at Cape Cod Community College.

Prof. Fernandez has twenty-five years of experience practicing law in Massachusetts. He represented financial institutions and government finance agencies in commercial and residential finance transactions. He had his own practice in Plymouth, Massachusetts for ten years. Before that, he practiced law in the city of Boston for fifteen years. He worked as in-house counsel for a state-sponsored affordable housing finance agency, managed the business department of a prominent minority-owned firm, and was an associate at two large Boston law firms. Also, he served on the Board of Directors for Habitat for Humanity of Greater Plymouth, Massachusetts. He was a volunteer teacher in Junior Achievement's Financial Literacy program, and a regular speaker at Homebuyer Education Workshops sponsored by South Shore Housing and Housing Assistance Corporation on Cape Cod.

Prof. Fernandez has an LL.M. from Boston University School of Law, as well as a J.D. from Northeastern University School of Law and a B.A. from Cornell University.

Made in the USA
Las Vegas, NV
31 May 2024

90575102R00187